REDS IN AMERICA

4 января

Цена 3 руб.

БЕЗБОЖНИК

№ 1.

РЕДАКЦИЯ: Советская площадь
Космодемьяновский пер., д. № 3,
тел. 1-99-62.

Орган М. К. Р. К. П
(большевиков)

A front page cartoon, reproduced in black and white, from *The Godless,*
illustrated anti-religious weekly published in Moscow by the Communist
Party of Russia. A careful study of the detail will disclose a particularly
vicious sacrilege, depicted in a style now called "advanced" or "Russian" art.
The translated caption reads: "Take, eat, this is my body." (*Matt. 26: 26.*)

REDS IN AMERICA

The present status of the Revolutionary Movement in the United States based on documents seized by the authorities in the raid upon the Convention of the Communist Party at Bridgman, Michigan, August 22, 1922, together with descriptions of numerous connections and associations of the Communists among the Radicals, Progressives and Pinks.

by

R.M. WHITNEY

WESTERN ISLANDS

PUBLISHERS

BOSTON   LOS ANGELES

The Western Islands edition of *Reds In America* has been reset from the original text. No editing of Whitney's text has been done except to correct typographical errors and to clarify a few sentences lest their exact meaning be missed by the reader. No corrections at all have been made in quoted material. The original Appendix F ("Concerning The Next Tasks Of The Communist Party Of America") has been incorporated into the text where it more properly belongs, and the original Appendix G is now headed "Appendix F."

Published by

WESTERN ISLANDS

BELMONT, MASSACHUSETTS 02178

Manufactured in the United States of America

CONTENTS

FOREWORD

Reds In America, by R.M. Whitney, first appeared in print in 1924. It then disappeared, almost for good, very soon thereafter. Yet this masterpiece of factual and documented history, which was so completely smothered and has been so little known, is basically one of the most important books of the Twentieth Century. The reader might ask, "How can a book nearly fifty years old have any 'relevance' to America's problems in the 1970's?" Let us try to answer this question in relation to the value and importance of the past itself.

The expression, "one cannot see the forest for the trees," is no less true because it has become one of the most overworked clichés in the language. It is true that people tend to become so involved in a part of a problem, or in everyday life, that they lose sight of the whole, and of the ramifications of the whole. This is particularly true of the life of the nation, or for that matter, of life on this planet. It is virtually impossible to step back and view the current happenings in one's country with the detachment that will permit an objective evaluation of the play of cause and effect in our daily national life.

But the lack of easy access to such knowledge does not lessen the effects that events have. The problem, nevertheless, is simplified by the fact that we do have basic concepts and beliefs that can guide us in sifting out the irrelevant from the important. Moreover, it is not unusual to have available a plan or outline that makes it possible to gain a clear insight into the present. One of the great tragedies of history is that people so seldom take advantage of such aids as are available.

The last ten years have seen the American dream turning into a nightmare: city blocks are burned, policemen are shot down in the streets, the flag is publicly desecrated, once great universities are seized by a handful of students who proclaim themselves revolutionaries. Patriotic citizens have tried to enlighten their fellow citizens as to the cause and the consequences of the present crisis. But petty perjudice, bias, and indifference have prevented too many citizens from clearly recognizing America's plight.

But what loyal American could fail to see the truth if a document predicting, or better yet, describing, the present crisis could be recovered from years past? *Reds In America* is such a document. The author was a newspaper reporter in a time when this title was one of distinction rather than opprobrium. Whitney's own deep and broad knowledge of the Communist Conspiracy, as well as his extensive and expert use of the documents seized by state and federal authorities in the 1922 raid on the secret Communist convention held near Bridgman, Michigan, give the reader an insight into the very core of the American Communist movement.

Reds In America is far more than a journalistic report on the raid of 1922. It is a carefully documented exposé of Communist activities in the context of the total conspiracy, presenting these activities in the light of what the Communists themselves planned for the future of America. For this reason, the fact that this book was written almost fifty years ago makes it more rather than less pertinent to our present crisis.

In *Reds In America* Whitney lays it out straight. He shows how by 1924 the Communists had already infiltrated every segment of American life: unions, education, religion, the armed forces, the government, political parties, women's organizations, the theatrical world (including the movies), and the civil rights movement. By 1924 they had in their ranks or affiliated with them priests, rabbis, and ministers, military officers, union bosses, movie actors, in fact "big names" from all fields. Whitney shows how people whom we have been led to respect today, were then known for their aid to the Communists — for example, Jane Addams, Charlie Chaplin, Felix Frankfurter, Carrie Chapman Catt, Upton Sinclair, and Charles P. Steinmetz.

The strength of the Communists at the time of which Whitney wrote is shown by the fact that the effects of the Bridgman raid of 1922, which might have been expected to have crushed them utterly, had already by 1924 been completely overcome. The Reds had developed a power base from which to drive for a conquest of the United States. The only things they had to fear were effective exposure, and legal suppression of their illegal activities. As of 1970, neither has yet occurred in anything near sufficiency.

But the picture is bleaker still. The Communist Conspiracy in the 1920's was not simply a collection of bearded, bomb-throwing fanatics. Whitney discusses this aspect of the Conspiracy, going into considerable detail about the Communist call for violent revolution. But as Whitney obviously realized this facet is by no means the most important. Because he was writing in a period immediately following the Russian Revolution — and in a period marked by many instances of violence in America — Whitney gives this aspect of the Conspiracy considerable space. The reader should keep in mind, however, that although the Communist party leaders of the 1920's called for violent overthrow of the American government, the real meaning and purpose of their words were quite different from the literal interpretation.

The leaders of the Communist party needed a group of hard-core followers on whom they could absolutely depend. The obvious recruiting ground was the unfortunately large group of politically criminal radicals that already existed in the United States. This element, exemplified by the assassin of President McKinley, the International Workers of the World, and the Haymarket rioters among many others, consisted of complete fanatics who would be useful in making up such a cadre. However, these radicals also had a long tradition of anarchism and violence. Realizing that immediate revolution in America was impossible and that victory could result only from tight organization and patient gradualism, the Communists set out to organize the radicals into a Red vanguard by replacing the belief in anarchy with a willingness to accept "iron discipline." Any attempt at the same time to replace the concept of violent revolution with that of patient gradualism would have been suicidal. So the Communists did the exact opposite: they preached immediate violent overthrow. By the time it became obvious that there was to be no revolution, most of the rank and file were so disciplined and so absorbed into the movement that they passed from the concept of revolution to that of gradualism without even knowing it. Later, this fraud and other factors did cause a split — the Trotskyite movement — but even this served Communist purposes.

The cry for violent overthrow also served as a conditioning to terrorism and as a cover for the Reds' more subtle attacks in the United States and elsewhere. When the American public of the 1920's realized that the Reds were calling for revolution, it was this aspect that received the greatest attention, rather than the real danger from their "boring from within" (an error Whitney did not make), and when in the 1930's it became obvious that the Communists could not overthrow the government, there was a tendency to dismiss the whole movement as crackpot but probably harmless.

Just as the cry for violent revolution is really a fraud, so also is the whole Marxist façade. Communism is not an uprising of the downtrodden masses, it is not Utopian socialism, it is not even true communism. The Communist Conspiracy is in fact a power grab by a clique of socially and financially prominent *Insiders*.

The Conspiracy was already seventy-two years old when it hired Karl Marx to write the *Communist Manifesto* as one part of its campaign to undermine and destroy Western Civilization. Communism has never been the whole of the conspiracy, and it was only in the early years of the Twentieth Century that it became the largest part of the whole. Although the *Insiders* had by then operated in the United States for at least a century, it was not until the Wilson Administration that they began to push publicly for the destruction of the United States, and it was then that they began assembling the machinery for the *open* assault. At the bottom the Conspiracy consisted of the Communist party with its captured unions, churches, social clubs, etc.; at the top it consisted of the wielders of power in financial, social, and political circles, such as Amos

Pinchot, Burton Wheeler, Felix Warburg, Jacob Schiff, Stuart Chase, William C. Bullitt, Christian Herter, John Foster Dulles, Allen Dulles, Frank A. Vanderlip, and A. Piatt Andrew. From the very beginning the attack was a pincer move: America was to be crushed between the "street revolution" at the bottom and the governmental imperium at the top.

Whitney's exposition makes clear that by 1924 the three major principles of the Communists' strategy were already being solidly employed: (1) It was their intention, even that early, to have the whole worldwide Communist revolution increasingly financed, directly and indirectly, by the American government; (2) a Communist system, and the absolute tyranny of a Communist regime, were gradually to be imposed, *from the top down,* on the American people – always by steps and measures supposedly designed to stave off Communism by promoting public welfare and prosperity; and (3) already the Conspirators were moving skillfully and insidiously toward inner control of both major political parties, which they were also seeking to make more and more alike. For thus their political victories could be won by manipulations of the party conventions, long before the Comrades had enough reach to win such victories at the polls.

This brilliant but simple strategy enabled the Conspiracy to spread its poison into every segment of American life. With the coming of the New Deal the Conspirators raised their power bloc into the structure of the federal government. The *Insiders* then began to extend their authority further and further down the structure of the nation, so that they now are approaching working control of the United States.

The present manifestation of the power of the Conspiracy should cause no surprise: the whole blueprint is to be found in *Reds In America*. But the greater truth which now emerges from *Reds In America* is one which would not have been so obvious in 1924. Communism is no more than a tool to be used by a powerful elite to seize all authority in their own hands. Since 1924 the *Insiders* have made great strides toward the ultimate goal of world domination. The danger is great and imminent. But all is *not* lost. If sufficient effort had been made in 1924 to expose the Communist Conspiracy for what it really is, the struggle would have been over decades ago. This was not done, but it is not too late to do it now. Although the enemy is much stronger, patriotic Americans are now much better informed. And *Reds In America* is a powerful new weapon in our educational arsenal. No loyal American, having once read this book, can fail to understand what has been happening for decades, what is happening now, and what is going to happen unless we wake up enough of our fellow citizens to the plain facts of the present crisis. For Whitney has put the whole blueprint of the Conspiracy squarely in front of us, without leaving any room for doubt.

Thomas J. Haas

INTRODUCTION

Better to be despised for too anxious apprehensions, than ruined by too confident security . . . .

The effect of liberty to individuals is, that they may do what they please: we ought to see what it will please them to do, before we risk congratulations, which may soon turn into complaints. Prudence would dictate this in the case of separate insulated private men; but liberty, when men act in bodies, is *power*. Considerate people, before they declare themselves, will observe the use which is made of *power*; and particularly of so trying a thing as *new* power in *new* persons, of whose principles, tempers, and dispositions they have little or no experience, and in situations where those who appear the most stirring in the scene may not possibly be the real movers.

— The Right Hon. Edmund Burke*

Turning over the pages of Burke's *Reflections,* the thought is constantly dominant — even if no other sources of information were at hand — that the points of similarity between the French Revolution and that which recently occurred in Russia far outnumber those of dissimilarity. The revolutionaries of France were as much adepts at the dissemination of catchwords and slogans as their Russian counterparts of a later day. Some of the rallying cries, as for instance "Liberty, Equality, Fraternity," have persisted in their psychic malfeasance even to the present, and the literature of the French Revolution abounds with phrases which crop out in the wordy exudates of Lenin and Trotsky. The correspondence of Jean Baptiste Carrier† has been recently published, and it is difficult to realize that the scenes of terrible cruelty which Carrier describes are not those in which the central figure is a Dzerzhinsky or a Moghilevsky or that Carrier's loathsome sacrilege is not that of a Bukharin.

---

*Burke, Edmund, *Reflections on the Revolution in France, and of the Proceedings in Certain Societies in London Relative to that Event.* In a letter intended to have been sent to a Gentleman in Paris. (Published October 1790.)

†E.H. Carrier, *Correspondence of Jean Baptiste Carrier.* John Lane Co.

1

The machinery of organized revolution which produced such a change in France has been well described by Mrs. Nesta Webster,* and the most startling truth is clearly brought out that the organization through which the chief conspirators accomplished their purposes of destruction was manipulated through *minorities, secretly organized, and ultimately influencing vast numbers of people who knew not the objective and cared less.* The direction of the movement, therefore, always came from the top. It must be admitted that the Revolution was only in small part a reaction against abuses, which were rapidly in the process of abatement, and which, such as they were, furnished talking points to the curbstone agitators. Mr. Theodore Roosevelt showed his keen historical insight and freedom from the influence of Carlisle's Prussianized history when he wrote to Mr. Felix Frankfurter, one of our modern revolutionaries:

> Robespierre and Danton and Marat and Herbert were just as evil as the worst tyrants of the old regime, and from 1791 to 1794 they were the most dangerous enemies to liberty that the world contained.

This organization of disorder in France carried its fighting front into foreign countries and counted upon reverberations as a part of its political capital at home. Friends of the Revolution in England, many of them fanatical in their devotion to the cause of democracy as pictured by its philosophers, organized, agitated, assembled, talked, and raised much money to help the cause along; so much so that many were of the belief that it was British government gold upholding the hands of the protesting party. As clearly defined but with less intensity, the same organized movement appeared in the United States. Its advent caused George Washington and his co-workers considerable anxiety, for they evidently could not understand its true significance. It can be said verily that the scars of that agitation are still apparent in our political life. They are the first deviations from the standard of a representative republican government as conceived by the framers of the Constitution, who were attempting to build something which could protect minorities against the liquid rule of a mob.

It was in contemplation of such things that Edmund Burke was prompted to write his *Reflections.* The times furnished an opportunity for a bit of wise political philosophy, just as applicable today with our eyes turned toward the Northeast as it was in the days of Burke when he was viewing events from the safe side of the English Channel. The lessons are all worked out, ready for study. As this book will show, we have with us a group of people numbering about 30,000 at the most, ninety percent of whom are aliens and cannot vote, who are closely bound by ties of a harsh discipline, fear of treachery, hope of loot, and of an easy future. They are ruled by a clever, more or less secretly organized minority. As a minority, this party hopes, or rather its minority leaders hope, to dominate an inarticulate and unorganized majority. It is this latter mass, in which it is so diffi-

*Webster, Nesta, *World Revolution.* Small, Maynard & Co.

cult to stimulate reaction, but in which reactions once stimulated are so difficult to stop, that was finally aroused in both France and Russia. The revolutionary leaders themselves know it, for we find William Z. Foster telling his fellow conspirators in the convention of Communists at Bridgman, Michigan:

> The fate of the Communist party depends on the control of the masses, through the capture of the trade unions, without which revolution is impossible.

There is a certain candor about this which is refreshing even if spoken to fellow Communists and in a secret session. Foster also said in the same speech:

> We no longer measure the importance of revolutionary organizations by their size.

Foster has evidently studied the history of revolutions and the psychology of minority control. Again he said:

> Communists get things done and paid for by others.

Quite so. Some of us have been watching the revolutionary movement for years, and with Foster, our opinion is unanimous that if the following three things happened, the movement in the United States would collapse in a hurry: (1) Cessation of governmental support to socialistic projects on the periphery of the revolutionary program. (2) Withdrawal of advertising support on the part of the several large corporations from quasi-Bolshevik magazines and other similar publications. (3) It is also suggested that benevolent old ladies and gentlemen (some of them not so very old either) clamber off the Bolshevik bandwagon and stand on a real rock-ribbed American platform, giving their funds to assist in maintaining the best government on earth as it was originally conceived. It is to be granted that the giving of money for an object thought worthy stimulates a satisfied feeling which is quite desirable, but it is equally true that starving children in Russia are not fed by the absent dollar – not at all. Up to this point at least, it is impossible to disagree with Mr. Foster.

But we must turn aside for a moment and determine just what kind of an organization this revolutionary party is. A line of thought is suggested by the Communists themselves. The Bridgman convention adopted a "Thesis on the Relations of Number One [illegal branch] and Number Two [legal branch]." It was written by a committee of which J. Lovestone, at that time executive secretary of the Communist party of America, was chairman, and must therefore be accepted as authoritative. It contains the following statement:

> The revolutionary party can avoid suppression into a completely secret existence . . . by taking advantage of the pretenses of "democratic forms" which the capitalist state is obliged to maintain. By this means the Communists can maintain themselves in the open with a restricted program while establishing themselves with mass support.

In other words, the revolutionary party assumes the pretense of democratic forms in order to secure the support of the masses, and this pretense is assumed only during the transitory phase which precedes the climax of a proletarian dictatorship. Things are said sometimes which do not work out in practice — especially with the Bolsheviks. Therefore, it behooves us to examine the machinery of world revolution and see for ourselves whether it is assuming the "pretenses of democratic form."

Authentic evidence is fortunately right at hand. Senator Henry Cabot Lodge addressed the Senate of the United States January 7, 1924, and gave a clear insight into the workings of world revolution right at its center in Moscow. Then followed the hearings before a subcommittee of the Committee on Foreign Relations of the United States Senate under the chairmanship of Senator William A. Borah, "pursuant to S. Res. 50, declaring that the Senate of the United States favors the recognition of the present Soviet Government in Russia," a resolution Introduced by Mr. Borah himself. Mr. Robert F. Kelley and Mr. A.W. Kliefoth, both of the Division of Eastern European Affairs, Department of State, testified and placed on record voluminous documents to back their conclusions.

The Russian Communist Party

This basic organization has never numbered more than 700,000, out of a general population of 120,000,000, and at the present time has about 387,000 members, largely confined to the urban centers. The party is highly disciplined, thoroughly organized, and is also a fighting as well as a political unit. Its members may be called upon to go anywhere, either singly or in numbers, in some respects resembling our own militia. New members are recruited after a probationary period of at least one year, often extending to five years, during which each candidate is subjected to the most rigid observation and trial. At the present time, no one can join who is not of the proletariat (urban industrial workers).

> At the party Congress held in April 1923, only industrial laborers were eligible to be enrolled in the party, and they must be seconded by two party members. All other applicants, it was decided, are to remain candidates for another year.*

Political reasons for limiting the membership to industrial workers are obvious.

> After admittance into the party, the new members must survive periodic combings of the party roster, during which their reports as practicing party members are minutely scrutinized . . . . The object of these cleansings is to eliminate all those who are not sincere communists.†

Members are penalized for the slightest infraction of rules, lighter offenses being followed by suspension or expulsion from the party, while greater trans-

---

*Speech of Senator Lodge, *Congressional Record*, January 7, 1924, p. 579.
†*Loc. cit.*

gressions are punished by those heavier penalties imposed under the statutes designed to discourage counterrevolution. Each member is pledged to propagandize against religion and is not allowed to enter a place of worship. Church marriage is a frequent cause for discipline. *Izvestia,* official organ of the All-Russian Central Executive Committee, published an article March 31, 1921, in which

> . . . notice was given to all members of the Russian Communist party in regard to the strict fulfillment of Article 13 of the Constitution of the Russian Communist party, which compels all members to carry on anti-religious propaganda.*

In return for such fealty to the party, members are carefully cared for in many ways. Shortly after the revolution, when food was scarce, members of the party were first in line during the distribution of food packages. They all have jobs under the government:

> *Senator Pepper.* I understand you to say that you did not know of any case where there was a member of the Communist party who is not also an office holder of the Soviet government?
> *Mr. Kelley.* Yes, sir.†

Naturally, this works both ways.

> There is not known a case of a single member of the higher governmental organs, either in the Federation or the so-called Russian Soviet Republic, who is not a member of the Russian Communist party.‡

Then there is the good old-fashioned Tammany method of getting the party heelers out of trouble. An official report of the Central Control Committee of the Russian Communist party, made at the last congress, states:

> All our work is carried on in contact with the courts and with the state political administration, in view of the fact that often in the courts there are pending cases of members of the party. The judicial organs inform us about the comrades in regard to whom there is judicial evidence. We acquaint ourselves with this evidence, as not infrequently there have been cases when comrades have been put into the dock solely as the result of personal intrigues. In such cases . . . we have raised the question of the expediency and advisability of a public trial in court, lest we undermine the party authority of our comrades.§

The party also has a "monopoly of legality" and no other political associations are allowed, under heavy penalties.

---

*Hearings of the Borah Subcommittee, p. 14.

†*Ibid.,* p. 16.

‡Speech of Senator Lodge, *op. cit.,* p. 578.

§The Central Control Committee of the Russian Communist party has the function of supervising and controlling the machinery of the party and of the Soviet government of Russia. Hearings of the Borah Subcommittee, p. 10.

> I refer to the fact that we are the only legal party in the country, and have, in this wise, as it were, a monopoly of legality . . . . Let us speak clearly — we have a monopoly of legality. We do not grant our opponents political freedom. We do not give the possibility of legal existence to those who pretend to compete with us.*

The All-Russian Congress of the Russian Communist party meets perhaps once a year, the last meeting having been the twelfth. It was held in Moscow April 1923, and another is scheduled for March 1924. The delegates are all hand-picked.

> *Mr. Kelley* . . . . [Exhibit] No. 21 is a translation from *Pravda*, May 12, 1912, a speech of Zinoviev, in which he points out that the delegates to the party conference Congress were carefully selected . . . . Selected by a small group of individuals . . . by the Central [Executive] Committee.†

The selections, we may be sure, are safe ones. Not much voting is done at these congresses. The business consists largely in listening to the reports of the "big chiefs," explanations of why things do not always happen just so, and exhortations to remain steadfast in the faith. The same individuals always do the talking, usually members of the Central Committee, or important members of the Soviet government. In turn, the Central Committee is elected by the Congress:

> According to the statutes of organization of the party, the supreme power in the party is exercised by the All-Russian Congress of the Russian Communist party, which elects an executive organ called the Central Committee of forty members, who, it is stated, should by preference be "laborers more closely connected with the proletarian mass."‡

The "laborers closely connected with the proletarian mass" are simply "fronts," for, as will be seen, when it comes to the matter of selecting the Political Bureau of the Central Committee, they are promptly forgotten. The Central Committee meets once in two months, and between sessions of the congress it holds supreme authority. With numerous proletarians on the committee it was, of course, difficult to transact business, so a Political Bureau is elected by the Central Committee.

> Attached to [elected by] the Central Committee, there is a Political Bureau of seven members who have grown skilled in directing political and economic work of our organs . . . . In the second place, the nucleus within the Central Committee, which has become expert in management, is already growing old and must be replaced. §

The following are given as members of the Political Bureau: Kamenev, Lenin, Rykov, Stalin, Tomsky, Trotsky, and Zinoviev; as alternates, Bukharin, Kalinin, Molotov, and Rudzutak.

---

*Hearings of Borah Subcommittee, p. 15, quoting Zinoviev in *Pravda*, April 2, 1922.
†*Ibid.*, p. 14.
‡Speech of Senator Lodge, *op. cit.*, p. 580, quoting *Pravda*, April 28, 1923.
§Hearings of Borah Subcommittee, p. 23, quoting report of Comrade Stalin, *Pravda*, April 19, 1923.

Lenin is now dead. Trotsky is reported more or less ill, and in disagreement as to policies with other members of the bureau. Tomsky and Stalin are not regarded as having predominating influence, owing to age and previous political history, though Stalin appears to be making rapid progress. Rykov is perhaps of next importance because of his skill along economic lines. He has been recently elected to fill Lenin's place. Kamenev, whose correct name is Rosenfeld and who married Trotsky's sister, is chief of the intellectual forces of the Bolsheviks, and is a close supporting second to Zinoviev (born Apfelbaum). Zinoviev is unquestionably, at this time, the dominating member of the Bureau. He is described as "most ruthless; it is he who by the offices he holds in the Communist party and the Communist International is at the head of all propaganda in foreign countries." "Party dictatorship," says Zinoviev, "is the lever which we cannot let out of our hands."

Relationship Between The Russian Communist Party, The Russian Soviet Government, And The Third (Communist) International

A rather lengthy description of the Russian Communist party machinery has been attempted for three reasons: in the first place, through it a small group of men, if not merely one or two, responsible to none but themselves, dominate, politically and economically, a large mass of people. The structure is that of minorities openly organized but of necessity secret. Secondly, the structure is characteristic of all communistic organizations. Finally, by a system of interlocking directorates, characteristic of radical and liberal organizations even in the United States, the Communist party machine dominates by its Political Bureau (Politbureau) the Russian Soviet government (including the Federation of Soviet Republics) and the Third (Communist) International. "The function of the Soviet government is to govern Russia; that of the International, to carry out the policy of the party abroad," both in the last analysis under the direction of the Political Bureau. A description by Lenin of the work of the Political Bureau is enlightening in many respects.

> The principal task of the Organization Bureau was the distribution of party forces and the task of the Political Bureau was the solution of political questions.
> Naturally this division is to a certain extent artificial, being understood that it is impossible to conduct any policy without making certain classifications. Consequently every question of organization assumes a political significance and among us has grown up the practice that the opinion of one member of the Central Committee is sufficient in order to have any particular question by virtue of this or that consideration held to be a political question.
> To attempt otherwise to limit the activity of the Central Committee would in fact hardly be of value and in practice could hardly be possible . . . . During the year much of the work of the Political Bureau has consisted of the current solution of all questions arising having relation to policy unifying the activity of all soviet and party institutions, all organiza-

> tions of the working class, unifying and striving to direct all the work of the Soviet Republics, all questions of an international, domestic and foreign policy, . . . each of us working in this or that party or soviet organization watches every day for any unusual developments in political questions, foreign or domestic.
>
> The decision of these questions, as it expressed itself in the decrees of the soviet power or in the activity of party organizations, was appraised by the Central Committee of the party. It is necessary to say that the questions were so many that it was necessary to decide them one after the other under conditions of great haste and only, thanks to the full acquaintance of members of the collegium, to the undertaking of the shades of opinion, and confidence was it possible to carry out the work. Otherwise it would have been impossible even for a collegium three times larger. Often it was necessary to decide conflicting questions by substituting a telephone conversation for a meeting.*

It is entirely conceivable that when the telephone was out of order, Lenin took upon himself the responsibility of making the decision. This relation, however, is not of so much interest to us as that which exists between the party and the Third (Communist) International. The organization schemes of both are practically the same, with slight differences in terminology. The Third International is the creation of Lenin who worked out the details in practice by utilizing the machinery of the Russian Communist party. Congresses are held at Moscow approximately every year, the last (at the time this is written) having been held in November-December 1922. Calls for its assemblage are issued by the Executive Committee, which has the power of seating the delegates and determining the number of delegates to represent each country. In turn, the Executive Committee is nominally elected by the congress, but the method of election raises the question as to whether it wasn't learned from political experience acquired in the Lower East Side of New York. Zinoviev, chairman of the Executive Committee, and unanimously elected president of the congress, is speaking:

> Unless there is objection, I will have the voting take place. I beg the comrades who understand German to sit alongside of the Russian comrades, to translate as well as they can to them. The voting will now take place. Has anyone any objection to this list? That appears not to be the case. The list is confirmed.†

And, thus, the Executive Committee, having nominated itself, took office until the next congress. Objection would have been futile, as the composition of the congress was dominated by the Russian Communist party elements, voting under unit rule. The congress agenda is prepared in advance, and consists largely of speeches and reports. The same persons appear, year after year. Voting is rarely attempted.

---

*Before the Ninth Congress of the Russian Communist party. Hearings of the Borah Subcommittee, p. 16.

†Bulletin of the Third Congress, No. 2, p. 19. Cited by Mr. Kelley before the Borah Subcommittee, p. 16.

And, after the vote was taken, in which, of course, the Russian motion was carried, Zinoviev remarks, "Comrades, this is the only vote during the whole Congress, and it is, after all, only a question of such a little thing."*

The Executive Committee of the Comintern† delegates the absolute authority vested in it to the Presidium, which it in turn elects. At present, the members of the Presidium of the Comintern, elected subsequently to the Fourth Congress, are as follows:‡

Bukharin	McManus	Souvarine
Katayama	Neurath	Terraccini
Kolorav	Radek	Clara Zetkin
Kusinen	Shatskin	Zinoviev

Little attention may be paid to those who are foreigners in Russia, as the Russian group dominates the organization and the foreigners are not often in Moscow anyway. Bukharin, Radek, and Kusinen are in immediate charge under Zinoviev, their names appearing on documents seized at Bridgman. Kusinen signs the orders that go out. Zinoviev is a member of the Political Bureau of the Communist party, and Bukharin is an alternate. "The Communist International is the chief channel of communication, organization, and agitation in the United States."

The Communist Party Of America

This is the American Section of the Third or Communist International.

It must always be remembered that the real revolutionary party — the American Section of the Third International — is the Communist party and that the legal party [Workers' party] is but an instrument which it uses to carry on its work among the masses.

And again:

The ruling of the Communist International must be accepted as obligating every member of the Communist party of America, minor-

---

*Speech of Senator Lodge, *op. cit.*, p. 585. The congress also had a presidium of its own which is in effect a "steering committee."

†Radicals generally have a habit of abbreviating the long names of their organizations. For instance, "Glavlit" refers to the Supreme Literature and Publishing Administration attached to the Commissariat of Education of the Russian Soviet Government, the bureau that has charge among other things of the press censorship; "Rosta" is the Russian Telegraph Agency, which exchanges news with Reuters and the United Press; "Tuel" is the Trade Union Educational League of William Z. Foster, a branch of the Communist party of America, to which is allocated the work of propagandizing and organizing within the trade unions. In the same manner, "Comintern" is an abbreviation of Communist International. "Presidium of the Comintern" is an expression often used, and refers to a small group of men within the Executive Committee which has ultimate authority, and which dominates the organization. The dominating group within the Presidium are members of the Political Bureau of the Russian Communist party.

‡Mr. Kelley before the Borah Subcommittee, Hearings, p. 40.

ity or majority, to work diligently in the immediate construction of a legal political party [Workers' party].*

This status is accepted by the American elements:

Even though the Communist party shall have come aboveground and acts as the section of the Communist International, the underground organization remains as the directing organ of the open Communist party. This status is to continue up to and through the revolution and to the establishment of the dictatorship of the proletariat.†

So that there is provision made for an illegal party to work as a secret minority within the open legal party. The relations between the two are considered in great detail both at the headquarters of the Comintern in Moscow and by the local leaders. No other relationship is thought possible for effectively carrying on the work of revolution in the United States.

The illegal Communist party . . . must continue to direct the whole communist work . . . .
The whole open work of all communists . . . must be directed by the Communist party . . . .‡
The entire membership of the underground party, the real Communist party, must join the open party [Workers' party] and become its most active element . . . . It must at all times hold positions of leadership in the legal party.§

And then again:

During the time when the Communist party operates, not under its own name and program in the open, but through a "legal" political party with restricted program and different name, the same principle is applied by having full control of such legal party in the hands of the Communist party.
This is accomplished by having a majority of all important committees composed of Communist party members, and by means of regular and compulsory caucuses of all the Communist party members within any legal unit, bound by the unit rule, a principle which will prevail in some effective form when the Communist party is itself in the open.
The convention of the Communist party must be held prior to the

---

*Instructions signed by Bukharin, Radek, and Kusinen. See Chapter 12.
†*Thesis on Relations of Number One* [illegal branch] *to Number Two* [legal branch], Appendix B. Written by J. Lovestone, executive secretary of the Communist party of America, and adopted by the Bridgman convention.
‡Report of the Adjustment Committee to the convention, written by Robert Minor, a member of the Executive Committee. See Chapter 1.
§Thesis, "Concerning the Next Tasks of the Communist Party of America," quoted in Chapter 12.

convention of the Labor [Workers'] party and determine all policies for the party and its open organizations.*

The absolute domination of the open party by the illegal party, the connections with the Communist International, are therefore shown. The Workers' party, however, is only one form of activity which is planned, and even the Workers' party has no monopoly in the political field. The presence of William Z. Foster at the Bridgman convention plainly indicated that his organization, the Trade Union Educational League, was designed to work in the field of labor as the Workers' party was designed to work in the field of politics.

> The general control of the No. One [illegal branch] within X [Trade Union Educational League] as within all other organizations must be in the hands of the party, and not in the hands of special committees.†

Within the ranks of conservative labor unions are to be established nuclei, here and there gradually winning over the more or less radical and discontented to a "red" platform and securing the benevolent neutrality of the conservatives. The plan does not call for the adhesion, in an organic sense, of large numbers of the labor union members, but for secretly organized minority groups. Acting through the labor union organizations, the Communist nuclei exercise an influence which reaches far beyond their immediate membership.

> The party must use its influence and strength in the trade unions to form delegated conferences of labor organizations. Such conferences decide on a general political campaign including all forms of political action . . . . Our members should initiate such action through the unions.
> In creating a united front for the working class for their economic struggles, the existing labor unions must remain the instruments of these struggles while the members of the Workers' party must be the instruments to unify these economic organizations.‡

The same methods of control are extended to the Communist press. As Foster expresses it, "one of the secrets of control is monopoly of the press," and provision is made that, insofar as possible, all editors of the Workers' party organs shall be members of the Communist party.

The convention of the Communist party at Bridgman was organized and carried on in true Bolshevik style. Little voting was allowed, care being taken to insure healing in the party dissensions early in the convention. Only true and trusted delegates were present, handpicked as it were. The program consisted principally of reports of committees, orders from Moscow to which the delegates themselves listened on the whole without much discussion. The convention had its presidium.

---

*Appendix B, *Thesis,* by J. Lovestone.
†Resolutions adopted by the Bridgman convention. See Chapter 1.
‡Appendix E. See also Chapter 11.

> Throughout the Communist movement of the world, the system of "presidiums" prevails, by which matters of necessarily secret nature are kept in the hands of the most reliable and most trusted members of the party. This is a necessary feature of a revolutionary organization.*

Secrecy of course is necessary to control, and the caution to observe it came from Moscow — the result of extended experience — emphasized by the local leaders.

> While coming out in the open, the Communist party must not make the mistake of being trapped in the open by exposing its national or district Communist party headquarters, or illegal machinery, its underground printing arrangements or the personnel of its Central Executive Committee . . . . †
> . . . The identity of members of No. One [illegal branch] working in offices or upon committees of No. Two [legal branch] , as well as their relations to No. One, must not be exposed . . . . Get used to speaking in terms that will not in any way reveal connections with No. One.‡

The Communist party of course has its Executive Committee and presumably it is elected in about the same fashion as those elected in Moscow. While the Bridgman raid on the party convention was a staggering blow to the revolutionaries, the latter have recovered their equilibrium rapidly and have transferred part of their work to the Workers' party organization. The Central Committee of the Workers' party is now composed of:

Alexander Bittleman	William Z. Foster
Earl R. Browder	Benjamin Gitlow
F. Burman	Ludwig Lore
J.P. Cannon	J. Lovestone
William F. Dunne	John Pepper
J.L. Engdahl	C.E. Ruthenberg

It also has its Political Bureau:

Browder	Lovestone
Cannon	Pepper
Dunne	Ruthenberg
Foster	

And it is perfectly safe to assume that this is the inside ring in the United States. John Pepper officially represents the Third International of Moscow in the committee and in the bureau. Pepper's correct name, i.e., the one under which he was born, is Pogány, and his Communist party name is Lang.

This picture is complete. For the time it is possible for the average man to gain a conception of the great political machine that controls the destinies of so

---

Thesis by J. Lovestone. Appendix B.
†*Ibid.*
‡Confidential bulletin written by Lovestone and sent to Communist groups throughout the country. See Chapter 1.

many individuals in Europe and that would extend its operations to the whole world. The lines of activity and the channels of thought are now an open book. To an extent never before dreamed of, the principles of secret, irresponsible, minority control have been brought to a magnificent perfection. Yet in the very perfection of its development lies the very danger to which it subjects society at large, the cancer-like infiltration into untouched fields. If one minority can build up and sway such a machine, why not another? That the leaders themselves have recognized this danger is apparent.

> The Thesis adopted by the Third World Congress on the subject of organization explicitly prohibited the formation of closed factions within Communist parties.*

Of course; the danger is much too real. Another minority might grab the machine.

It borders on the silly to say that this ponderous organization has been erected for the purpose of bringing about a proletarian dictatorship. That sort of slogan may be sufficient to keep the proletarian busy with his thoughts while the leaders twist his nose, for "it is necessary for victory to bring about common 'mass action' of workers who are not yet communists." The climax of a proletarian dictatorship is somewhere else. The problem is to locate it, evaluate it, and see to whose interest the movement contributes.

If we take a glance over the field of international politics, we find bonds of sympathy between world revolution, which is international, and more particularly Germany, which is national. Internationalism has never been anti-German for the reason that Germany has now been "bolshevized" these many years. It has been and is now being ruled by an irresponsible minority. A constant watch on the events of the past few years discloses too many points of sympathetic contact between the leaders of Moscow and Berlin. Policies are shaped to conform to common objectives. Under present circumstances there can be no Communist revolution in Germany, no matter how many times it may be walked out as a threat. Under the new economic policy in Russia, Communism is abandoned and has gradually been superseded by a socialistic form of government which in general lines is the exact duplicate of that which exists in Germany. Is that the real objective of the world revolutionary movement, the struggle for a proletarian dictatorship? The temptation to belief is great when the "stream of thought" among the revolutionaries is all in one direction: "The German steam hammer and Soviet wheat will conquer the entire world."†

It seems that the time has come to seriously consider the question: Did the Entente win the war only to lose to the sneakery of a back-stairs thief?

---

*Taken from a newsletter service sent out by Brooks, representative of the Communist International in this country. See Appendix D.
†Slogans for the sixth anniversary celebration of the October revolution written by Comrade Stalin and published in *Pravda*, Oct. 27, 1923. Hearings of the Borah Subcommittee, p. 64.

The preparation of the material for this book has been of absorbing interest. Much of it appeared in the *Boston Evening Transcript* over a year ago, and there have since been many bitter attacks and withal much praise. The attacks give little concern because of their source, radicals of every hue, from Reds to parlor pinks, from the American Civil Liberties Union, a most subversive organization, to members of Congress who pretend to be patriots and while hiding under the cloak of "progressivism" are in reality playing the game of the world revolutionaries. The pacifists have been particularly virulent, as if they believed in fighting to obtain peace. Praise has come from labor leaders among others who believe in the open publication of the truth, realizing that it hits none who are still loyal to the tenets of those who founded this Republic.

There are many to whom credit should be given for assistance and advice, and with them I would share the honors. The publication of *Reds In America* in this form would not have been possible without the material cooperation of the American Defense Society and its Board of Directors. Under the greatest difficulties this organization is attempting to preserve to our succeeding generations America as we found it, and this book is one of many evidences of its work. I am also greatly indebted to Mr. William E. Brigham, Washington correspondent of the *Boston Evening Transcript,* who has been of much aid and comfort because of his determined stand for Americanism and his insistence that the American people know the truth of the radical situation. My appreciation is also expressed to Mr. Fred Marvin, editor of the Searchlight department of the *New York Commercial,* who wrote the chapter concerning the trials of the Communists at St. Joseph, Michigan, following the raid at Bridgman. Thanks are also extended to Dr. Harris A. Houghton of New York, who has given me valuable suggestions, and who, at my request, corrected the final proofs. The officials of the Department of Justice, especially Mr. William J. Burns, Mr. John Edgar Hoover, and Mr. George F. Ruch, have also been particularly helpful with advice and friendly criticism.

My earnest hope is that this book will be helpful to those students of the science of government who are still befogged in the trackless sea of "liberalism" as now defined, and that it will ultimately prove to be a permanent contribution to the bibliography of loyalty to American institutions.

R.M. WHITNEY

Washington, D.C.
February 1924

CHAPTER ONE

The Raid At Bridgman

The most colossal conspiracy against the United States in its history was unearthed at Bridgman, Michigan, August 22, 1922, when the secret convention of the Communist party of America was raided by the Michigan Constabulary, aided by county and federal officials. Two barrels full of documentary proof of the conspiracy were seized and are in possession of the authorities. Names, records, checks from prominent people in this country, instructions from Moscow, speeches, theses, questionnaires — indeed, the whole machinery of the underground organization, the avowed aim of which is the overthrow of the United States Government, was found in such form as to condemn every participant in the convention.

It is now known and can be made public to what extent this movement, inspired from Moscow and directed by Lenin and Trotsky, has grown since the first seeds were sown a few years ago. The seriousness of the menace may now be measured for the first time. The ramifications of the organization are now known. It can be stated with authority that the Workers' party of America is a branch of this organization, placed in the field by orders direct from Moscow and supported by the illegal branches of the Communist party. It is known that agents of the Communists are working secretly, through "legal" bodies, in labor circles, in society, in professional groups, in the Army and Navy, in Congress, in the schools and colleges of the country, in banks and business concerns, among the farmers, in the motion picture industry — in fact, in nearly every walk of life.

These agents are not "lowbrows," but are keen, clever, intelligent, educated men and women. They are experts in their several lines. Their programs, which are now known, show that their plans for inciting the Negroes, the farmers, the clerks, the workmen in industry, members of Congress, employees in government departments everywhere, to violence against the constituted authorities, have been drawn with almost uncanny appreciation of the psychology of each

15

group, with facts and figures so manipulated as to appeal to those approached, with false premises so cleverly drawn as to fool almost anyone.

The names of persons interested directly or indirectly in this movement are astounding. They range from bricklayers to bishops, and include many prominent official and society people. It must be understood that by far the greater number of these people do not know to what they are lending the use of their names and influence or to what they are giving their money. They have been approached to give aid to the Workers' party, or to the many relief organizations which have sprung up disguising Communistic activities, or to the forward-looking, "advanced" schools of political thought. They do not know that their names are on what are known in the secret circles of the Communists as "sucker lists," comprising the names of people who have given to one or another of the various "causes" which are manipulated by the Communists, and who can, if properly approached, be induced to give again.

These are not idle words. The plans and programs of the Communists contain the proofs. But for the length of the documents they might all be printed in full. They are worth the study of all true Americans, for by suggestion and innuendo, they are designed to bring about the moral annexation of the United States to Russia, and by direct words they show that Lenin and Trotsky, with their precious group in Moscow, control the secret as well as the open work of the Communists of America in all its ramifications. The coal and railroad strikes of 1922 are striking examples of the opportunities offered the Communists for making and abetting disorder. For the Communists thrive on disorder. Trouble is a rallying cry for them. They deliberately "plant" their agents in labor unions for the purpose of inspiring disorder. Their creed is to make capital out of strikes, riots, and every other form of popular unrest. Their plans for the coal and railroad strikes, which were so extensive a feature of 1922, were laid in 1921. Their sympathizers attend church meetings for the purpose of presenting arguments to weaken the faith of members of the church. They preach free love, the nationalization of women and children, and openly proclaim that the breaking up of home ties is an advance in civilization.

Many of the leaders of this movement in the United States are foreigners who cannot speak the English language. In the ranks are large groups of non-citizens whose sole reading is the radical papers printed in their native language. Communist literature includes thousands of books, pamphlets, magazines, and newspapers printed in various editions to meet the requirements of their foreign readers; fully a half score of languages other than English are found in this literature. Much of the scheming is done by these foreigners, but a part of it, and practically all the putting into effect of the results of the conspiracies, is the work of native Americans.

The raid at Bridgman will go down in history as one of the most important events in the war against radicalism and world revolution. Seventeen delegates to the convention were arrested on the spot and others were later apprehended in different parts of the country. All who were there have been identified by the records that were captured, which answer any pleas of alibis. The place of the convention was an ideal one. It was in a wooded valley on the estate of Karl Wulfskeel, less than a mile from Bridgman and about twelve miles from St. Joseph and also from Benton Harbor. Small hills surrounded the meeting place, from which lookouts could keep watch and give warning of the approach of strangers. The grove in which the convention was held is close by a few cottages, which the owner was accustomed to rent to summer campers and which served to house the seventy-odd delegates to the convention. The spot could be reached only by a wagon road, not in good repair, so that swift automobiles could not travel with sufficient speed to prevent flight.

Watchers were also stationed in the town of Bridgman to note and report the presence of any strangers, and on August 21 this foresight yielded its rewards. Word was also received from Chicago of a raid in that city on the offices of William Z. Foster, who was in attendance at the Bridgman convention in his official capacity as head of the Trade Union Educational League. Foster and some of the higher-ups from Russia and the United States escaped during the raid, but later seventeen were caught. Foster himself was arrested the next day in Chicago, and denied that he had been at Bridgman — but the authorities had the minutes of the meetings, including roll calls to which Foster had answered "present," and the text of the speech delivered by Foster. Denial was useless.

Preparations had been made, as is always the case at the illegal meetings of the Communists, to hide the records in case of discovery. In this instance a hole had been dug back of one of the cottages, into which were dumped typewriters, mimeograph machines, adding machines, the private papers of the delegates, and the official records of the convention when the authorities swooped down upon the conspirators. They are called conspirators advisedly, for the purpose of the Communist party of America is to overthrow the government of the United States by violence, by armed revolution, and to make this country like present-day Russia.

It is interesting to note that every member of the Communist party has what is known as a "party name," by which alone he is known to the other members. Rule No. 12 of the regulations governing the meetings at Bridgman states that "no one shall disclose or ask for the legal name of any person present." The identity of many members is unknown, although the party name of practically every member is now on record.

The delegates who were in attendance at this illegal annual convention of the Communist party of America came from all parts of the United States. There were also present honored guests (albeit in an official capacity) from Moscow, bearing instructions from their chiefs, Lenin, Trotsky, *et al.,* and they gave explicit orders as to what should be done in this country, looking to its overthrow. There were present besides Foster: C.E. Ruthenberg, three times candidate for mayor of Cleveland; Ben Gitlow, the New York labor leader; Ella Reeve Bloor, who says she has been arrested more than a hundred times for radical agitation among workers; Robert Minor; J. Lovestone; Ward Brooks, direct representative of the Communist International of Moscow; Rose Pastor Stokes, whose spectacular radical career is well known; William F. Dunne, candidate for governor of New York on the ticket of the Workers' party, a "legal" branch of the "illegal" Communist party, and many others. The seventeen arrested at or near Bridgman were Thomas Flaherty of New York; Charles Erickson, Charles Krumbein, Eugene Bechtold, and Caleb Harrison of Chicago; Cyril Lembkin and W. Reynolds, Detroit; William F. Dunne of Butte, Montana, and New York; J. Mihelic, Kansas City; Alex Ball, Philadelphia; Francis Ashworth, Camden, New Jersey; E. McMillin, T.R. Sullivan, and Norman H. Tallentire, St. Louis; Max Lerner, Seattle; and Zeth Nordling, Portland, Oregon.

The convention was called to order on the afternoon of August 17 by Comrade J. Lovestone, secretary to the Central Executive Committee. Lovestone, whose party name is L.C. Wheat, had just returned from a trip to Germany where he secured $32,000 from the International Propaganda Bureau. At the head of this organization is Karl Radek, the notorious Bolshevik who has been identified with the Communist movement since the time of the Brest-Litovsk Treaty and whose real name is Tobiach Sobelsohn.* The International Propaganda Bureau was organized for the specific purpose of pooling and distributing all propaganda funds so that the money could be quickly placed where most needed. A definite proportion of the funds collected in the United States is sent to this bureau in Berlin, a definite proportion being retained for direct propaganda work here.

The convention was quickly organized, committees appointed, and the work begun. William Z. Foster figured largely in the organization, he having been seated as a fraternal delegate by virtue of his position as head of the Trade Union Educational League. Comrades Ben Gitlow and Caleb Harrison were chosen chairmen by the "Presidium," or governing body, of the convention.

The regulations governing the convention, drawn by the ground committee, illustrate the efforts made to prevent the proceedings from becoming known outside the secret circle. All persons were forbidden to leave the grounds without permission of the grounds committee, and if granted this permission they were required to register when leaving and report when returning. "No person shall mingle with strangers," reads Rule No. 4, and the next one provides that no persons shall be allowed to send messages or mail letters. Rule No. 6 reads, "No incriminating literature or documents shall be kept in baggage or in rooms. All such matter must be turned over to the committee every evening. The grounds committee must arrange for the safe keeping of this matter."

The rules prescribed the time lights should be out, what time the delegates should get up in the morning, and when they should bathe and that "all persons going in bathing must wear bathing suits." Lest some trace of their plans become

---

*Webster, Kerlen, Beckwith, *Boche and Bolshevik*, p. 27, Beckwith.

known, it was forbidden to write on tables, seats, or any part of the premises, and all were prohibited from "throwing away papers or written matter of any kind"; it was provided that "all written notes, not longer required, must be handed to the committee for destruction." Roll calls were held three times a day to guard against spies getting in or leaving, and all grants to leave the grounds were to be reported at every roll call.

Following the organization of the convention and the adoption of the rules and regulations, Comrade Ward Brooks of Moscow addressed the convention in German. Notes taken in English by Comrade Max Bedacht, a member of the Central Executive Committee, were found among the buried records. At the outset of his address Comrade Brooks admitted that "for the first time since the Third International" the party was faced by really serious problems. He said:

> The revolutionary situation immediately following the Russian Revolution gave its impress on the Communist International. It was thought that we were really at the beginning of the world revolution. Some say that this crisis will be the final one. Others that it will be followed by a period of prosperity.

Evidently prosperity is not to be desired, for the Communist movement thrives on the dissatisfaction of the masses. Throughout their literature and in all their speeches the Communists stress "class struggle," preaching always the need of creating class consciousness as a step toward the "struggle." Comrade Brooks's explanation of the present situation follows:

> The situation is really that although the economic situation is bettering, still the political consciousness and the class struggle are sharpening. Capitalism has no way out to regain complete health. The situation in the Entente is such that England and France are constantly at odds. America is at odds with the rest of the world. This leads to a great complication of interests. Thus the revolutionary movement is solidifying. Ireland endangers the position of Great Britain on the Continent.
> Germany is the greatest proletarian power, with seventy per cent urban population. The bourgeoisie cannot for any length of time hold power. The slogan of a proletarian government by the German Communist party is not artificial, but is based on the desires of the proletariat. Germany is the seed of Europe. France is so closely connected with Germany that an uprising in Germany would ultimately lead to a revolution in France.

Comrade Brooks went on to report on conditions in Italy, Hungary, Czecho-Slovakia, Poland, Finland, Japan, and Russia, painting the picture in brilliant colors for his American hearers, turning every defeat of Communist plans to victory by twisting the significance of the developments which led to the defeat and claiming the results as satisfactory to the Communists. Among other wild claims he made was that Russia herself had contributed ninety-nine per cent to the relief of the famine sufferers of that country. Then he turned to America:

The American situation. What has happened? Much and better. The Communist party in America sees more concretely, more definitely, its goal and also sees the methods. The tactical questions were never so intensively discussed as during the last year. This will fit them to take the lead in the class struggle. As far as results go nothing is to be seen yet. Are we better or worse off than we were last year? Better, because the party exists and knows why it exists. It is more fit for the purpose of the Communist party than it was last year.

Inasmuch as they were among themselves at Bridgman, there was no need of pretending that the work of the Communists was legal. The differentiation of the legal and illegal branches was made clear, and the fact that the illegal branch is regarded as the more important and the controlling branch was plainly stated. For it is in the work of the illegal branch of the organization that the violations of the laws of the country are committed, the conspiracies fathered by Moscow and imposed upon the party in America are carried out. The report of the Adjustment Committee, of which Robert Minor was chairman and of which Brooks and Reinstein of Moscow were among the members, consisted of revolutionary resolutions, which were adopted, as follows:

1. To multiply tenfold the activities of the whole membership of the Communist party in the trades unions is not only a question of the life and death of the party, but, alongside of another form of the work among the masses, the best counterbalance against controversies that tear the party to pieces.

2. The road to revolution in America leads over the destruction of the power of the yellow leadership of the American Federation of Labor. This aim can be accomplished only through work within the American Federation of Labor for the conquest of this organization. Therefore it is the main task of the Communists to work in the American Federation of Labor.

3. The main goal of the Communists in their trades union work is the unification of all organized labor into one federation.

4. The work in the independent unions must be carried on in the above spirit. The necessary and right amalgamations (not artificial ones) of independent unions within a certain industry or in local councils should be influenced by the Communists so that they are not carried through in a separatist spirit against the American Federation of Labor but as a step toward the general unification of labor and in support of the work within the American Federation of Labor.

5. The tendency for the formation of a national federation of independent unions or the amalgamation of local councils into a competing federation against the American Federation of Labor is harmful.

6. The existing councils wishing to affiliate with the Red Trades Union International should not be discouraged but should be attracted under the condition that they support the trades union program of the party.

Illegal Party Must Continue

1. The illegal Communist party must continue to exist and must continue to direct the whole Communist work.

2. The open work in all forms and especially in No. Two* is the main task of the party.

3. A legal Communist party is now impossible. Should conditions change, only a convention can change the party's policy.

Relations Of One And Two†

1. According to the thesis of the Second World Congress of the Communist International the role of the Communist party in the Proletarian Revolution is, "The Communist party is the organized political lever by means of which the more advanced part of the working class leads all the proletarian and semi-proletarian mass."

2. The Communist party in its revolutionary outlook does in no country feel itself bound by the existing laws forced upon it by the bourgeois class state; not only in the historic revolution which it strives to bring about and which naturally cannot be carried out legally, but also in its activity in the period of preparation does the Communist party and the fighting proletariat come in open conflict with bourgeois justice and the organs of bourgeois state apparatus. Whether in spite of these facts the Communist party can exist as an open party, tolerated by the enemy as a so-called legal party, or whether it must exist as an illegal party, depends upon a number of circumstances which differ in various countries and from time to time. Even an open Communist party must be armed for the eventuality of exceptional laws against it, and also for the carrying out of many permanent tasks it must maintain an illegal apparatus. The present situation in America makes the existence of a legal Communist party, as it exists in Germany, France, Italy, etc., impossible. In spite of all differences America belongs in the category of countries like Finland, Poland, Rumania, Jugoslavia, where the Communist party must be illegal. In spite of the fact that lately an extension of the possibilities of legal activities has taken place, prospects for the possibilities of an open Communist party within a reasonable length of time do not exist. The American illegal Communist party, therefore, is and remains the Communist party, the only section of the Communist International in this country.

3. The centre of gravity of the Communist party lies in its open activities. The whole open work of all Communists in the legal political field, in the trades unions and all other organizations, and in the press, must be directed by the Communist party. The directions of this whole open work will not lead to a neglect of the illegal party work but, quite the contrary, will instill the party with real life and give its work political significance. It will direct its attention to the great problems of the struggle of the proletariat. It will establish the real connections between the party and the masses and their struggle. If in the future No. Two should become a revolutionary mass party which can openly and unrestrictedly operate as and call itself a Communist party, then the present underground organization will become an illegal apparatus within that party and must be adapted to the new situation and new functions. For the practical carrying out of these policies the following rules must be observed:

---

*The legal branch.
†Illegal and legal branches.

A. In all their activities the Communists are subject to the directions and discipline of the party.

B. Every member of the Communist party is in duty bound to be active in No. Two.

C. The Central Executive Committee will see to it that the directing body of No. Two will be subject to its guidance in the composition of its membership as well as in the execution of the political directions of the Central Executive Committee. All meetings of the No. Two must be prepared for by the No. One. This is especially important for the conventions of the No. Two which, under present conditions, must be preceded by a convention of the No. One.

D. The same holds true for local party committees.

E. The meetings of party committees of No. One as well as the organizations and groups of No. One must be devoted, along with inner organizational questions, mainly to discussions of plans of action in the open work. These meetings must not duplicate and thus hinder the open work but must become the driving force of the open activities.

F. The No. Two shall be recruiting ground for the No. One and must be the constant source of new forces.

G. No member of the No. One is allowed to neglect No. One work but must be in constant touch with the illegal organization. This must give the members backbone and direction for the open work.

H. The Central Executive Committee publishes monthly an illegal organ for the discussion of important party questions to be distributed among party members and sympathizers. By actual work the Central Executive Committee must keep in constant touch with the membership so that its decisions are not carried out by purely mechanical means, but also and more important, by a thorough understanding of party policy and technique on the part of the membership.

I. The publication of illegal propaganda and agitational literature for mass distribution shall be adapted to political necessity whenever the legal possibilities are exhausted.

To Proletarian Dictatorship

1. The program of the No. Two must be short. A manifesto which in short, concise sentences, not in the form of a narrative or a syllogism, contains the declaration of principles.

2. The red thread of the program is the idea and the practice of the class struggle. In this connection mass actions should be dealt with. This part must be American; it must deal with partial struggles of the American masses as well as with the general struggle of the thirty million of American workers. In this portion must be stated the basic elements out of which our trade union tactics are developed. The fundamentals of the United Front should be here expressed.

3. The political part must lead up to the climax of the proletarian dictatorship. This formula appears in contradistinction to the dictatorship of the capitalists. American democracy must be analyzed. Rule of the thirty million for the overthrow of capitalism as against rule of Wall Street for the conservation of exploitation. Soviet rule as the historic form of a proletarian regime in the transformation period.

4. One or two sentences may be inserted in a fit place dealing with the yellows and reformists and against the policy of compromise.

Centrists In The Workers' Party

The Workers' party was organized to comprise not only Communists but also sympathizers who, although not yet clear-cut Communists, gravitate toward Communism and accept the moral and political leadership of the Communist International and the Communist Party of America. From that point of view the decided non-Communists and anti-Communists (that is, opponents of the existing Comintern), especially when they belong to the caste of leaders, are not a desirable element in the Workers' party, but are a disturbing and at times even a dangerous element. Even though at a certain period of development we are forced to accept such elements on account of their important following, we must do everything in our power to win this following for us as quickly as possible and to destroy the influence of the non-Communists .... To the question of whether it would be better for us if they go sooner or if it were better they go later, we answer: at the present moment an open breach would mean a split, a weakening and compromising of the as yet extremely weak party. They may therefore remain; but even now already our Communist work within the Workers' party must be doubled and trebled as well as our propaganda for the Workers' party.

Especially dangerous are the positions of power of the centrists and half-centrists in the daily papers. This condition must be remedied immediately. First by organizational measures to get this press absolutely in our control; secondly, by the open criticism of their mistakes in the official organ of the Workers' party, which latter organ must be absolutely in our control; thirdly, by the establishment as soon as possible of an English daily paper.*

The "Coordination of Communist Activity in the Americas"† was discussed at length as a thesis presented to the convention. The chief point made in this thesis was that the Communists of the United States must take the lead in all Communist activity in the Latin American republics because they brand the Latins as backward, lacking in intelligence and in no way strong enough to accomplish anything without the support of the organization in this country. The capitalists of the United States were condemned utterly because they have invested so much money in Latin America, but no credit, naturally, is given for the work of aiding the countries to the south of the United States by giving employment to the people and by developing the natural resources. This extension of capital for use in Latin America is called "imperialism" by the Communists and the warning is sounded that the American capitalists are thus extending their influence for the purpose of finding labor to import into the United States to break strikes. It is also stated in this thesis that:

> The introduction of an exotic capitalism into Latin American countries has opposed to a backward and unripe proletariat the highly developed bourgeoisie of the most powerful capitalistic nation in the world, with the military resources of the United States at its command. The fight is

---

*This daily Communist paper was recently established in Chicago.
†See Appendix A.

unequal. Isolated, the Latin American workers cannot hope to defend their interests successfully against their mighty adversary. They need us as well as we need them. A proletarian revolution anywhere in Latin America is well nigh impossible until there is a revolution in the United States. Wall Street, with its billions of dollars imperilled, would crush it immediately. American imperialism, economic and political, is the instrument of exploitation throughout the western world. In Latin America, as in the United States and Canada, the Class Struggle is a struggle against Wall Street.

Throughout the minutes of the convention, and also in all Communist literature, the letter "X" is used to refer to the Trade Union Educational League, of which William Z. Foster is the head and organizer. This is done in order to aid Foster in his efforts to avoid conflict with the authorities and to make the American people and his opponents in labor union circles believe that it is not connected with the Communist movement. Foster was a member of the committee which drew up the resolutions of the relation of the Communist party to the Trade Union Educational League, adopted by the convention. These resolutions provide specifically that the illegal branch of the party must always be in control of the League. They read as follows:

1. The party recognizes the "X" as one of the most important factors for the revolutionizing of the trade and industrial unions and therefore will take all the necessary measures in order to develop and strengthen it through the active participation of the membership of the party in its work.

2. The formulation of the trade union policies by the party must be based upon the closest contact of the party with the experiences of the trade union nuclei.

3. The general control of the No. One nuclei within X as within all other organizations must be in the hands of the party and not in the hands of the special committees.

4. Contact must be established between the executive committees of the party and the executive committees of the X.

5. No. One nuclei within the X must be made to function regularly.

The most important event, in the eyes of the delegates, was the speech of Foster himself before the convention. His hostility to Samuel Gompers and to the American Federation of Labor, of which Foster is a member, was shown in his address. He told of the work done among the railroad workers and the miners leading up to the strikes of 1922. He counseled violence in overthrowing the government of the United States. He told of his dealings in person with the authorities in Moscow and how the leaders in Russia understood the situation in this country. His speech in part follows:

The fate of the party depends upon its control of the masses. The trade union work is one of the most important things in order to get control of the masses. The influence of the masses can be measured by the amount of control we happen to have in the trade union work in all countries. We have seen the Socialist party here go to pieces, more so than in any other country of the world. The Socialist party in Germany suffered, but not like the Socialist party here. It is practically outside the labor movement. There is nothing left of it.

One of the prime reasons is that the Socialist party in this country never understood the importance of industrial work; never had an industrial policy. It seemed to go along on the idea that the Socialist party should be an organization of citizens in general, and did not realize that the foundation had to be the workers, and not only the workers but the organized workers. The Socialist party never realized that the key to the working class lies through organizations that carry on bread-and-butter, everyday struggles. The consequence was that the Socialist party has wavered ever since it was formed. The Socialist party never crystallized itself. It fell into the hands of Debs, and Debs has been a man who never really grasped the significance of mass organizations. As a consequence, the Socialist party developed a wing that stood for dual organizations, a left wing. The right wing stood for working in trade unions in mild milksop fashion. They used the trade unions merely as vote-getting machines. They did not attach first-rate importance to them. The left wing, led by Debs, Haywood, and others, had the idea of dual organizations, the right wing had an idea of going along in trade union work mildly.

The result was a compromise between the two positions. They endorsed the principle of industrial unionism but failed to direct the active work or attempt to put it into practice. The Socialist party had an industrial program, but they failed because of lack of organized effort. When the war came along, the Socialist party took a stand against the war. The result was that Gompers by controlling strategic points was not only able to sway the masses in favor of the war, but the whole working class as well, and the Socialist party failed to realize the necessity of entrenching itself in these masses and found itself at the end of the limb, amounting to nothing. The whole working class turned against it because it was foolish enough to allow their unions to remain in the hands of the bureaucracy. The split that came along completed the job because of their faulty industrial policy. They could have withstood solidly but, because they had no backing of the workers, they collapsed.

The Communist party is not going to make the same mistake. This laying so much stress on the importance of trade union work is one of the most helpful features of the movement. When we lay stress on the importance of this work, we realize that we must capture the trade unions if we want to get anywhere. Different Communists differ as to the importance of capturing the unions in the revolutionary struggle. Some say that the trade union does not amount to anything; that it is just a neutral organization and will never become a revolutionary unit. Others say that it is one of the really revolutionary instruments of the workers and will function as such in the revolutionary struggle. Syndicalists take the position that trade union work is the only thing. Although we may differ as to the positive value of the trade union work, we must agree with the negative, namely, that it is absolutely impossible to have a revolution in the country unless we will control the mass trade unions. This fact alone should justify the policy that the Communist party of the United States is working out. If we wish a revolution, we must have their support.

After our delegation came back from Moscow last year, it brought with us a program which we thought was a good practical program for this country, and we want to tell you this — a lot of people say that those in Moscow do not understand the situation. I want to dispute that. I found in the Red Trades Union International and in the Communist International and generally in Moscow, a deep understanding of the fundamentals of our situation in this country. I can say that I found a better understanding of the general fundamental situation in America than we can boast of here. It was a peculiar thing to find men like Radek and Lenin telling American revolutionary organizations that their industrial policy was wrong. Radek said, "Your delegation that you had here at the previous congress of the Communist International seemed to be too anxious to get away from the trade unions." They do not know details but understand basic principles of trade unionism, and these fellows were too anxious to find excuses to run away.

Radek knew that these fellows were wrong because of his general knowledge of the international situation and fundamentals of the labor movement. Radek stated that every policy that we are now undertaking we should put into effect. Every leading man in Russia took that position. The important thing is that we finally arrived at a practical foundation for a trade union policy in this country. We came back with this policy and started to put it into effect. It was laid before the Central Executive Committee and endorsed and also before the No. Two and endorsed, and we were instructed to undertake to organize the Trade Union League. We began in February. The program initiated was to simultaneously set up groups in all parts of the country. It was a very good conception and should have worked out better than it did, but unfortunately most of the people were not clear and did not get as good results as should have been gotten.

However, we succeeded in establishing branches of the League in practically all important centres of the country. Some of these branches are small, but I think we have reached the point of development where we no longer measure the importance of revolutionary organizations by size. In some places where there are only one or two men, more results are obtained than where they have larger organizations which spend time fighting and not doing real work. We formed this League, but in forming it we were under a great disadvantage. We did not dare to say it was a Communist organization. It was necessary to camouflage to a certain extent, and for that reason it had to start differently. The ideal way to have started this League was to call a national conference and there adopt a program, endorse the Red Trades Union International program and send it out broadcast. We were unable to do that because it would immediately have been labeled Communist. The alternative was to start it and have the Chicago League function as the national organization until it had union connections established and could call a national conference. That has been the proposition up to the present time. The Chicago League served as the national organization. We picked its executive board which mapped out a policy and served as a national organization. We have now reached the stage where we can call our national conference.

Before I touch on the conference, I would like to say that we started this League with an idea to making it a paying organization, but we had to abandon this idea. In spite of the financial loss, we had to give it up, because the American labor movement is in such a state and the bureaucracy is so ruthless and so weak that we run a great danger of expulsion for dual unionism, and it was necessary to have an organization that did not carry cards but more of a diffuse proposition so that they could not put a finger on it and clean it out.

In France they started out with a policy of accepting affiliation from organizations endorsing the program. It was a left bloc organization. The program was very general in character, to overthrow the yellow bureaucracy. The affiliations from local and national unions and sympathetic ones eventually resulted in the fact that the bureaucracy was able to charge them with having a dual labor movement, and convinced the rank and file and the French trade unions that the R.S.C.* was in reality a dual labor movement, and not only convinced a great portion of them that that was the case, but also convinced the leaders of the R.S.C. themselves that it was an inadvisable thing.

The reason urged for the split was that it was a dual organization. Before the split occurred, the R.S.C. abolished the proposition of accepting affiliations and therefore their organization, to some extent, was on the same basis as the Trade Union Educational League, but it was too late. The fight was made and even by stopping the affiliations it did not have the desired effect of taking away the unions. When the R.S.C. was formed it in many respects was analogous to our own League except that it was dominated by syndicalists, and the Communists were in a minority, whereas in the United States the League is in the hands of the Communists. They paid no attention to excepting dues when discussion on fundamental policy was adopted. Afterwards they found out that it was a great handicap. We decided to accept neither affiliations nor organizations without dues, but rather function in a more advanced manner, at least until we were well intrenched on a firmer basis without danger of expulsion. We have succeeded in making an inroad into a number of organizations. In fact, I find that the American trade union movement is very receptive to a great deal of the program.

The situation on the railroads: we have carried on work not only in the mining districts, but were particularly successful in the railroad trades. To show the ripeness of the American trade unions for this kind of proposition, to concentrate on explaining the situation will be as good as any. We started out with the railroads with a program of industrial unionism. There are sixteen organizations on the railroads. We started out with laying stress on the proposition of industrializing the situation, and started a movement for amalgamation. The trade unions connected with the Trade Union Educational League were instrumental in sending out several thousand letters through local unions. In the face of the convening of the railway employees' convention, we sent out a letter with the idea of industrial organization to the rank and file and delegates to that convention (500), ninety-eight per cent being highly paid officials getting from $400 to $700 a month, more than the presidents. When the convention came together, Knudson and I spoke to as many delegates as we could and the result was that between sending out these letters and one meeting, we set up a stampede among the delegates of the convention and had a majority on record for our program.

*Revolutionary Socialist Committee (France).

This shows conditions as they were at the convention. Samuel Gompers came to Chicago for the purpose of spiking the League and preventing it from having any effect on the convention, and he held a public meeting and advanced the League as being financed by Moscow and out to destroy the unions. He sent a man there to address the workers. He was denied the right to speak to the convention, but in spite of all that, we succeeded in stampeding these under-officers for that much of the program. Could that happen in France or any other country where a lot of fellows could stampede a convention of high-paid officials? It could not be done. In no other movement in the world is there such a thing. If we were able to stampede the majority of this convention, what can we do with the rank and file? The president of the railway employees' department issued a challenge to me to the effect that these people who talk industrial unionism should help them get down to something concrete and something definite.

We drafted a program for industrial unionism and sent out 11,000 copies to every trade union in America. This cost the party absolutely nothing. It was so organized as to pay for itself. The trade unions in Minneapolis and St. Paul raised the money and circularized all the railroad unions in the country. We knew that the strike was coming along and tried to be on the job. The strike occurred with the result that there was the great object lesson of bosses using one section to defeat the other. The leaders were cowards and did not dare tell the men that the brotherhoods were at work. It fell upon our League to show the men this. We were the only element in America to point out the lessons of this strike. The leaders did not dare to mention it and we did. The result has been that our propaganda has run like wildfire through the railroad men of the country.

So far in the railroad situation we have merely talked industrial unionism to them. We have not raised the issue of the Red Trade Union International and various other issues. If we have not raised them our enemies have and in the campaign wherever the officials have taken a hand in it, they said that the Trade Union Educational League is purely a Communist organization, and the rank and file know definitely whom its program has come from and what is involved. In such a desperate state, and destitute of leadership on the part of any of the officials, they are accepting it anyhow. During the strike I could go before them and talk anything at all. The wall has broken and we have succeeded in getting a grip in these organizations and have got them coming our way. We have got to break the monopoly of the press.

The bureaucracy of the trade unions has got the press which is one of the secrets of control, and we must try to aim at that — the breaking of the monopoly of the press, and with the great volume of sentiment we could succeed.

I am not trying to overstress the importance of industrial trade unionism. The workers of America are ready for new ideas. There is nothing to be got from the old machine and if we will go to them, they will listen to what we have got to say. In our conference we should be very careful about the program that we adopt. As far as I am concerned, we should adopt a clear-cut revolutionary program. Adopt a proposition endorsing Russia and endorsing the dictatorship of the proletariat in Russia. Adopt a resolution calling for the affiliation with the Red Trade

Union International without qualifications. Adopt a program calling for industrial organizations, and adopt a revolutionary program as the basis of our work. Popularize it and let it be spread broadcast. It is a strange thing that some of our men who are most extreme radicals left us and advocated the idea that we go careful on the industrial field. It is a strange situation, but natural.

The relations of No. One and No. Two (the illegal and legal branches of the party) to each other was set forth in a thesis that was adopted by the convention.* It was prepared with great care by an important committee of which J. Lovestone, executive secretary of the party in America, was chairman. It provides for the permanency of the illegal branch, setting forth explicitly that even after the Communist party becomes strong enough to come out in the open the illegal branch will be necessary to direct the conspiracies of the party. It says at the outset, in discussing the "necessity of a Communist party":

> All experience in the modern class struggle proves that the working class can emerge victorious only after developing an organ of leadership in the form of a highly disciplined Communist party, thoroughly conscious of revolutionary principles and tactics. The first task of the Communists is, therefore, to develop such a party.

The authors of this thesis point out that while education and propaganda are necessary in preparing for the final great armed revolution, it is more important that all Communists have a major task in the "participation in all the struggles of the workers as the most active force." The inciting of "masses," not individuals or even small groups, to violence is held to be the chief effort to which the Communists should lend themselves. It holds that "the leadership of the masses of the exploited can be attained only by directly engaging in all their struggles together with the masses of the workers." It then urges that political organizations are necessary and states that "in America it has become the most urgent, immediate task of the Communists to secure a public, open, so-called 'legal' existence as an organization." The significance of the following paragraphs is obvious.

> A truly revolutionary (i.e. Communist) party can never be "legal" in the sense of having its purpose harmonize with the purpose of the laws made by the capitalist state, or its acts conform with the intent of capitalist law. Hence, to call a Communist party "legal" means that its existence is tolerated by the capitalist state because of circumstances which embarrass the capitalist state's efforts to suppress it. The revolutionary party can avoid suppression into a completely secret existence only by one or both of two means:
>   a. By taking advantage of the pretenses of "democratic forms" which the capitalistic state is obliged to maintain. By this means

---

*See Appendix B.

the Communists can maintain themselves in the open with a restricted program while establishing themselves with mass support.

b. (Later stage) By commanding such mass support among side masses of workers that enable them to proclaim publicly their final object in the revolutionary struggle and manoeuvre openly to attain this object regardless of the desire of the capitalist state to suppress it. It is necessary at the present time (and circumstances make it the most urgent immediate need) to resort to the first of the before-mentioned methods of open contact with the working masses; which means to maintain an open political party with a modified name and a restricted program.

The thesis continues:

A legal political party with such restrictions cannot replace the Communist party. It must also serve as an instrument, in the complete control of the Communist party, for getting public contact with the masses. It must mobilize the elements of the workers most sympathetic to the Communist cause, with a program going as far toward the Communist program as possible while maintaining a legal existence. It must, with a course of action in daily participation in the workers' struggle, apply Communist tactics and principles, and thus win the trust of the masses, and prepare them for the leadership of the Communist party.

Again it is declared that:

The overthrow of the capitalist system can only come through the overthrow of the capitalist state. To accept this view is to accept the certainty that the capitalist state will find itself in violent conflict with the masses led by the Communist party. While the capitalist state retains the governmental machinery, and as the struggle grows sharper in approaching the final struggle, the capitalist state will inevitably strike again and again at the revolutionary party in the effort to destroy it. After the Communist party shall have established itself in the open, it must be prepared for and must expect to be driven out of a "legal" existence from time to time. The Communist party must at all times be so organized that such attacks cannot destroy it. It must perform its functions of leadership in the class struggle no matter what tactics the ruling class adopts — open as far as possible, secretly as far as it must.

For this reason, it argues, the underground machinery of the Communist party, that is, the illegal machinery, is not merely a temporary device, but is for permanent use.

There is never a time, previous to the final overthrow of the capitalist state, when a truly revolutionary party does not have to perform a considerable amount of work free from police knowledge and inter-ference. The Communist party will never cease to maintain its underground machinery until after the establishment of the dictator-ship of the proletariat in the form of the Workers' Soviet Republic.

It is held to be necessary for all members of the legal party to become members of the No. One or illegal part of the party, and it is impressed upon all members of the No. One to be supporters of the legal political party. Then the thesis urges activity in the work of the Communist party caucuses, in the ranks of trade unions, constantly striving to alienate conservative members of the unions from their conservative ideas, thus increasing the sphere of influence of the radicals in the union ranks until they become all-powerful.

The Pittsburgh District presented a thesis complaining of lack of action at the present time. This thesis said that the party was not thinking enough of its immediate work in America, was relying too much on instructions and orders from abroad (meaning Russia), and that it was and always must be largely in control of foreign elements because the English-speaking workers always get the easiest jobs. It says: "The Communist party is not organized for itself and for the satisfaction of idealists, but we are a rough fighting organization, aiming to bring about a mass movement in this country led by us."

Comrade Lovestone also presented "a brief statement of the progress and aims of the African Blood Brotherhood," which calls for a liberated race, "liberated not merely from alien political rule, but also from the crushing weight of capitalism"; absolute race equality, "political, social, and economic"; the fostering of race pride, "fellowship within the darker races and with the class-conscious and revolutionary white workers"; higher wages and lower rents. The entire program is intended to incite the Negroes to attain by violence the ends specified.

The work of the World War Veterans was also highly commended by Lovestone, who presented to the convention the constitution and bylaws of the organization and a declaration of principles which has many revolutionary features. It declares its unalterable opposition to any form of compulsory military training, and to "any interference, official or unofficial, with any right secured by us by the first amendment to the Federal Constitution." It also expresses sympathy with, and states that the organization shares the aspirations of, "the people of India, Egypt, Ireland, and Russia."

The split in the Communist party of America in December 1921, when three members of the Central Executive Committee broke away from the majority members and continued publishing their illegal paper under the same name as that used officially by the party, *The Communist,* was taken to Moscow for settlement. Each faction sent representatives to Moscow, and the authorities there decided in favor of the majority, ordering the minority faction to return at once to the fold and the majority faction to receive them without prejudice. This in explanation of the following messages received from Moscow and read to the convention. The first of these, a cablegram, reads:

BOTH SALESMEN RETURNING HOME WITH FULL IN-
STRUCTIONS FROM BOARD DIRECTORS STOP POSTPONE
STOCKHOLDERS MEETING UNTIL THEY ARRIVE STOP
ACKNOWLEDGE RECEIPT.

This cablegram was signed "Block and Company" and apparently relates to business matters. "Block and Company" are Comrades Jake Cannon and Bittleman, agents for the majority faction sent to Moscow. They, of course, are the "salesmen." The "board of directors" is the Comintern or governing body of the Communist Third International, and the "stockholders meeting" is the convention at Bridgman. If it had been postponed the raid might not have taken place. The second message was a radiogram, also apparently a business message, which reads:

HENRY CURTIS DOW COMPANY INSTRUCTED QUIT USING
OUR FIRM NAME AND TRADEMARK STOP THEY MUST DIS-
SOLVE AND REJOIN OUR COMPANY IMMEDIATELY OR LOSE
THEIR STOCK STOP JOHN IS WIRING THEM TO QUIT COMPETING
AND ATTACKING OUR BUSINESS STOP YOU MUST ACCEPT
THEM WITHOUT PREJUDICE AND POSTPONE SHAREHOLDERS
CONFERENCE SO THEY CAN PARTICIPATE.

"Henry Curtis Dow" are the party names of the minority members who seceded from the Central Executive Committee; the "firm name and trademark" are the Communist organ. "John" is John J. Ballam of Winthrop, Massachusetts, who was sent by the minority leaders to Moscow.

Comrade Lovestone then read from the "newsletter"* sent out from the party headquarters with instructions to "rush to every group" the information that "Comrade Cook, member of the Presidium of the Comintern and the Presidium of the Red Trade Union International, has been ordered to return home (from Moscow) immediately, with full instructions from the Communist International," and urging all districts to hold themselves in readiness to call hurried meetings to hear the instructions. He says in this newsletter that the Central Executive Committee, by a vote of five to five, had decided not to postpone the Bridgman convention in spite of instructions to do so. This was doubtless because of the preparations already made for holding the meetings and the difficulty of disseminating the news of the postponement without letting the secret be known.

The imperative need of a "united front" of the workers was also presented by Comrade Lovestone in a thesis on political activity.† After stating that "a united front of labor, a solid phalanx of the working class drawn up in battle against the forces of the capitalist state is the prerequisite of the victory of the proletariat," he declared that the groups of workers already in the labor

*See Appendix D.
†See Appendix E.

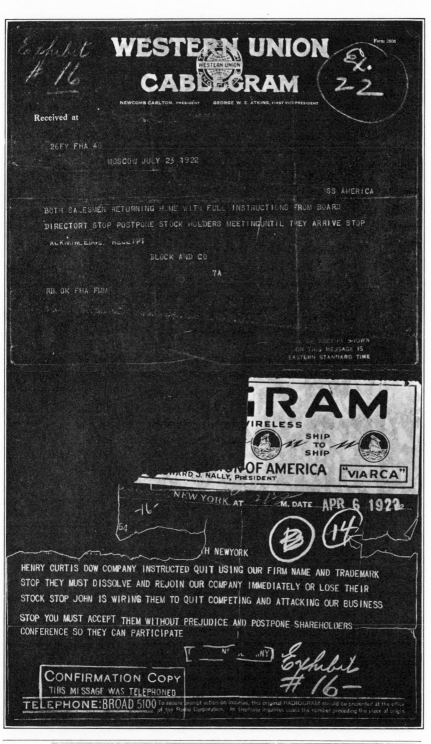

WESTERN UNION CABLEGRAM

Form 2606

NEWCOMB CARLTON, PRESIDENT   GEORGE W. E. ATKINS, FIRST VICE-PRESIDENT

Received at

26FY FHA 40

MOSCOW JULY 25 1922

SS AMERICA

BOTH SALESMEN RETURNING HOME WITH FULL INSTRUCTIONS FROM BOARD
DIRECTORT STOP POSTPONE STOCK HOLDERS MEETING UNTIL THEY ARRIVE STOP
ACKNOWLEDGE RECEIPT

BLOCK AND CO

7A

RD. OK FHA FMM

THE TIME OR RECEIPT SHOWN
ON THIS MESSAGE IS
EASTERN STANDARD TIME

RAM
WIRELESS
SHIP TO SHIP
OF AMERICA "VIARCA"

WARD J. NALLY, PRESIDENT

NEW YORK AT 2/5 M. DATE APR 6 1922

64   -16-

H NEWYORK

HENRY CURTIS DOW COMPANY INSTRUCTED QUIT USING OUR FIRM NAME AND TRADEMARK
STOP THEY MUST DISSOLVE AND REJOIN OUR COMPANY IMMEDIATELY OR LOSE THEIR
STOCK STOP JOHN IS WIRING THEM TO QUIT COMPETING AND ATTACKING OUR BUSINESS
STOP YOU MUST ACCEPT THEM WITHOUT PREJUDICE AND POSTPONE SHAREHOLDERS
CONFERENCE SO THEY CAN PARTICIPATE

Exhibit # 16

CONFIRMATION COPY
THIS MESSAGE WAS TELEPHONED

TELEPHONE: BROAD 5100 To secure prompt action on inquiries, this original RADIOGRAM should be presented at the office
of the Radio Corporation. In telephone inquiries quote the number preceding the place of origin

Cablegrams sent by the Executive Committee of the Third (Communist) International to the convention of the Communist Party of America in session at Bridgman,
Mich. The messages have been decoded in the text.

organizations, and independent groups of workers, must unite to attain this end. Without mentioning names, he referred repeatedly to the "treacherous leaders" of organized labor who have fought the idea of the labor party, and cautioned that because of this the word "labor" must be kept out of the name of the new party. He approved support of the labor organizations when they have united on an independent candidate for office, but warned against lending support to the labor unions when the latter are supporting the candidate of any other party.

"The basis for a united political front," he said in announcing the program for the coming elections in the United States, "which will embrace the working masses, has not yet been created in the United States. To enter into a political federation with existing political organizations, none of which has the support of the masses of the workers, would be to negate the possibility of creating a real united front of the workers politically. The Workers' party will, therefore, as a rule, nominate its own candidates in the coming elections and carry on its campaigns independently."

In referring to the platform, he said: "The platform must raise as the issues of the campaign immediate questions of the class struggle, such as unemployment relief, the open shop, the use of the injunction against the workers, opposition to industrial courts, etc." He also said that special permission may be secured from the Central Executive Committee to place a candidate on the ticket of an existing working class political organization if it is impossible to launch an independent ticket.

An exhaustive report of the activities of the party, especially in relation to the organization itself, followed. This report bitterly assailed the minority trouble-makers, and precipitated a scorching debate, but documents found by the authorities show that this trouble was settled by the resignation of the three trouble-makers and the election of Robert Minor, A. Wagenknecht, and E. Browder in their places. This was in obedience to the mandate from Moscow, and resulted in the unification of the party in America. This settlement of factional fighting within the party was followed by the issuance of a "special bulletin," one copy to be sent to each group in the country, with the injunction to "read this carefully: study each point thoroughly; and then make sure this is put into action." The bulletin deals with the relations of the members in legal and illegal work of the party, and states that the organization is enlarging its scope of work, and that new responsibilities are imposed on each member. The features of the conspiracy laid bare in this document, with the injunction of secrecy, are foreign in nature to the American mind, but are part and parcel of the communist work.

The bulletin says:

All members of the No. One must join the No. Two, and activities of the latter are to be broadened as extensively as possible. We have no room for anyone who does not participate whole-heartedly. No. One must be strengthened by all possible means. No liquidators will be tolerated and all rights must be watched. Every member of No. One must submit to an iron discipline in both No. One and No. Two. If anyone is called upon to do a certain task, he or she must carry it out unflinchingly.

All addresses of connections of No. One must be kept in code, and all incriminating material is to be kept absolutely safe; if possible outside of the place where you live. All records of No. One must be kept safely and the identity of the members of No. One working in offices or upon committees or in units of No. Two, as well as their relations to No. One, must not be exposed .... All groups are to have alternate captains. All branches are to have alternate organizers ....

We must endeavor to have a majority of our members on all important committees, and all our members to fill the offices of No. Two .... Use nothing but the real names in No. Two. Get used to speaking in terms that will not in any way reveal connections with No. One. Do not discuss any of the specific affairs of No. One in meetings of No. Two.

Under the head of "Industrial Activities" the bulletin says:

The proper conduct of this line of activities is dependent upon the alertness and understanding of our forces, and must be controlled and guided by No. One — the same principle applies here as was laid down before, that all decisions as to policies and fundamental principles, as well as tactics, are to be decided upon by No. One before being carried out in No. Two. We must organize nuclei of members of No. Two, and work as a unit within these nuclei, and become a live factor in all the activities; but at all times keep our forces intact. We must endeavor to create left wing militant groups within the labor organizations in which we must also become the leading factor.

The end of this illegal, secret, mysterious convention came suddenly. On the afternoon of August 20, William Z. Foster saw on the grounds a man he recognized as a government official. Within a half hour Foster was on his way to the railroad station at Bridgman with several of the other delegates. He did not warn his comrades but promised to send more watchers from Chicago. The next day the watchers in the town of Bridgman reported the presence of Chicago detectives arriving in town. In view of these facts the Presidium decided to end the convention that day and so notified Comrade Caleb Harrison, who was presiding. The Presidium called a special meeting for the final proceedings, which were rushed through with machine-like speed. It was then night, and no raid had come, but the delegates were warned of their danger, the grounds committee advised everyone to leave, and the records, private papers, etc., were buried in the hole already prepared for such an emergency. But there was no train they could take from Bridgman before evening, so many of the delegates decided to stay in the grove. During the night, several made their way carefully out of danger, and in the morning the officers gathered in those who were left.

CHAPTER TWO

In Political Fields

Existing political parties in the United States are more loosely organized than ever before in their history. There is little party discipline, and political consciousness which involves deliberate consideration of party principles is non-existent or at a low ebb. Therefore, political contests resolve themselves into personal contests, and the tendency is toward a government of men rather than a government of laws. Many causes have contributed to bring about this state of affairs, but there has been no more potent one than that of the Communist-radical movement itself. The objective is best illustrated by the present political situation in England, where party lines are more or less completely obliterated and there has risen a workers' party controlled by a secretly organized minority, with Moscow always in the background giving moral aid and financial assistance. In other words, the realignment has been along class lines. In the development of this realignment in the United States, the revolutionaries have approached the objective by both direct and indirect methods. There has been the formation of a direct action political party called the "Workers' party," which is absolutely dominated by the illegal Communist party, and in turn by the Third International at Moscow. With the capture of the documentary evidence at Bridgman, the political manipulations of this alien group are now thoroughly understood. There can be no further doubt as to either the objective or the methods that are being employed.

But of the insinuating methods used under the cover of respectability and regularity, methods in which secrecy is a prime requisite for success and which will eventually bring about revolution by legislative enactment, or pave the way for revolution by force, only too little is generally understood. One difficulty which retards understanding of this angle of the problem is the necessarily complicated machinery which has been set in motion to accomplish the result. Few people stop to square details with general principles. The fact that there is now in Congress a bloc which is bent on carrying out the detailed behests of the

Communist party, repudiating at the same time the name by which the movement should be designated, and that this bloc is itself built up on class lines, is not an accident but the best evidence of design.

Until that time has arrived when a workers' or labor party has been built up with sufficient strength to carry elections under its own name, the gradual disappearance of the regular party lines may be expected. It is a situation which presents very little natural opposition to those who would use the machinery of party government for subversive purposes. In fact, it favors the entrance of radicals into the political field through regularly established channels. The radicals have a positive program as opposed to those more conservative who have either no program or one that is more or less neutral. They have a positive advantage which is difficult to overcome, and all of which is quite in harmony with recognized psychological laws.

When a radical, having received the approval of the Republican or Democratic party machinery, is presented to the electorate, the citizen must vote in the last analysis for or against the Flag, which in times past has stood for certain definite principles. There is no middle ground. The choice is usually made with no such thought in mind, for to make it a conscious thought, there would be required a knowledge of men and events, a grasp of the principles and science of government, and the use of careful analytic powers such as few possess. Consequently, mere inaptitude for political thought, which is a common characteristic, favors the election of the more dramatic figure or the one who has a positive program, no matter how fantastic or opposed to sound principles that program may be.

The Communist party of America has presented candidates for office many times to different electorates, under the legal emblem of the open political organization known as the Workers' party. In the raid upon the illegal convention at Bridgman, William F. Dunne, who at that very time was a candidate of the Workers' party for the governorship of New York State, was arrested. He was a member of the Central Executive Committee of the Communist party of America, and by virtue of such membership, he was one of ten who controlled the Communist movement in this country under direct orders from the Executive Committee of the Third International at Moscow. He is still (1924) a member of the Executive Committee of the Workers' party. It is not at all likely that Dunne could ever be elected as governor of New York on any ticket. The Communist party of America does not number more than 30,000 persons throughout the whole of the United States, and a majority or more are aliens, not naturalized. To hope that as a party with this numerical strength the Communists could carry an election is fatuitous even to them. The danger does not lie in this direction. A proper conception of the strength of the Communist party in the political field can be attained only by recognizing the fact that a large number of people and their political leaders are believers in political and economic projects which are a part of the Communist party program developed by the Third International at Moscow, but which in detail are not recognized by them as part of a definite and inclusive program. It is not permissible to call such persons "Communists," no matter how closely their ideals approximate those of the Communist party. One may include them within the definition of the word "radical," but that word in reality means little. The meaning of "progressive" has been utterly perverted, and its use to cover a socialistic-communistic political movement can best be expressed by "a shorter and uglier word" familiar to everybody.

The objective of the Communist party is political and economic control of the country through manipulation of an uneducated minority, using the idea of communism as a means to an end. Those who are cleverly directing the policies are certainly aware of the fact that all history shows the futility of communism as a political system, and this raises immediately the question of their sincerity. But in the accomplishment of this objective, the leaders are quite ready to use many things and people at this time which, as their plans develop, would be of little or no use to them later. To the Communists, present usefulness of a project may depend on many factors, such as the simple tendency to upset established customs or institutions, inherent possibilities or value for agitation or the promotion of unrest, violence, and crime; the breaking down of family life; or the decrease of the authoritative influence of religion. All or any would contribute to a state of flux or an instability of which world revolutionaries would take full advantage. The time for radical change in anything is not now.

Therefore, the political influence of the Communist party extends far beyond the confines of its own membership, permeating the minds and controlling the thought of large numbers who would violently resent the implication that they were Communists. The subversiveness of the Communist party does not lie so much in the violence which it threatens as in the insinuation of ideals and ideas which are undermining our representative republican form of government. When these facts are taken into consideration, the strength of the Communist party in political fields immediately assumes a monstrous aspect. Under our present definition of the word "radical" we are justified in regarding radicals as conscious or unconscious tools of the Communist party, helping in the cause of world revolution, brushing aside the question of the willingness of the tools to be used.

The warning has gone forth from the headquarters of both major political parties that there is danger of radicalism in their respective ranks. The warning was entirely justified. The voter has no protection against the insinuation of personages on political tickets whose ideas do not square with those of the men who were the founders of the Republic. Insinuations of this sort, operating through the formation of nuclei, are not confined to the political field. Agents are planted in labor unions, social and society circles, and eleemosynary organizations for the purpose of gradually securing the adhesion of dissatisfied individuals and factions for the support of the Communist cause, or at least to secure the non-opposition of the more conservative. This is done precisely and with design as a part of a plan. Again, in the field of politics, some candidates for office running on "regular" tickets have the direct and secret support of the Communist party and its friends, whose backing results from definite promises. Other candidates, however, be it said to their credit, stand squarely for honest Americanism and against the cohorts under the Red banner which would destroy the American government, home, and church.

In formulating a judgment as to the activities of the Conference for Progressive Political Action, due regard must be paid to all that has been presented above. As an organization, it has chosen to assume a name which misrepresents its political objective. It has made the gesture of refusing to seat delegates from the Workers' party, which is the legal branch of the illegal Communist party. Its political program parallels that laid down by the Moscow overlords in the "Next Tasks of the Communist Party of America" (see Chapter 12), and carried to its logical conclusion would lead to "workers' control." The program, therefore, is simply a means to an end. Even the Executive Committee of the Third International at Moscow has no word of criticism for the Conference for Progressive Political Action, for in discussing this organization in its thesis, "The Workers' Party on the United Front" (Appendix E), it says in effect that in the field of general politics now covered by the Conference, the methods used are not applicable in the field of labor. From a technical standpoint it may not be possible to designate the Conference for Progressive Political Action as an important "front" for the Communist party, or to place it along with the Friends of Soviet Russia as an open, legal branch of the Communist party of America. But, as a matter of fact, the "Conference" is doing exactly the work which the Communist leaders at Moscow have evidently allocated to it, whether the personnel of the "Conference" is aware of that fact or not.

To call it a socialist organization as opposed to communist is specious, for in a thesis on tactics adopted by the Third International, the Moscow group rightly says: "The realization of socialism is the first step towards the communist commonwealth."

Following is something of the history and personnel of the Conference for Progressive Political Action, which has succeeded in attracting the adherence of a part of the following of the late Theodore Roosevelt.

Townley and the Non-Partisan League, having stolen the machinery of the Republican party in North Dakota, were finally driven from power through operations of the recall. In July 1921, Non-Partisan leaders left over from this defeat and Socialist party leaders of the more radical types met in Detroit and passed the following resolution:

Be it Resolved: That the incoming national executive committee be instructed to make a careful survey of all radical and labor organizations in this country with a view of ascertaining their strength, disposition and readiness to cooperate with the socialist movement on a platform not inconsistent with that of the party.

As Fred R. Marvin pointed out:

> This survey was made and it was found, as every one knows, that there was a vast amount of unrest, distrust, ill feeling, and class consciousness; that the farmers were disgruntled at the fall in prices; that the workers were sore at the cut in wages; that the consumer was of the belief that somewhere along the line he was not getting a square deal; that business was in a bad way; that the persistent use of the term "profiteer" had caused the people to believe every business man dishonest and unfair; that the railroads, after being returned to their owners, were having a hard struggle to function properly; that money was tight, etc. In other words, they found the very foundation upon which they hoped to lay their campaign for political control most favorable.
>
> Committee meetings were held in November 1921 and it was agreed that any conference of all radicals called by the socialist party would fail of its purpose. In consequence the call was not issued at the instigation of radical leaders of some labor organizations, which had been drafted into the great socialist scheme to nationalize the railroads of the United States, under the name of the Plumb Plan. The actual call was headed by William Johnston of the International Machinists' Union, the leading union in the 1922 railroad strike, and bore the name of LaFollette's organization, the People's Legislative Service of Washington, of which Johnston is secretary and treasurer. Johnston is a socialist and an ardent advocate of the present Russian form of government.[*]

It was obvious that, to make the Conference effective, the interest of the radical farmers must be aroused. To this end, it was no accident that Ben Marsh, working with Townley from the latter's headquarters in Washington, on the day that Johnston sent out his call for delegates from all radical movements to meet in Chicago on February 20 and 21, 1922, sent out another call to the known radical farmer movements to send delegates to Chicago on Saturday, February 18, 1922.

Both conferences met according to plan. Townley with his Non-Partisan League, the LaFollette organization of farmers in Wisconsin, Marsh's organization known as the Farmers' National Council, and a few radical Granges and farmers' unions, had delegates present. Marsh and Townley dominated the meeting. Marvin again tells the story:

> They proceeded with the usual socialist harangue of damning capitalism, and charged all defects in farming from short crops to grasshoppers to Wall Street. The socialist scheme of stealing party organizations was endorsed. The name adopted for the amalgamation of all radical farmer movements was the United Farmers National Bloc. A pronounced radical

---

[*]Fred R. Marvin, *My Country, 'Tis of Thee,* p. 8, Beckwith.

was made president, and the present vice president of the Non-Partisan League was made vice president. Then the delegates of this convention in body moved over, Monday, to the radical convention called by Johnston, in keeping with the socialist resolution to which reference has been made.

In this Monday convention, February 20, 1922, were to be found delegates from every radical movement in the United States, and while the newspaper reports said the I.W.W. and the Communists were excluded, yet it would appear from later articles in the *New York Call*, the leading daily Socialist paper in this country, that they were not excluded, but were present.

Here again the system employed in the alleged farmers' meeting was adopted. Fiery speeches were made by radicals of all kinds. Capitalism was blamed for all human ills. Soviet Russia was lauded. The man who pays the wages was condemned as tyrannical. The plan of the socialists to unite under one common head all radical movements in the land was approved. But no party name was adopted, since it was not proposed to act as a party, but rather to adopt the Townley scheme of "stealing" party names through going into the primaries of one of the old parties — the plan so successfully employed in North Dakota and Wisconsin. The names "radical," "socialist," "labor," "farmer," "industrial," etc., which had been used in the past were dropped, and there emerged an organization known as the "Conference for Progressive Political Action," to be directed, until the next convention, to be held after the election this fall, by a committee of fifteen.

This conference agreed that in the states which were to be attacked through the system of stealing party names, local conditions should govern action — that is, in one State it might operate under the name of "the People's Reconstruction League" and in another under some other name, or it might operate without any accepted name — just work to "steal" one of the party names.

This is the organization that is, today, directing socialist and radical activities in a large number of states, including Colorado. The dropping of every name employed in the past and adopting the term "progressive" is deceiving a large number of loyal persons . . . .

That the movement is of radical origin and not for the good of the people, the State, or the nation is clear. First, referring back to the resolution adopted by the socialist convention, upon which resolution the call for the conference that formed the Conference for Progressive Political Action was based — remember that a similar call in 1907 by the same elements resulted in the formation of the I.W.W. Further, from the time of the issuance of this call, socialist and radical papers had much to say of the good that would result. Johnston was lauded in the socialist papers for his action and the purpose was unanimously endorsed. For several weeks preceding the convention, the *New York Call*, at that time the leading socialist paper in the country, contained much laudatory comment on the proposed gathering.

At that time the confederation known as the Conference for Progressive Political Action consisted of the following organizations:

1. The "Big Four" Railroad Brotherhoods.
2. Railroad crafts, which are a part of the American Federation of

Labor and which include the United Brotherhood of Maintenance of Way Employees and Railway Shop Laborers, the International Association of Machinists, the International Brotherhood of Blacksmiths and Helpers, the Sheet Metal Workers, the Brotherhood of Railway Electrical Workers, the Brotherhood of Railway Car Men, the International Brotherhood of Boilermakers, the Order of Railroad Telegraphers, the Brotherhood of Railway Clerks, the International Brotherhood of Stationary Firemen and Oilers, and the Brotherhood of Railroad Signal Men.

3. The United Mine Workers, affiliated with the American Federation of Labor.

4. The Amalgamated Clothing Workers, an open, legal branch of the Communist party.

5. The Non-Partisan League, composed largely of farmers in the Northwestern States, which has received the sympathetic endorsement of the Communist party of America.

6. The Farmers' National Council.

7. The Farm Labor party, later merging into the Federated Farm-Labor party.

8. The Women's Trade Union League.

Of the original National Committee of the Conference for Progressive Political Action, William H. Johnston was the chairman and Warren S. Stone the treasurer. Some of the personal histories and connections of the committee members are given here:*

William H. Johnston, Washington; president, International Association of Machinists; lecturer, Rand School of Social Science; National Advisory Committee, National Labor Alliance for Trade Relations With and Recognition of Russia; National Council, League for Industrial Democracy; secretary-treasurer and member of the Executive Committee of LaFollette People's Legislative Service; vice president, People's Reconstruction League; Board of Directors, Labor Publication Society; Executive Committee, American Civil Liberties Union. Has been accused of saying that he "sees great advantage in the establishment of a soviet government in the United States."

Warren S. Stone, grand chief, Brotherhood of Locomotive Engineers; member of the National Council, People's Legislative Service; member of Committee on Primaries of same organization; organizer of Labor Banks in Cleveland and New York. As grand chief of the Brotherhood, he is responsible for the political activities of its official journal and its ultra-radical editor, Albert F. Coyle.

William Green, Indianapolis; secretary, United Mine Workers of America.

Sidney Hillman, New York; president of the Amalgamated Clothing Workers; has visited Soviet Russia and obtained concessions for the re-establishment of the clothing industry in that country, capitalizing this by selling stock to workers in this country; Defense Committee, I.W.W. The Amalgamated has been shown to be an open, legal branch of the Communist party of America. Of the documents seized at Bridgman, one

---

*See *Railway Review* (Chicago), January 27, 1923.

was a report to Moscow of the work of organizing nuclei in trades unions by the Communists, in which it was stated: "At best the prospects of our influencing the labor movement (in the United States) are mainly in the predominantly Jewish organizations like the International Ladies' Garment Workers, Amalgamated Clothing Workers, Hat, Cap, and Millinery Workers, etc."

Joseph A. Franklin, Kansas City, Kansas; president, International Brotherhood of Boilermakers, Iron Ship Builders and Helpers of America; member, National Council, People's Legislative Service; member, Executive Committee, People's Reconstructive Service.

E.J. Manion, St. Louis, Missouri; president, Order of Railroad Telegraphers; chairman, Nominations Committee, Conference for Progressive Political Action; member, National Council, People's Legislative Service.

Edward Keating, Washington, D.C.; editor, *Labor*, official organ of the Conference for Progressive Political Action; former member of Congress from Colorado. Of *Labor*, it has been said: "It is one of the most radical and untruthful publications published. Its advocacy of violence is persistent. There is nothing too scurrilous and even defamatory for it to print regarding public officials and even the President of the United States. Its untruthful campaign against the Supreme Court could not be equalled even if openly presented by the Communist International and its well-trained corps of propagandists. Indeed, the language appearing in *Labor* and in foreign Communist papers impels one to believe the writing is that of one and the same person."*

Morris Hillquit (Misca Hilkowicz), New York; national secretary, Socialist party of America; joint publisher of *New York Call*, Socialist and pro-Soviet daily paper, now defunct; instructor and lecturer, Rand School of Social Science; national council, League for Industrial Democracy; National Committee, American Civil Liberties Union; one of the original founders of the Intercollegiate Socialist League; contributing editor, *Labor Age;* chairman, Committee on Organization and Finance, Conference for Progressive Political Action. (See also Lusk Committee Report.)

Benjamin C. Marsh, Washington, D.C.; managing director, Farmer' National Council; managing director, People's Reconstruction League; publicity representative, Plumb Plan League; advocate of Single Tax and nationalization of public utilities.

Jay G. Brown, Chicago; national secretary, Farm-Labor party; formerly secretary of the National Committee for Organizing Iron and Steel Workers, a position once held by William Z. Foster. He was also a former I.W.W. organizer and was a director in Foster's Trade Union Educational League, a branch of the Communist party of America, and Friends of Soviet Russia, legal branch of the Communist party of America.

George H. Griffiths, Minneapolis; National Non-Partisan League.

Fred C. Howe, New York City; National Committee, American Civil Liberties Union; special writer, Federated Press; Board of Directors, Cooperative League of America; former Commissioner of Immigration (under President Wilson) at the Port of New York, "a position from which he resigned following a Congressional investigation into his alleged neglect of duty and radical activities because of his unauthorized action in releasing alien radicals held for deportation by the Department of Justice" (Congres-

---

*Fred Marvin, writing in the "Searchlight" department, editorial page of *New York Commercial,* January 4, 1924.

sional Record of 66th Congress, pp. 1522, 1523); chairman, Committee on Resolutions and member of National Council, People's Legislative Service; contributing editor, *Labor Age;* Defense Committee, I.W.W.; organizer, School of Thought, Siasconset, Nantucket, Massachusetts.

Miss Agnes Nestor, Chicago; Women's Trade Union League, an organization which is regarded by the Communist party of America as a part of its united open front against capitalism; assistant director, Bryn Mawr Summer School for Women Workers in Industry, Bryn Mawr College; Advisory Committee, Workers' Education Bureau of America. Among her other radical activities during the past twenty or more years, Miss Nestor with Mrs. Raymond Robins organized an agitative parade in Chicago designed to stimulate public interest in the release of Big Bill Hayward, on trial for murder. The *Chicago Tribune* at the time called it an "anarchist parade."

Basil M. Manly, Washington, D.C.; for many years a radical lobbyist; director, People's Legislative Service; author of publications distributed by the Rand School of Social Science; contributing editor, *Labor Age,* a weekly radical paper which is the successor of the *Socialist Review,* official organ of the Intercollegiate Socialist Society; former member of the War Labor Board and of the National Industrial Conference Board under President Taft; Defense Committee, I.W.W.

The above list comprises the names of those who directed the destinies of the Conference for Progressive Political Action as originally made up. There have been some resignations among those who regard themselves as among the more conservative, and the following members have been added:

D.B. Robertson, Ohio; president, Brotherhood Locomotive Firemen and Enginemen; member, Committee on Resolutions, People's Legislative service.

James H. Maurer, Harrisburg, Pennsylvania; president, Pennsylvania State Federation of Labor; president, Labor Publication Society of Chicago, publisher of *Labor Age;* member, National Executive Committee, Socialist party (1921-1922); chairman, Workers' Education Bureau of America; member, National Advisory Committee, National Labor Alliance for Trade Relations With and Recognition of Russia; lecturer, Rand School of Social Science; member, National Committee, American Civil Liberties Union; member (alternate), Board of Directors, Co-operative League of America.

Benjamin Schlessinger, New York; president, International Ladies' Garment Workers of America, subsidiary to the Amalgamated Clothing Workers, an open, legal branch of the Communist party of America.

H.F. Samuels, Idaho; farmer and merchant.

D.C. Dorman, Montana; farmer; member, National Council, People's Legislative Service; member, Executive Committee, People's Reconstruction League; national manager, Non-Partisan League; secretary-treasurer of the Montana State organization of the C.P.P.A. "Dorman swore that he did not believe in the Constitution and was opposed to the Flag of the United States; that the Flag was nothing but a rag, or words to that effect, and that the Government was no government at all and should be destroyed." (Affidavit of Judge L.J. Palda, case of Ray McKaig vs. Frank Gooding, reported in *New York Commercial,* Oct. 20, 1923.)

J.B. Laughlin, Boxchito, Oklahoma; president, Oklahoma Farm Labor Union of America.

Alice Lorraine Daly, South Dakota; Non-Partisan League.

John M. Baer, Washington, D.C.; former member of Congress from North Dakota; cartoonist for *Labor* and other radical publications; member, National Council, People's Legislative Service.

Here then is a group of people, some of whom are known Communists at heart if not in fact, others having direct connection with the Communist party of America both through personal contact and by virtue of their leadership in organizations recognized as a part of the united front of the Moscow cohorts in the United States. The constituent organizations of the Conference for Progressive Political Action comprise a membership of about two million members, it is claimed, and it is certain that *Labor*, its official organ, reaches readers to the number of approximately a million and a half. That it is well financed is shown by the fact that, as a paper, *Labor* costs much more than it brings in; that the Washington office employees of the Conference number more persons than are employed in the headquarters of either the Republican or Democratic National Committees; and that it has just purchased a plot of ground in Washington on which to erect a four-story marble and limestone building. A publicity fund has been raised for the purpose of furnishing speakers and disseminating literature, and for supporting the Federated Press, which is so closely allied to the Communist party of America as to be regarded by the Communists as their official press association. Several officials of the Federated Press are known to be active Communists. It supplies radical news and propaganda to more than two hundred daily and weekly newspapers in the United States, according to statements by its officials.

The Conference for Progressive Political Action is now rapidly organizing through the middle and far West for the 1924 campaign. Inasmuch as stealing of party names was endorsed at the second Cleveland convention, it is certain that the future activities of the Conference will include "boring from within" the organization of whatever party happens to be the strongest locally. In states that are Republican because most of the voters have the Republican habit, this organization seeks to control Republican nominations. In states where the Democratic habit prevails, the aim is to make the nominations radical. In short, the words "Republican" and "Democratic" have no significance to these political pirates. For instance, in counties, conservatives are satisfied with nominations for strictly local offices and give help to radical candidates for Congress and other legislative positions in trade for such support.

The method of organization is about as follows: A county chairman is selected in each county, being picked because of his ability to organize and spread propaganda. The choice is made by the leaders and not by the local members of the organization. This chairman then selects four vice chairmen, one a wage-earner, one a farmer, one an ex-serviceman, and one a woman. If the county is strongly unionized, then the first vice chairman must be a member of a labor organization that has in no wise antagonized the people. The ex-serviceman is to be a member of the Legion if possible, and if not possible, one is picked from the Spanish-American War Veterans.

The farmer vice chairman is selected from the leading organizations of farmers. If the Farm Bureau is the most influential, then he is selected from this group. If he has been prominent in the dominant political party, that fact is an added qualification in considering his fitness. If he has been prominent in the opposite party, he can give as a reason for change the fact that he has no hope for the salvation of the farmer through the action of the party he is leaving. The fourth vice chairman is always a woman, preferably someone prominent in lodge or church work, with extensive acquaintance and organizing ability. She must be intelligent enough to grasp a talking acquaintance with the slogans of the Conference; one who can make a handy speech and who because of her personality and activity has a personal following.

In the two years of its existence, the Conference for Progressive Political Action, with frankly communistic connections and with a program which parallels in many respects that of the Communist party of America, has succeeded in accomplishing this:

It has crystallized the small amount of radical sentiment to be found in the national legislature at all times; furnished this nucleus with aid and comfort; given it a standing by forcing upon it a positive program; disciplined it, thereby giving it the advantages which are bound to accrue from such measures.

It has backed this element in its home districts and secured re-elections; added to its strength by influencing the election of other radicals; and brought the whole group to a point where, by voting *en bloc* on certain matters, it exercises the functions of a majority party, notwithstanding the fact that its members were elected (with two exceptions) on regular party tickets.

In 1922, the Conference for Progressive Political Action endorsed for senatorships, among others, the following:

McKellar of Tennessee	Ralston of Indiana
Frazier of North Dakota	Swanson of Virginia
Kendrick of Wyoming	Howell of Nebraska

In 1923, the Conference endorsed:

Dill of Washington Wheeler of Montana Ashurst of Arizona	Democrats
La Follette of Wisconsin Brookhart of Iowa Norris of Nebraska	Republicans
Shipstead of Minnesota Johnson of Minnesota	Farm-Labor party

All the candidates named were elected. In addition the Conference claims to have secured the election of Governor Sweet of Colorado and Governor Walton of Oklahoma, both Democrats. Preparations for the 1924 campaign are being enthusiastically pushed.

Literature of the organization is sent into every state where there are to be elections, advocating the choice of selected candidates and declaring its adherence to certain radical policies. In many instances it is known that the supporters switched from one party to another, voting for one candidate in the primaries and another at the elections. This is exactly what was done in Pennsylvania; the radical element, backed by the Conference, was solidly behind Burke in the primaries, but its followers were later instructed to vote for the Democratic candidate at the election.

In the declaration of principles there is an appeal for action, with many arguments taken from the code of the Communists. It is a part of the Communist work here to make similar appeals through legal channels with the intent of alienating Americans from the Flag as a step toward the proletarian dictatorship to be established here following the exact pattern of that now existing in Russia. This declaration refers, on Communist lines, to "a long record of injury and usurpation," and says in part:

> The history of recent years is a history of repeated injuries and usurpation by the servants of this oligarchy in both the dominant parties; all having as their direct object the establishment of an absolute tyranny and plutocratic dictatorship within these United States. Life, liberty, and happiness all have been sacrificed upon the altar of greed. To prove this let facts be submitted to a candid world.
>
> They have stifled free speech, throttled free press, and denied the sacred right of assembly. They have used the Federal Reserve System, controlling the life blood of the nation's credit, as an instrument to deflate and crush farmers and independent business men and cause nationwide unemployment. They have obstructed every honest effort to relieve the distress of agriculture thus caused and have used every influence to secure betrayal of the farmers' interests.
>
> They have conscripted 4,000,000 men and boys while they permitted corporations and individuals to extort unconscionable war profits and have sacrificed the soldiers' just demands for equitable compensation to the dictates of Mellonism and the selfish interests of tax-dodging capitalists and profiteers. They have abolished the taxes upon excess profits of corporations and have reduced the taxes upon incomes of millionaires. They have used the army and the troops and police forces of States and cities to crush labor in its struggles to secure rights guaranteed by the Constitution.

Playing directly into the hands of the Communists in agitating radical legislation, the Conference for Progressive Political Action puts forward as its platform startling proposals affecting taxation, court proceedings, and government ownership, which are worthy of the efforts of the cleverly tricky

Communists, whose method of procedure is to advance any kind of theory to effect changes, in the belief that the more changes made, the easier it will be to bring about the great change, the establishment of the Dictatorship of the Proletariat. Among the proposals in this remarkable platform is one providing that any decision of the Supreme Court of the United States may be reversed by a vote of Congress. Thus, distasteful court decisions may be nullified as soon as the radicals can get control of Congress — and the fight for this is now being waged.

Another provision is that all dwellings, farmhouses, farm machinery, farm improvements, household furniture, and tangible personal property be exempted from state and local taxation, and that all funds be raised by taxes levied on incomes above a certain amount, business profits, and corporations. Unemployment and old age pensions and a federal workmen's compensation insurance fund are also advocated. This would result, they believe, as do the Communists, in breaking up what they love to call the "capitalist state." The Plumb Plan for government ownership of railroads and other public utilities is naturally included in the platform, and the Conference is now practically the only source of propaganda in this country for nationalizing of the railroads.

Not satisfied with the plan to nullify decisions of the Supreme Court by vote of Congress, the platform of this group of radicals advocates state legislation providing that no act of any state legislature shall be declared unconstitutional if any one member of the Supreme Court casts his vote in favor of the constitutionality of the measure. This, of course, would tend to weaken the safeguard that the courts of the country give to all citizens, and would bring the entire judicial system of the country into disrepute, so that the coming of the proletarian dictatorship would be made easier. New banking features are also advocated which would tend to concentrate the savings of workers in a way which would permit of their being used more readily and in greater amounts for the provocation of unrest and other unwise purposes. This is included in the proposal advanced for the organization under government charter of cooperative banks with full banking powers designed especially to enable farmers and factory workers to mobilize their own resources.

Also advocated is a provision that laws be enacted prohibiting interference by Congress, either by means of injunctions or in any other way, with the right of labor to organize, strike, picket, boycott, and otherwise "to carry on industrial controversy by peaceful means." The Communists include violence in strikes as a cardinal principle, and now this alleged Conference for Progressive Political Action seeks to restrain the government from the use of the only judicial means of preventing violence in labor warfare aimed at the government.

Constitutional amendments in all states, and federal legislation, are also advocated, permitting cities and other units of government to own and operate all classes of public utilities, including markets, cold storage plants, coal, and food supplies; and authorizing cities, counties, and other units of government to issue bonds to raise the money to purchase these public utilities and supplies. This is just what the Communists are working for in their illegal political organizations as a preliminary step to the overthrow of the government by force of arms.

The next step taken by this group of radicals is to catechize every nominee to Congress. A questionnaire is prepared and sent to all candidates for Congressional election, without regard to party affiliation, before each election. A copy of this questionnaire is sent to every labor union member and every other person in sympathy with the labor union and radical movement, with the request that the local unions and all local radical and so-called progressive organizations take the matter up in their meetings and besiege the Congressional nominees with the questions. These questionnaires are headed with the peremptory demand, "Answer must be Yes or No!" In substance, they read as follows:

1. If elected to Congress will you work and vote to repeal the Esch-Cummins railroad law?

2. If elected to Congress will you work and vote against the ship subsidy and subsidies of all other special interests?

3. Do you believe that five men on the Supreme Bench who have not been elected by the people, and who cannot be rejected by the people, should be permitted to nullify the will of the people as expressed by their representatives in Congress and the Executive in the White House?

4. If elected, will you work and vote for a Constitutional amendment restricting the power of the Supreme Court to nullify acts of Congress?

5. If elected, will you work and vote against compulsory arbitration and all attempts to destroy and restrict the rights of labor to organize, bargain collectively, and strike?

6. Will you work and vote for a clean-cut federal statute prohibiting federal judges from issuing injunctions in industrial disputes?

7. Will you work and vote to reinstate the taxes on excess profits and maintain the taxes on big incomes?

8. Will you work and vote against a sales tax on the food and necessities of the poor?

9. Will you work and vote to reduce appropriations for the Army and Navy to a pre-war basis?

10. Will you favor increased federal appropriations for education?

11. Will you work and vote for a special tax on war grafters and profiteers to pay the soldiers a just compensation?

12. Will you work and vote for a law to take the profit out of war by manufacturing battleships, munitions, and other implements of war in government plants only?

13. Will you work and vote for a clean-cut corrupt practices act which will put an end to Newberryism?

14. Will you work and vote for the abolition of child labor and a constitutional amendment for that purpose if necessary?

The public exposure of the Workers' party of America as a branch of the Communist party resulted in the refusal of the Conference of Progressive Political Action to seat delegates from the Workers' party in the Cleveland

The Red Napoleon

Joseph Pogány, known in the Hungarian Communist party as Schwartz, his alias in the United States being John Pepper and his American party name Joseph Lang, is the representative of the Third (Communist) International of Moscow on the Executive Committee of the Communist party of America. He was present at the illegal convention of the Communist party at Bridgman, Michigan, but succeeded in escaping capture. A check for $25.00 signed by Bishop William M. Brown of Galion, Ohio (Episcopal), made payable to "Joseph Lang" and similarly endorsed was found on the grounds after the raid.

Pogány was originally an Hungarian journalist, and has a long career in promoting world revolution to his credit. The following has been written of him by an eye witness: "He is still suspected of having been the ringleader of the gang which murdered Count Stephen Tisza; he was responsible for the agitation which, during the Károlyi régime, made the reorganization of the army impossible; and it was he who led the demonstration against the War Ministers, Count Festetich and Batta, which ended in the resignation of those 'last shadows of the ancient régime.' It was Pogány who protested against the proposed preventive measures against the Communists in February and March, 1919; and it was he who led the 'naval' detachment when it liberated Béla Kun-Cohen from his confinement in the barracks of the First Honvéd Regiment in Ullői-út, and who later on, after the fight in Conti-utca, helped to prepare the way, both actively and passively, for the final 'triumph' of March 21. His share in the work of demoralizing the army predestined him for the post which he obtained, that of Commissar for War."

Under Béla Kun-Cohen's regime, Pogány in the space of four short months became successively Commissar for Foreign Affairs, Commander-in-chief of the Red Army and Commissar of Education. He was known to be heartily in sympathy with the reign of terror as instituted and maintained by Szamuelly and his army of "Lenin boys."

During this period, there was an enforced production of Pogány's play "Napoleon" in Budapest. This with his ponderous physiognomy and nimble mentality secured for him the sobriquet of the "Red Napoleon" or the "Bolshevik Napoleon." When Hungary was finally liberated from alien rule, Pogány escaped to Russia and, with Béla Kun-Cohen, presumably remained there for the following two years.

Pogány-Schwartz-Pepper-Lang was known to have arrived in America a few weeks before the Bridgman Convention, with orders from Moscow for American Communists and with instructions to take charge of the revolutionary forces in this country. How he entered is not known, and for that reason his presence here is illegal — an alien revolutionary. His first appearance was at a meeting of a radical Jewish Federation in the Bronx from which there was a hasty exit. It appears that during this secret meeting, a blundering policeman entered the hallway of the building and began to ask innocent questions. The janitor, knowing what was going on, gave the alarm and those present disappeared down the fire escapes to meet again in another place. After the Bridgman raid Pogány disappeared, but was known to be in correspondence with Communists as late as December 1923, when it was variously stated that he was in Canada with Béla Kun-Cohen or in Chicago.

Pogány speaks Hungarian, German and Russian but no English. His articles in the Communist party publications are forceful and it has been said that when he writes, it is with an authority and knowledge of the technique of revolution and with an eye single to future events that is not equaled. A critical examination of his literary work gives plain evidence that its more radical thought is usually deleted to avoid conflict with the authorities.

convention (1922), but the Conference's work is greatly favored by the Communists because of its efforts to disturb the functioning of the government.

It is frequently difficult to link individuals and organizations with the actual illegal Communist machine, but it is known that many members of the various labor unions, as well as of the American Federation of Labor, are members of the Communist party. The Brotherhood of Locomotive Engineers, whose president, Warren S. Stone, is treasurer of the Conference for Progressive Political Action, issues from its headquarters at Cleveland a publication called *Brotherhood of Locomotive Engineers Journal,* of which Albert F. Coyle is "acting editor and publicity manager." On July 18, 1922, Coyle, who is a Yale man, wrote to Robert Minor, at present a member of the Central Executive Committee of the Communist party of America, a letter beginning, "Dear Comrade Minor," in which he states that he is trying to make the *Journal* "a real voice of the producing classes, interpreting to them the big social, political and economic movements of the day," and refers to a meeting with Minor at the 1920 convention of the Intercollegiate Socialist Society.

This is but one of many such connections that unite individuals prominent in labor union circles with the Communists. The principles of many of the union leaders, as expressed in their public and private statements, coincide with remarkable fidelity with the principles of Communism. It is, indeed, no secret that the radical wing of the American Federation of Labor, led by William Z. Foster, is allied with the Communist party of America and is controlled by the "underground" or illegal organization of that party. The fight between Samuel Gompers and Foster for leadership of the American Federation of Labor is the reason adduced by many for Gompers' alleged conservatism — combating the pronounced radicalism of Foster being the only means by which he could retain personal independence. Foster's Trade Union Educational League agencies, through which the illegal party works, is controlled absolutely by the Communists.

Directly associated with these organizations making up the Conference for Progressive Political Action is the National Federation of Federal Employees, which is affiliated with the American Federation of Labor and in which are a number of Communists. These Communists are keeping well under cover and their membership in the Communist party is not known to the rank and file of the Federal Employees' organization. This federation is composed of various unions made up exclusively of federal employees who are members of the American Federation of Labor. It is their boast that no member of Congress dares go against the wishes of the National Federation of Federal Employees if he desires to hold his position in Congress.

These unions are composed not only of postal clerks, rural letter carriers, and railway mail clerks, who make up the best-known of federal employees' unions, but also of organized county agents, engaged in agricultural extension; all employees in public land offices; employees in irrigation, reclamation, forestry, and like work; all those connected with Indian work, particularly with Indian schools; and every other line of activity in which government employees are interested.

The Federation of Federal Employees has shown its strength and influence on more than one occasion. It is even a bit boastful about its power with Congress, and it was this boastfulness that attracted the attention of the Communist party and led to the "planting" of Communists in federal employ for the purpose of getting control of the organization. The Federation has successfully resisted all attempts at any reorganization of federal bureaus that would result in the decrease of the number of employees. It succeeded in forcing the House of Representatives to reject a report by the Committee on Appropriations against the continuation of a $240 annual bonus to government employees. This bonus was first allowed employees during the war to offset the increased cost of living. The Appropriations Committee reported in 1922 in favor of a reduction of this bonus upon the ground that the cost of living was lower and there was no longer a need for giving employees a bonus over and above their fixed salary. The American Federation of Labor immediately got behind the Federation of Federal Employees and succeeded in forcing the House to reject this attempted economy, restoring the bonus for the fiscal year and appropriating for it $36,287,000.

Many bodies which appeal to "forward-looking" individuals, or to philanthropists, or to the sympathies of right-thinking people, are in the field endorsing candidates for office. Ostensibly their purpose is to aid the suffering or to uplift the downtrodden; but in reality their work is in furtherance of the work of the Communist party in America. Among them are organizations with high-sounding names like the All-America National Council, the Non-Partisan Relief Committee, the Society for Medical Aid to Russia, the League for Industrial Democracy, the American League to Limit Armaments, and the American Union Against Militarism. All the openly pacifist organizations, which sponsor such movements as "No More War Day," and which are trying to influence Congressmen and candidates for Congress, are directly or indirectly branches of the illegal Communist party and their work is being controlled, though some of them may not know it, by the Communists in secret and illegal meetings. The list of such organizations in the United States is so long that a mere enumeration of them would fill several pages.

The Workers' party of America is the open political branch of the Communist party of America, and every member of the official Workers' party is a member of the illegal branch of that organization. But the Communists are clever enough to know that they cannot yet win elections through their own political party. Accordingly they have instructed their members to support other candidates when no Workers' party ticket is in the field; and that party has no open candidates as yet (1924) in Congressional elections. But these workers are also instructed to "make themselves felt" in order to acquire prestige in the minds of the candidates they support. In this way they believe they will gain more strength in the campaigns. But it must be borne in mind that at all times every member of the Communist party in America is bound to obey the orders of the illegal party and to be entirely controlled by it in his political as well as his industrial activity.

Both Communists and every other breed of radicals were ready to make capital out of the bonus question, however it might be decided by the government. If the bonus were approved, they would attack the action as an imposition upon the people of the country and an effort of the "capitalist" state to rob the poor. If disapproved, that action would be attacked as a capitalistic effort to defraud the ex-soldiers of their just due. The "Conference," like the Communists and all other radicals, makes friends with all dissatisfied portions of society. It takes the losing side on every public question in order to make capital out of the fact that the side lost, and its supporters, therefore, are believed to be hostile to the authorities.

Those who are familiar with the workings of the Communists are aware that the United States is in jeopardy. They are not fearful if the people of this country awake to the danger. But the enemies of civilization, both those in the Communist party and those on the fringe, who are playing with fire in their support of Communist theories, are at work to effect the overthrow of this government. They are working cleverly, insidiously, and are willing to take plenty of time to accomplish their ends, but their main purpose, the goal toward which they are striving, is the destruction of church, home, and state in America and the raising of the Dictatorship of the Proletariat, controlled by Zinoviev and his gang in Moscow, to take the place of the government of the United States.

CHAPTER THREE

Schools And Colleges

"Give us one generation of small children to train to manhood and womanhood and we will set up the Bolshevist form of the Soviet Government."

This statement, made in 1919 by Mrs. Marion E. Sproul, a Boston school teacher, has become the guiding light of the Communist party of America, has been adopted officially as a slogan of the party, and is being used throughout the United States by the secret, illegal organization for the purpose of alienating the American youth from the precepts of this country and the teachings of a century and a half of democratic government. Public and private schools, colleges, and universities are the feeding ground of the "intellectual Communists," and the agents of the party have been deliberately "planted" in the educational institutions of the United States for the purpose of making converts of the young. Even in grammar schools of the larger cities of the country the children have "nuclei" of Communism, frequently encouraged by radical-thinking teachers.

Dr. William B. Bizzell, president of the Texas Agricultural and Mechanical College, told the Dallas County Teachers' Institute in 1922 that "Red radicalism is stalking over the prairies of Texas," little knowing that at that instant the Communists were supporting students in his own and other colleges of that state. The Soviet Government of Moscow paid the expenses of sixty-five Russian students in a single college in the United States — and their first duty is to the Communist International, which specifically provides that they shall make use of every opportunity to make converts of as many of their associates as possible. One of the chief features of the Communist party's program in the United States is to send promising young men and women to the institutions of higher education to fit them for future work in the Red movement aimed at the destruction by violence of the government of the United States and the substitution for it of a dictatorship of the proletariat, subordinate to the Moscow regime.

55

Radicalism in colleges is nothing new. It has existed since such institutions have been known. It has always taken one form or another, usually on religious lines, for adolescence likes to believe that its mind is untrammeled by convention. For generations educators have been familiar with that period of mental revolt in the college youth which made him proclaim himself an atheist or an agnostic — some kind of "free-thinker." It is a stage that has been so common as not to be alarming. For when college days passed and the youth emerged into a sane, practical world which is not particularly interested in religious technique as long as right living governs the people of the earth, this period passed and the college-bred youth took his proper place. But today, when the Communism-fed student leaves college he does not step out into a sane world, but into the ranks of the Communist movement, which is watching him and waiting for his arrival to assign him to definite work for the propagation of the work of the party.

Aside from the recognized schools and colleges, every city now has Communist classes, attendance upon which is compulsory on the part of even little children, who are forced by law to attend public school a certain number of hours each day. These classes usually meet at night, and all that is taught is Communism. Attendance is usually all the "homework" the children have to do. Active Communists, frequently college graduates, conduct them. There is a bit of fun mixed with these studies, so that, for the youngsters, the work will not become irksome. Ridicule is heaped upon religion, home ties, and especially upon the government, in the form of Communist songs which are taught to the children. A sample of such songs will show the nature of all of them. A typical verse reads:

> A patriotic churchman in his den, in his den,
> A-fishing after gold and men — Red flag comes along,
> His holiness he cocks his eye, lets out a snort, and then — oh my!
> Golly, golly, what a roar! Blood and gore! How he tore!
> Golly, golly, how he swore at the Crimson Rag!

Another song taught the children concludes with the verses:

> I've got the rebellion in my heart,
> It's bred in flesh and bone.
> A rebel I will be
> As long as men shall men exploit
> On either side of the sea.
> While right upon the scaffold lies,
> And wrong upon the throne,
> I'll be a blooming rebel, sir,
> A rebel to the bone.

The drift from liberalism to radicalism and finally to Communism is gradual and easy. Many college professors who were liberal in their views and teachings became radicals almost without its being known, and some of them, doubtless, without knowing it themselves. Others, however, and in this group must be listed some of the leading "liberal" lights of the greatest universities in the country, knowingly preach and teach radicalism, which is seized upon by the Communists for ammunition with which to further their ends. Men like Felix Frankfurter and Zacharia Chaffee, of Harvard; Frederick Wells Williams and Max Solomon Mandell, of Yale; and many others in different schools and colleges throughout the country – these men are too wise not to know that their words, publicly uttered and even used in classrooms, are, to put it conservatively, decidedly encouraging to the Communists. It is of men like these that James H. Collins wrote in the *Saturday Evening Post:*

> The spread of radicalism in our colleges is perhaps most marked of all. The cartoon type of radical, with his whiskers and bomb, has a very limited field of activity – any policeman would arrest him on sight. The college radical, on the contrary, can move in every circle. It is not easy to explain him. Sometimes he is a self-seeker and loves notoriety. Again, his hostility to society is based on envy. Ambitious but lacking energy, he hates people who succeed through energy, and sours on life. Some of this intellectual radicalism is attributed to the materialism of the age, Socialism and similar philosophies being based on the material concept of history. Other observers charge it up to slipshod teaching of history and economics, students lacking the solid grounding that would put superficial radical theories in proper perspective . . . . The teachings of a radical college professor may have great influence. In one college recently some of the students made a demonstration when a radical professor was dropped from the faculty . . . . Never having worked with his hands, nor mingled with wage-earners, nor been creative or constructive in any way himself, the intellectual radical sees nothing difficult in the revolutionary program of first tearing everything down and then building from the ground up, entirely new.

In a Los Angeles high school one of the teachers constantly taught hatred of capital and took the side of labor in a definite attempt to instill in the minds of her pupils the propriety of such hatred. Finally, when she openly declared that the United States was behind Russia, Germany, and Italy as progressive countries, one of the pupils publicly protested, because, as he pointed out, "there is revolution or civil war in each of these countries." But that teacher continued for some time after this incident expounding her theories to the youth under her charge.

The spreading of propaganda in rural districts has been a subject of study by the Communists since the organization of the party. In certain parts of the country where there are colonies of foreigners gathered under Communistic influence, radical plays are put on in schoolhouses by amateur, home-talent performers. Occasionally trouble arises when a patriotic schoolteacher discovers that meetings of what had been thought to be clubs, or societies for social intercourse, were in reality Communist meetings under the direction of the Third International through the Communist party of America. One such incident may be cited as an example.

A colony of Finns, thirty-three families in all, of whom only three families were American citizens, is located about twelve miles north of Deer River, Minnesota. The company which located this colony confined its efforts entirely to Finns and made particularly attractive offers to the colonists. Fifty dollars secured a farm for each family and subsequent payments were to be nominal. The thirty non-American families are Communists, and they undertook to give a play at the rural schoolhouse for the benefit of the Friends of Soviet Russia. The teacher, Mrs. G.M. Smith, learned of the nature of the organization, called the Suoma Raatagen Club, under the auspices of which the play was to be given. She discovered that the play was simply Red radical propaganda and refused to assent to the use of the schoolhouse for that purpose; but the Finns overrode her by getting permission from the county school superintendent. Mrs. Smith attended the entertainment and forcibly prevented the giving of the Red play or taking up of a collection for the Friends of Soviet Russia. Singlehanded she drove them from the schoolhouse when they began to shout, "We are Reds! We are Bolsheviks!"

The Communists are constantly grooming some of their shining stars for positions in the faculties of our colleges. The pay of the teachers in all parts of the country, both in public and private institutions, is so small that many able men are unable to accept positions as teachers. But the small salary is no deterrent to the Communist or the radical of any stripe, who joyfully accepts places where he may elaborate his views and teach real radicalism to the impressionable youth in his classes. His salary is frequently supplemented by funds from the Communist treasury, sometimes camouflaged under the cloak of "contributions" as a testimonial to his clear thinking as expressed in his lectures.

The dissemination of radical, or as they term it, liberal propaganda in institutions of learning, particularly in universities and women's colleges, has been a pet scheme of the radicals and their friends for years. There is hardly any university of size in the country today which does not have at least a branch of the National Student Forum, or its predecessor, the Intercollegiate Liberal League, or the League for Industrial Democracy. These are direct descendants of the Intercollegiate Socialist League, which went out of existence when "Socialism" became too mild a term to satisfy the radical tendencies of many members. The frequent changes in name are characteristic of all organizations affiliated with the Communists, who alter their names and addresses in an effort to hoodwink the authorities and fool the public, a proceeding in strict accord with the orders of Nicolai Lenin. The Intercollegiate Liberal League was born at Harvard, April 2, 1921, and it was a result of the activities of the Socialist and later the Liberal League that developed the "modern intellectuals," or as they are better known, the "parlor Bolsheviki." There is so much in the teaching of radicalism that appeals to the mental processes which invariably accompany certain periods in the life of every student that it is not surprising that the Communist party and the many inconspicuous individuals who are satisfied that they should be leaders and have no better means of attaining notoriety have grasped the opportunities offered as a business proposition, as the Socialists did before them. Many are really capitalists, others are plain parasites.

It is safe to say that no institution of learning in the country has been so thoroughly saturated with "liberal" activity as has Harvard University. This institution has stimulated such a spirit of democracy among the students of the past generation that the radicals have had a more fertile field in which to work at Harvard than in a less liberal establishment. The professors themselves have not been inactive in the encouragement of the movement, and the names of several of them appear prominently in the roster of American liberals and are known in the "illegal" circles of the Communist party of America. These professors, as well as the professors of many other colleges, number known Communists among their personal friends, and are frequently found speaking from the same platform even with members of the Central Executive Committee of the Communist party of America. It is impossible that men of their intelligence should not know that they are advocating what the Communist party desires but cannot use in public propaganda because their own words would be discounted. Prominent radical speakers have been brought to speak at meetings of the Harvard liberals from all sorts of organizations, among them men who are actually paid agents of the Communist party.

Prominent in the organization of the Intercollegiate Liberal League were men notorious as radicals, as well as men whose patriotism and Americanism cannot be questioned. The latter, of course, did not realize to what they were lending their aid. It is inconceivable that Dean Briggs would in any way permit himself to be identified with a movement whose chief object is to overthrow the government of the United States by force of arms. And yet Dean Briggs was one of the speakers at the meeting to organize the Intercollegiate Liberal League, in which the Communists were interested. Roger N. Baldwin, head of the American Civil Liberties Bureau, a "conscientious objector" who served a prison term as a "draft dodger" during the war and an intimate friend of the most radical of Communists, was one of the organizers. Another was the Rev. John Haynes Holmes, whose anti-American activities during the European War were so pronounced that his New York church had to be watched by officers of the government, and whose writings were used by the Germans as propaganda with which they sought to break down the morale of the Allied soldiers.

Harry W.L. Dana, known in Communist circles as one of the most effective radical agitators, was also active in the organization of the Intercollegiate Liberal League. Professor Dana, who was dismissed from Columbia University because of his radicalism, said as far back as 1918 that he would be glad to aid in whatever way he could in furthering the cause of Soviet Russia in America, and from that time on has been issuing pronouncements on the "class war." Yet he is considered a leader in the radical collegiate group. Among the others participating in the organization of this league were Augustus Dill, of *The Crisis;* Francis Neilson and Walter Fuller, of *The Freeman;* Donald Winston, of *Young Democracy,* and representatives from a number of other colleges. Dean Briggs and President H.N. MacCracken of Vassar College were among the speakers, and by their presence lent aid to the movement. The Rev. John Haynes Holmes, in his speech on that occasion, urged the students to "identify themselves with the labor world and there to martyr themselves by preaching the gospel of free souls and love as the rule of life." He predicted a revolution, and said: "If you want to be on the side of fundamental right you have got to line up on the side of labor."

According to the *Literary Digest* there were, in 1921, organizations of the Intercollegiate Liberal League in 250 colleges and universities in this country. At about the time when the Harvard Liberal Club's application for membership in the Associated Harvard Clubs was rejected because of its radicalism, a thorough investigation of the club and the league was made. In the report it was shown that some outside agency was financing the establishment of the league and the various clubs and their activities. From the report of this investigation it is possible to quote one paragraph, which reads as follows:

> It would appear that the Harvard Liberal Club, Harvard Students' Liberal Club, and the Intercollegiate Liberal League may be the means devised and about to be used as propaganda agencies by radical movements not yet disclosed. The Russian theory of instilling sympathetic ideas in the younger generation while they are still in school is well known, and after a brief examination . . . it appears more than likely that the system is being put into execution among college students in this country. Such a plan of radical activity is most patently dangerous, as the students at that age, while mentally keen, active, and alert, have not yet formed their permanent characters and are at a formative period in their mental development, during which they are particularly susceptible to the influence of older minds, especially those of their masters whom they are accustomed to look up to as fountains of authority, wisdom, and guidance. Under those circumstances, with men like Felix Frankfurter, Roger Baldwin, and others behind such a movement, its potentialities for evil at once appear to be tremendous.

The retention of Professor Frankfurter at Harvard has called forth a great deal of criticism from men in public affairs, Harvard graduates, and others. When he was counsel for President Wilson's Mediation Commission in the Mooney case, in California, he had the temerity to try to influence Theodore Roosevelt in the work he was doing in the endeavor to aid Mooney. This drew from the ex-president, whose Americanism has never been questioned by friend or foe, the following letter, the existence of which few people know of:

I thank you for your frank letter. I answer it at length because you have taken and are taking . . . an attitude which seems to me to be fundamentally that of Trotsky and the other Bolsheviki leaders in Russia; an attitude which may be fraught with mischief to the country.

As for the conduct of the trial, it seems to me that Judge Dunne's statement which I quoted in my published letter covers it. I have not been able to find anyone who seriously questions Mr. Dunne's character, judicial fitness and ability, or standing. Moreover, it seems to me that your own letter makes it perfectly plain that the movement for the recall of Fickert was due primarily, not in the least to any real or general feeling as to the alleged short-comings on his part, but to what I can only call the Bolsheviki sentiment. The other accusations against him were mere camouflage. The assault was made upon him because he had attacked the murderous element, the dynamite and anarchy group of labor agitators. The movement against him was essentially similar to movements on behalf of the McNamaras, and on behalf of Moyer and Haywood. Some of the correspondents who attacked me frankly stated that they were for Mooney and Billings just as they had been for the McNamaras and for Moyer and Haywood. In view of Judge Dunne's statement it is perfectly clear that even if Judge Dunne is in error in his belief as to the trial being straight and proper, it was an error into which entirely honest men could fall.

But the question of granting a re-trial is one thing. The question of the recall is entirely different. Even if a re-trial were proper this would not in the least justify a recall — any more than a single grave error on your part would justify your impeachment, or the impeachment of President Wilson for appointing you. Fremont Older and the I.W.W. and the direct action anarchists and apologists for anarchy are never concerned for justice. They are concerned solely in seeing one kind of criminal escape justice, precisely as certain big business men have in the past been concerned in seeing another kind of criminal escape justice. The guiding spirits in the movement for the recall of Fickert cared not a rap whether or not Mooney and Billings were guilty; probably they believed them guilty; all they were concerned with was seeing a rebuke administered to, and an evil lesson taught, all public officials who might take action against crimes of violence committed by anarchists in the name of some foul and violent protest against social conditions. Murder is murder, and it is rather more evil when committed in the name of a professed social movement. It was no mere accident, it was the natural sequence of cause and effect that the agitation for the recall of Fickert, because he fearlessly prosecuted the dynamiters (and of course no human being doubts that Billings and Mooney were in some shape or other privy to the outrage), should have been accompanied by the dynamite outrage at the governor's mansion. The reactionaries have in the past been a great menace to this Republic, but at this moment it is the I.W.W., the Germanized Socialists, the anarchists, the foolish creatures who always protest against the suppression of crime, the pacifists and the like, under the lead of the Hearsts and La Follettes, and Bergers, and Hillquits, the Fremont Olders and Amos Pinchots and Rudolph Spreckels, who are the really grave danger. These are the Bolsheviki of America, and the Bolsheviki are just as bad as the Romanoffs, and are at the moment a greater menace to orderly freedom. Robespierre and Danton and Marat and Herbert were just as evil as the worst tyrants of the old regime, and from 1791 to 1794 they were the most dangerous enemies to liberty that the world contained. When you, as representing President Wilson, find yourself obliged to champion men of this stamp, you ought, by unequivocal affirmative action, to make it evident that you are sternly against their general and habitual line of conduct.

I have just received your report on the Bisbee deportation. One of the prominent leaders in that deportation was my old friend Jack Greenway, who has just been commissioned a major in the army by President Wilson. Your report is as thoroughly misleading a document as could be written on the subject. No official writing on behalf of the President is to be excused for failure to know, and clearly to set forth, that the I.W.W. is a criminal organization. To ignore the fact that a movement such as its members made into Bisbee is made with criminal intent is precisely as foolish as for a New York policeman to ignore the fact that when the Whyo gang assembles with guns and knives it is with criminal intent. The President is not to be excused if he ignores this fact, for of course he knows all about it. No human being in his senses doubts that the men deported from Bisbee were bent on destruction and murder. If the President through you or anyone else had any right to look into the matter, this very fact shows that he had been remiss in his clear duty to provide against the very grave danger in advance. When no efficient means are employed to guard honest, upright and well-behaved citizens from the most brutal kind of lawlessness it is inevitable that these citizens shall try to protect themselves. That is as true when the President fails to do his duty about the I.W.W. as when the police fail to do their duty about gangs like the Whyo gang; and when either the President or the police, personally or by representative, rebuke the men who defend themselves from criminal assault, it is necessary sharply to point out that far heavier blame attaches to the authorities who fail to give the needed protection, and to the investigators who fail to point out the criminal character of the anarchistic organization against which the decent citizens have taken action.

Here again you are engaged in excusing men precisely like the Bolsheviki in Russia, who are murderers and encouragers of murder, who are traitors to their allies, to democracy, and to civilization, as well as to the United States, and whose acts are nevertheless apologized for on grounds, my dear Mr. Frankfurter, substantially like those which you allege. In times of danger nothing is more common and nothing more dangerous to the Republic than for men to avoid condemning the criminals who are really public enemies by making their entire assault on the shortcomings of the good citizens who have been the victims or opponents of the criminals. This was done not only by Danton and Robespierre, but by many of their ordinarily honest associates in connection with, for instance, the "September massacres." It is not the kind of thing I care to see well-meaning men do in this country.

Sincerely yours,
(signed) Theodore Roosevelt

The writings of Lenin, Trotsky, or other high priests of Communism, as well as those of Marx and Engels, have been and undoubtedly still are used as textbooks, or as prescribed reading, in classes or clubs in Wellesley, Vassar, Smith, Yale and many other colleges, and trouble is constantly occurring in various state universities in the West where radicalism is being taught or studied. In all these colleges, also, Communist propaganda prepared with a view to being placed in the hands of students is secretly circulated among the students. From time to time this secret work of the Communists becomes known publicly through the indignation of some thoroughly aroused American student into whose hands the propaganda falls by mistake. However, this does not often happen, for the Communists are very careful to place such literature only in "safe" hands.

Upton Sinclair made, in 1922, a tour of the United States, lecturing wherever he could on radicalism, ostensibly gathering material for a new book on education. Before his departure from his home in Pasadena, California, he was entertained as guest of honor at a dinner given by Mrs. Kate Crane Gartz and Prince Hopkins, known as radicals, although standing high in Pasadena society. Representatives of all classes of radicalism from Communism to theoretical Socialism, society men and women, and motion picture stars and producers were present. It was entirely radical in its personnel and intended to be. In telling of his then projected trip, Sinclair said that there were "capitalist spies" in practically every school and college in the country, reporting any teacher expressing liberal thought. "This perfect network of spies," he said, "has created such a fear among school and university teachers" that nearly all his letters of inquiry remained unanswered, thus forcing him to visit the institutions in person in order to get information for his book, in which he proposed to tell all about the sinister influence and domination of the reactionaries and of Wall Street finance and capital over the educational system of this country. The radicals present appeared to believe all that Sinclair told them, and there was much indignation expressed because objection was being made to the teaching of radicalism in the schools of the United States. And yet this radical teaching is backed by the illegal Communist party of America and by the Russian Soviet government of Moscow.

Judge J.H. Ryckman was another speaker. He dwelt upon the "terrible persecution" of the I.W.W. radicals in California and said that but for the assistance given by some wealthy radicals, mentioning Miss Fanny Bixby Spencer and Miss Esther Yarnell, well-known in California society, who have given bail for many of the radicals arrested in the West, the syndicalist movement, sponsored by the Communists, would have been wiped out in that state. Gaylord Wilshire, a prominent Los Angeles radical who boasts of his connections with the Communist movement, delivered an ultra-radical speech, full of sarcastic and scathing vindictiveness against American democracy, saying that a mixture of syndicalist principles and Communist tactics was the only salvation for this country. These speakers are mentioned for the reason that this was the ammunition to be used by Upton Sinclair on his tour of American colleges in making addresses to students.

After Sinclair had started his tour he wrote friends from San Francisco saying that *Hearst's Magazine* had accepted his latest novel, *Mobland,* and ascribing this good fortune to the fact that Norman Hapgood, known for his radical tendencies, and connected with the American Civil Liberties Union, had shortly before been made editor of that magazine. On May 21, 1922, a small private meeting of a number of radical and "progressive" public school teachers of Pasadena was held, at which letters from Sinclair were discussed. He had written from Chicago that at Madison, Wisconsin, he was received in a very friendly spirit and had held several successful meetings. At the University of Chicago, he wrote, he had been given a small auditorium in which to lecture, and so many students could not get in to hear him that the meeting was adjourned to out-of-doors, so that all could hear. "Generally speaking," he wrote, "I am very much pleased to find so many Socialists and adherents of other anti-capitalistic systems among the college professors, and I am quite sure that if we could only make these men feel reasonably sure of economic independence there would be a great wave of radical thought sweeping through all our schools."

On this tour Sinclair was entertained by and addressed several local clubs associated with the Intercollegiate Liberal League, and at other places his meetings were held under the auspices of the "Cosmopolitan Club" of the college. The Cosmopolitan Club movement is one which has been investigated and found to be engaged in spreading radical propaganda in practically all institutions in which it has been introduced. There are branches in Coe University, Columbia, Cornell, Drake, Iowa State, Harvard, Massachusetts Institute of Technology, Oberlin, Ohio State, Ohio Wesleyan, Purdue, Radcliffe, Syracuse, Union College, Vanderbilt, William Jewell College, Worcester University, Yale, and the Universities of California, Chicago, Illinois, Indiana, Kansas, Michigan, Missouri, Nebraska, Oregon, Pennsylvania, and Wisconsin.

These clubs include active Communists as well as radicals of other types and are unquestionably supported, at least in part, by the Communist party. In their membership are many foreigners, the ostensible object of the clubs being to foster international friendship. In some cases radical professors are the active leaders in these clubs, although usually active Communists who are undergraduates are the leaders. They frequently have as speakers members of the Communist party of America who never miss an opportunity to make converts.

As Upton Sinclair made his tour of the country and worked either directly or indirectly for Communism, so Lillian Reiseroff of Cambridge, Massachusetts, made her way from East to West, working directly for the Communists, and organizing in schools and colleges, among her other activities, branches of the Young Workers' League of America, a part of the Communist organization supported as one of the "legal" portions of the radical party. Miss Reiseroff made her way to the Pacific Coast and at Seattle found Sidney E. Borgeson, who while attending the summer school at the University of Washington was very active as a member of a number of local radical organizations. These two worked together in college circles and left together for Minneapolis, where Borgeson said he was to be employed as an instructor at the University of Minnesota, and where Miss Reiseroff was to engage actively in organization work for the Young Workers' League.

The Communists have not been slow to seize upon the fact that practically no efforts are made, outside of the public school system, with its more or less lax laws relating to attendance at certain ages, to furnish children of foreign birth and children of the working class with educational facilities. This lack of attention on the part of the American public has given the Communists an excellent opportunity to organize night schools for the teaching of Communism. Among the documents found at Bridgman were many referring to the work on the education and early training of the youth on Communistic lines. Much of this work is done by the Young Workers' League, which has been organized all over the country in a remarkably short time.

A single example of how the Communists work in the schools and colleges will suffice to explain many recent activities in such institutions. In 1922 sixty-five Russian men and women applied for admission to the United States from Mexico as students. They said they wished to matriculate at the University of California for study. The United States government permitted them to enter, believing them anxious to attend the University of California for educational purposes only. As a matter of fact the sixty-five were sent by the Russian Soviet government to Mexico to facilitate their entrance to this country. They were financed by the Communists in Moscow and carried on well-organized Communist propaganda on the Pacific Coast under the direction of the Third International of Moscow. They made a number of converts among the students of the University, according to a well-informed visitor to the Coast. They also acted as advisors to the organizers of the Young Workers' League in Pacific Coast states.

The Young Workers' League is an outgrowth of the Young People's Communist League and the Young People's Socialist League, and was organized for "legal" propaganda purposes. The reorganization was effected by the Executive Committee of the Workers' party and the installation of the various circles was in charge of the national secretary, Oliver Carlson, alias E. Connelly, alias Edwards. He is a member of the Communist party of America, of which the Workers' party is the open or "legal" political branch. The purpose of the Young Workers' League is "to educate the members, the young workers, to understand their position in capitalist society, to show them the stupidity of seeking to climb higher, and to map a course of action for their emancipation." Among the organizers of the League were such persons as Walter Bronstrup, Mrs. Margaret Prevy, Mrs. Sadie Amter, Max Kaminsky, and D.E. Early, all well-known in Communist circles.

The headquarters of this League is, at the time of this writing, at 208 East Twelfth Street, New York City, and the country is divided into districts with an organizer in each district. Classes are held in many cities for the instruction of the young people and their elders along Communistic lines. The following is quoted, as an example, from a report of the organization in Roxbury, Massachusetts:

> Meetings are held every Sunday evening. Classes have been opened in economics and psychology and are attended. Harry W.L. Dana and Mrs. Antoinette F. Konikow, of No. 52 Chambers Street, Boston, are lecturers at these classes. Leo Golosov, of Dorchester, was formerly in charge of the organization and he has since been in Russia. Louis Marks, of Dorchester, is now at the head. Recently copies of *Youth,* a Communist paper, were distributed at one of the meetings.

This is only a sample of the work done in many localities in addition to the work among the children. The Communists are using the schools regularly as places of meeting for older students of Communism, as well as for children of tender years. In the classes such materials as "The A.B.C. of Communism," "Fundamental Principles of Communism," "Theses and Resolutions of the Communist International" are read and studied. *Youth,* the publication just mentioned, was the official organ of the League until March 1922, when the *Young Worker* became the official organ.

From a convention call issued by the national secretary of the Young Workers' League, the aim of the organization is given in the following words: "Our aim is to be the abolition of capitalism by means of the Workers' Republic, a government functioning through the power of the proletariat to the exclusion of all other classes, as the first step toward the establishment of an international classless society, free from all political and economic slavery." International Liebknecht Day was first celebrated by the Young Workers' League of America in January 1922, when international meetings were held in almost every important city in the United States. A joint convention was held in New York in April. It was announced that all organizations subscribing to the convention call and sending delegates must agree to merge into the Young Workers' League. Conventions were also held in Brooklyn in May, and in Chicago in July, of the same year.

Bearing in mind that this organization is chiefly interested in educating first the young and then their elders in Communistic lines of thought, and that an effort has been made to lead the public to believe that the Young Workers' League is not connected with the Communist movement, it is interesting to read the following communication, dated Moscow, June 27, 1922, and addressed to "the National Executive Committees of the Communist parties," which was found with other documents at Bridgman when the Communist party convention was raided:

> Dear Comrades: In agreement with the Executive Committee of the Comintern, the Executive Committee of the Young Communist International decided to launch an energetic campaign of the youth for the united

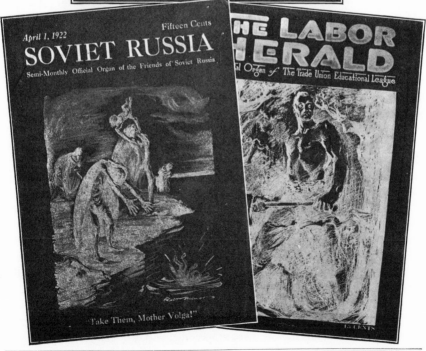

A group of Communist publications in the United States. *Soviet Russia, The Labor Herald,* and *The Young Worker,* on the right William Z. Foster of Chicago; on the left, Robert Miner.

front of the proletariat. For this purpose it decided to convene a World Congress of Juvenile Labor.

In order to prepare the proletarian youth for our campaign, it is of utmost importance that the Communist parties with their press support us in the most extensive manner. This is especially necessary because the whole action is closely connected with the united front policy of the Comintern in the next [near?] future.

We have already informed the National Executives of our League in order that the editors of the party organs may support us. With consideration to the immense significance of this forthcoming action and its effect on the Social Democrats and Centrists, we ask you, the National Executive Committees, to instruct the editors of your organs to grant sufficient space to the publications of the National Leagues as well as to the international publications. With Communist greetings of the Executive Committee of the Young Communist International.

In a circular marked "strictly confidential," sent from Moscow June 24, 1922, the National Executive Committees of the Communist parties in the various countries of the world were told that "recent events in the international labor movement render necessary a revision of our tactics in the problem of the 'proletarian united front and juvenile labor.'" It is then stated that the youth must not be made to carry on their fight for the united front alone but that all branches of the Communist party in each country must work together for the united front under the direction of the National Executive Committee of the Communist party. "The slogan of the united front will for a long time," the circular says, "be the underlined principle of all activities."

"Recent events in the international labor movement" refers to the refusal of the Socialist Internationals to surrender to the Communists in the matter of calling a world labor congress, to insist upon all labor working with the united front movement for the establishment of the proletarian government of the world. Because of this opposition the matter was dropped for the time being and the Executive Committee of the Young Communists' League in Moscow, upon direction from its superiors in the Soviet government, shifted the movement to the various national organizations instead of trying to make it a solid world movement.

It is interesting to note the care with which this work in America, as is the case in all other countries, is mapped out in Moscow. One of the documents found at Bridgman contains the proceedings of the Young Communist International at Moscow, when, under the leadership of Zinoviev, programs for the future were arranged and the work specified for the branches all over the world. In each country the youngsters must be instructed as to the form of government in that country and given points for argument against its maintenance. Care must be taken that the study and work shall be interesting to the youth. A few paragraphs of these proceedings will be illuminating.

In view of the fact that almost all of the practical arrangements of the Leagues have an educational character (evenings of groups, lectures, discussions and entertainment evenings, excursions, etc.), and that in all other departments of work an increase of the educational endeavors is necessary (training of officials), the systematic improvement of this sphere of activities must be paid great attention to. The organization of this work (elaboration of plans, discussion of the active workers providing new forces and material) must in any case be transferred to a special department of the Executive Committee and the branch committees.

The performance of the task imposed by the Second Congress — that of basing educational work on the problems of the day — is only possible if the active members of the leagues know the elementary principles of the Marxian theory. In order to enable the members to acquire this knowledge, political elementary instruction must be given. All young workers entering the Leagues must as far as possible during the first year of their membership be provided with elementary political knowledge.

Then the work is mapped out in detail, taking them through grades, much as is done in our public school system, until they are developed, full Communists, when they are admitted to active membership in the party and assigned to work. A part of this future work is given as "agitation and propaganda" among youth not of Communist families. The proceedings say:

The patient, persistent and systematic enlightenment of the broad masses on juvenile labor on the character of our opponents, along the practical lines of their daily activities, must become the basis of this agitation and propaganda work. So far as the bourgeois youth organizations are concerned, it is the task of the Young Communist Leagues to expose their class character, to fight the Church, to carry on a strong, elastic anti-religious propaganda, to lead a ruthless fight against militarism and to unveil not less ruthlessly pacifism and political neutrality. They must, furthermore, be able to sharpen the class antagonism in these organizations where proletarian and semi-proletarian elements are organized.

In the resolutions adopted by the first national convention of the Young Workers' League of America, organized by the Young Communist League pursuant to instructions from Moscow and held in May 1922, it is distinctly stated that "in the struggle of the working class against the capitalist class the laboring youth does not hold any special position; the class struggle is a conflict between but two classes — the working class and the capitalist class." The resolutions at this convention endorsed Soviet Russia and "demanded" its recognition by the United States, approved the stand of the World War Veterans against "the avowed foe of the working class, the American Legion," and endorsed the Friends of Soviet Russia and all other Communist branches and efforts.

The call for this convention was officially endorsed by four branches of the

Young Women's League, in Chicago, Detroit, Boston and New York. A single paragraph from the resolution on education, adopted by the Young Communist International and approved by the convention in America, tells the extent of the work of this organization:

> With the change in the character and intensity of the class struggle must come about a change in our method of agitation. This field must be subdivided under these two headings: first, education within the organization; second, propaganda and education among the masses.

It has been seen that the machinery of the Communists for gaining converts and trained workers embraces all stages and degrees of education, from the poor youngster who has to work selling papers, running errands, or in any other way, through the Communist night schools, the public schools, colleges and universities, even to professorial chairs in the higher institutions. In addition to this, the names of all radicals who, by word or deed, lend encouragement or endorsement to the Communist movement are used in the propaganda work of gaining recruits to the Communist army. Whenever a college professor, a government official, a big businessman, or any individual whose name carries distinction in any line of endeavor, carelessly or with intent expresses an opinion which can be construed as favoring, even in a limited sense, the aims of the Communists, such words are seized upon and used for propaganda purposes, especially in endeavoring to win over young men and women, in college or out, to the Communist party. Thus it is that correspondence between the late Charles P. Steinmetz, the electrical genius, and Lenin was broadcasted throughout the English-speaking world and was translated into many languages for propaganda purposes. It was given out by Lenin.

Steinmetz, who had for many years been known as an enthusiastic intellectual socialist, expressed to Lenin his admiration of the Russian Soviet government in the "building up of socialism and economic reconstruction," and offering his services "to assist Russia in the technical sphere and particularly in the matter of electrification in a practical way and with advice." Lenin's reply was a studied attempt to furnish material for propaganda, writing of "the necessity and the inevitability of supplanting capitalism by a new social order" and using other hackneyed phrases familiar to those who study revolutionary literature. Lenin also took occasion to refer to the lack of recognition of the Soviet government by the United States as a prime difficulty in the path of accepting the Steinmetz offer of assistance.

CHAPTER FOUR

Radical Publications And Literature

The number of radical publications issued in the United States, including those published abroad and circulated in this country, almost trebled in the year 1922. This is due to two facts: the tremendous growth of the Communist party and its "legal" branches in America, and the fact that a number of radical publications suspended after the raids by the authorities in December 1920 and January 1921 resumed publication in 1922. There are known to be at least 227 radical publications in foreign languages and 73 in English issued in the United States; there may be others, for many of them are printed secretly and circulated surreptitiously, and it is more than probable that some such papers find their way only into the hands of those whom they are intended to reach. In addition to these, there are 269 papers printed abroad in various languages, including English, and imported into the United States in large quantities, as well as 42 papers published in Argentina, Canada, Chile, Cuba, Mexico, Puerto Rico, and Uruguay, which are brought in increasingly large quantities to this country to aid in the drive of radical propaganda. This is a total of 611 periodicals known to be circulated among the people of the United States, directly or indirectly aimed at the overthrow of this government.

In addition to the daily papers, weekly magazines, and monthly reviews included in the above list, books are published and circulated for children and adults, all of them very cleverly presenting propaganda for the purpose of instilling Communism in the minds of the readers. Most of these books are prepared in Russia and many of them are printed abroad, being brought to the United States by smugglers. Picture post cards, some of them of high artistic merit, are also secretly brought to this country, and efforts are constantly being made to give them wide distribution; but as these post cards are unmailable under the laws of the country, they are usually confiscated. No attempt is made, however, to distribute the books except from hand to hand, and through the underground organizations of the Communist party. The subtlety and excellence

71

of these books are worthy of commendation but for the message they bear — that the government of the United States must be overthrown and the Dictatorship of the Proletariat established. Several different volumes of fables, imitating the Aesop classics, especially designed for little folk, are widely read by Communist children and the children of radicals of other stripes.

Many of the Communist books, also, may be obtained at public book stores. Care is taken in the preparation of these books — this refers solely to the reading matter for mature people — to make them accord with the laws of the United States so that the propaganda may be more widely distributed. These volumes are largely philosophical and bear on industrial conditions. But the single moral pointed, the single lesson conveyed, is that all capitalistic governments must be overthrown by violence, and Soviet governments, patterned after and under the direction of the central Soviet government at Moscow, established.

At first the Communist, anarchist, and other radical papers published in this country were crude affairs, frequently printed on coarse, brown paper and typographically barbarous. But today these papers are excellently printed, many of them on better paper than is used by most metropolitan newspapers, and the make-up and typography are of a nature that would please the most exacting journalist. Colors are frequently used — though this applies exclusively, perhaps, to magazines and pamphlets. And whereas the reading matter in the early publications was crudely put together, usually nothing but the most blatant excoriation of this government and praise of the Soviet regime, and almost invariably showing ignorance of composition and of English, the present publications are excellently written in blameless diction, and present their propaganda message in far more insidious and interesting style. In fact, some of their newspapers and magazines are fascinating in their cleverness. The chief propaganda articles are logically constructed (on false premises, to be sure) and the best American in the world would have to be on his guard to keep from falling into agreement with the writer. These publications are well illustrated with cartoons and photographic reproductions and have various departments, even columnists and jokes, all carefully built to further Communist propaganda.

One excellent series of pamphlets is entitled "Children's Stories of Soviet Russia" and is issued by "Friends of Soviet Russia Famine Scout Clubs of America." This is patently an effort to make use of the boys' and girls' scout organizations, and the pamphlets are purely a Communist organ for the dissemination of Communist propaganda through the Communist "legal" branch known as Friends of Soviet Russia. They are profusely illustrated, with covers in colors, and contain a number of stories about and for children. The blow at capitalism is struck at the outset in the following paragraph, as a preface to the stories:

> The rich capitalists all over the world tried to crush the government of the Russian workers and farmers. They blockaded Russia. They crippled her factories and destroyed her farming machinery and made Russia fight

for her life at a time when she was beginning to make life happy and free for all workers and their children. Then came drouth, starvation, and death for millions.

Radical periodicals are published from Boston to Los Angeles, from Seattle to Florida. The place of publication of the most radical is unknown; they simply appear. They are printed in many languages, including, besides English, Armenian, Bulgarian, Croatian, Czech, Danish, Estonian, Finnish, French, German, Greek, Hungarian, Italian, Lettish, Lithuanian, Polish, Roumanian, Russian, Slovak, Slovenian, Spanish, Ukrainian, and Yiddish.

Many of the papers, such as *The Communist,* the official organ of the Communist party in America, are printed in various language editions. The editors of the different editions attend a regular round table at which the editor-in-chief dictates the general policy to be followed in each article. This policy is discussed by the polyglot circle and the translations are made to conform, not in words but in sentiment, to the policy dictated. The same is true of the books, pamphlets, circulars, posters, and magazines, which appear in many languages, directed to bringing about the one definite result. This part of the Communist party work is thoroughly organized and is progressing without a hitch. These publications are practically all the reading matter the foreigner in the United States gets. They are carefully prepared to keep his mind alien to the interests of the United States, and are devoted to inspiring and maintaining interest in the "class struggle," which is preached to him continuously from the time of his arrival in America. His only companions, frequently his only associates, speak his language, and here are a newspaper, a weekly and a monthly magazine, and even books in his native tongue. There is little in reading matter that falls into his hands to urge him to become an American because everything he wants in the way of reading matter is furnished him in his own language. And therein lies the seriousness of the foreign press situation in the United States. With few exceptions, the reading matter that comes to the foreigner's hand in his own language preaches either openly or by innuendo the "necessity" for the violent overthrow of the United States government.

The radical press was largely concerned with the strikes of 1922, as was to be expected. The radical and labor press was interested in the period of unrest as an example of the larger, broader fight between capital and labor in which the strikes were regarded as but preliminary, although very important, battles. Characteristic is the sentiment expressed: "Capitalism is advancing; Labor is on the defensive." The coal and rail strikes were not only in part the fault of the owners and operators, according to this press; they were entirely so – an unprovoked assault upon the living rights of the workers. Hence, also, the almost universal plea for the united front, the general strike, as the only hope against the unity of purpose and power of the enemy, the ultimate end, of course, being "the complete abolition of capitalism." Certain of the editorials in recent numbers of the Communist and other radical press on the strike situation are very bitter. If they do not in actual words urge measures of direct action, words are scarcely needed in the light of the inflammatory picture painted. To assert, as one of them does, that "The bourgeoisie stands in a fighting line — ready to shoot you down like dogs," and then add, "To give in means — Death! To struggle means — Life! Struggle!" does not require more in the way of exhortation to forcible resistance.

As Moscow is the headquarters of the entire Communistic movement, all important orders affecting Communism throughout the entire world come from that city. Berlin is one of the chief, if not the chief, subordinate headquarters, for it is in the latter city that the governing body of the parties in Western Europe and America sits and directs the work done in those two important sections of the world. The propaganda work in the United States has its headquarters in Berlin, always, of course, under the supreme authorities in Moscow. Early in the summer of 1922, Jay Lovestone, secretary of the Central Executive Committee of the Communist party of America, brought from Berlin $35,000 for propaganda work in this country. Later, A.A. Heller* of New York, representative of the Supreme Soviet of People's Economy in the United States, received $48,000 from Berlin for the same purpose. This latest consignment of gold was for work in connection with the drive of the Friends of Soviet Russia for additional funds, the major portion of which goes into Soviet coffers in Moscow.

Bearing in mind that the United States, then, is fed with Communist propaganda from Berlin, it is interesting to know that this propaganda is prepared at the Berlin headquarters in English, printed on sheets on one side only and thus distributed, so that the English radical papers can reprint it simply by using shears and paste in its preparation. This material is also furnished to the foreign language press here in whatever language is desired, and in the same way. The Berlin organization is no secret abroad, for the *Deutsche Allgemeine Zeitung* published an excellent chart of the ramifications of the organization with the following interesting article:

> The chart shows the organization of the Bolshevik propaganda as spread throughout Europe. Its management is being conducted by the propaganda bureau, which is a division of the All-Russian Central Executive Commit-

---

*Mr. Heller was commercial attaché in Ludwig Martens' "Russian Soviet Embassy," prior to Martens' departure from this country under pressure. *Who's Who in New York,* issue of 1918, states: "Heller, Abraham Aaron, Gen'l Mgr. Internat. Oxygen Co.; b. Minsk, Russia, October 1874; s. Lazarus and Sarah (Chautin) Heller; ed. public schools Moscow, Russia, and New York; m. Edith Spectorsky, Dec. 1902, N.Y.C. Children, Anna, Lyndal, Mireille. Organized in 1893 firm of L. Heller & Son (importers of precious stones) and in 1906 opened European office at Paris, France. Formed Internat. Oxygen Co. in 1910, and is now treasurer and Gen'l Mgr. of same. Mem. Executive Board Compressed Gas Mfrs. Ass'n, Dir. Rand School of Social Science. Recreations, farming, golf. Clubs, Twilight, Inwood Country. Residence, 9 W. 68th St., and Bernardsville, N.J. Address 115 Broadway, N.Y.C." The International Oxygen Co. received large contracts during the War to supply the Army and especially the Navy with oxygen and other chemicals.

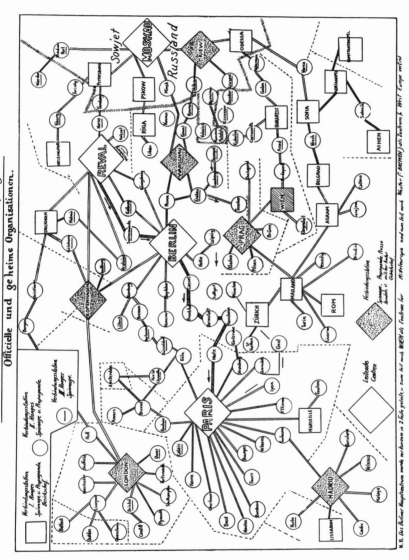

Schematic diagram of the Bolshevik propaganda organization taken from the *Deutsche Allgemeine Zeitung* of Berlin. At that time the propaganda in America was directed largely through the Berlin headquarters but latterly orders have been received direct from Moscow.

tee, having as its object the propaganda within the country, in the army and abroad. The latter is divided into two sections: the Eastern and the Western. The Eastern section consists of eight groups, those of China and Korea, Japan, India, Afghanistan, Turkey, Persia, Caucasus, and the nomadic nations. The Western section embraces, outside of the European countries, the United States of America. The propaganda bureau is headed by the propaganda committee, the members of which are Zinoviev, Radek, Chicherin, Lunacharsky, Krassin, Litvinov, and others. The committee is again divided into an Official Section, containing the diplomatic and commercial delegations abroad, the press bureau, the news agency "Rosta," and a number of wireless stations, as well as the secret sections A and B, conducting a special information and communications service under the management of a member of the Extraordinary Commission, the Cheka. The official section is conducted by Litvinov in Reval. Here are the printing offices, the information bureaus, and warehouses for goods that will be required, should *rappochement* with other countries be perfected.

Litvinov also has charge of the Central offices in Helsingfors, Riga, Kovne, Prague, Vienna, Rome, Stockholm, Copenhagen, London, and Berlin. The Russian money for the feeding of the chest of the Russian missions is being forwarded by Litvinov either directly to those offices or to Berlin for further transmission. It also is being used for the support of the Communist groups, mainly those in Vienna, Prague, and Berlin.

Berlin is ranking first among the Bolshevik central offices. It is overrun with Soviet agents. Its head is Wigdor Kopp, with his secretary, Stomuniak. The main offices are located in the Massenstrasse, Nr. 9. With this there are connected further separate bureaus constituting together an enormous administrative apparatus. The Berlin office is supporting the paper, *Rote Fahne,* and is conducting the Red press bureau in the Muenzstrasse, 24, issuing reports which are being scattered in enormous quantities through Europe and the United States. The office is directed by the German Communist, Anna Geier. The Berlin central office disposes of vast funds. It is obliged to maintain, however, an army of agents, informers, couriers, clubs, newspapers, etc. Kopp also is subsidizing a shipping company; his real name is Kopelevich. He places great confidence in the organization "Peace and Work," which is managed by Professor Stankevich and the journalist Golubsov, endeavoring to reconcile the Russian émigrés with the Soviet government.

The secret sections are working by means of strikes, sabotage, provocations, and economic crises. Their Central Office is administered from Moscow and is under the direction of Zinoviev, Dzerzhinsky, Kamenev, Kursky, and others. Every foreign country has there its representative. Among them there is the Englishman, MacLean, who was arrested recently in England during the demonstrations of the unemployed. The main and sub-arteries are indicated on the chart. Seven of them are connecting Moscow with the centres of Europe. [The United States comes directly under Berlin. — Author.]

The second place after Berlin is Prague. It is the connecting main between Moscow and Paris. The office in Milan is directing the Italian, the Swiss, and the Yugoslav districts. Offices of similar importance are situated in Rome, Zagreb, Belgrade, Sofia, Adrianople, and Constantinople, all of which are directed from Adrianople. Roumania is under special direction of Rakovsky in Kiev. The well-organized Western sections of Zurich and London under the management of Rubalsky are worthy of mention. London is a subdivision of the Paris section and is receiving special attention from Moscow. Toulouse is connected with Spain, while Belgium and Holland are connected with Paris.

This enormous organization could not be changed or overthrown in a night. Changes of individuals might take place but they could not disturb the entire structure. The organization of the Bolshevik propaganda as outlined here is working for the only great goal for which it has been created, which is Universal Revolution.

While the Berlin organization, with the multitude of tentacles outlined above, serves to direct the attitude of the papers of the United States, and various other countries as well, along lines of the general Communist movement, editors of the radical newspapers are permitted great freedom in handling their local situations and problems. Every strike, every political disturbance, every racial clash is seized upon to promote the cause of radicalism and to serve as grounds for an attack upon the "capitalistic" state and form of society. On these lines the radical press in the United States leads the world, for the Communists abroad have passed the stage of development where they have to be continually aroused. The foreigner in the United States, dependent in large measure for his information and almost entirely for his reading matter upon the radical press, needs to have his mind concentrated on his "wrongs" in order to keep him at the proper pitch of rebellious feeling.

Therefore, the radical press pursues its tireless course with steadily increasing skill in fastening upon those issues in the industrial and political life of the United States which lend themselves, often neatly enough, to the cause of radicalism. The characteristic feature of this attitude of blame, contemptuous or ironic, as the case may be, is that never by any chance is a fair or good word, even an extenuating word, said for the existing state of things. Never by any chance is an effort made, never even a suggestion, to improve things as they exist; the sole aim and object is utterly to destroy the present social system before considering the moves that will have to be made in effecting the establishment of the Dictatorship of the Proletariat in America. Everything that is, is wrong, they say; all is black, and there is no relief or betterment in sight because relief and betterment are not to be looked for in a cesspool of iniquity. Read their press day after day and its influence will not be denied. A blatant chauvinism might be proof against it. An intelligent appreciation of this press, pro and con, is not to be gained by belittling it. How a full sympathy with it must be nourished and strengthened by regular reading, it is disconcerting to think.

The proletariat of the United States, the Communists and other radical leaders believe, has passed the stage where wild excitement is necessary to waken workers to an appreciation of what they must do. Accordingly a change appears in their press. In 1920 the efforts of press and agitators were devoted to exciting the workers to radicalism in thought and deed. The most inflammatory appeals were printed and broadcast by every way that could be found in which the law could be evaded. But today the propaganda is far more insidious. The minds of the workers have been filled with the necessity of overthrowing the government by violence and now they are being trained to the work which is regarded solely as preliminary to the great "mass action." That is why the united front is being preached and stressed on every occasion. *Freiheit,* the daily organ of the Jewish Federation of the Workers' party, the "legal" branch of the Communist party of America, in discussing strikes editorially, said in the autumn of 1922:

> The right to work has no meaning to them [the employers] when they lock out the workers, reorganize the factories, have the work done outside (in order to deprive their own workers of work), and demand for themselves the right to discharge employees. The worker is to them of lesser value than a machine.
>
> A machine is not thrown out when there is not enough work to keep it going. The worker, however, who creates all the wealth for his employer through the sweat of his brow, is thrown out in the street when there is not enough work to keep him busy.
>
> We are not discussing this with the railroad companies or other employers. We do not want to preach morals to them. We only want that the workers themselves conceive fully the "sacred right to work."
>
> The workers will acquire the right to work with the abolishment of the rights of the employers over the industries and with the substitution of the dictatorship of the masters with that of the workers.

As an example of the radical press's efforts to keep the spirit of the workers up to fighting pitch, a couple of paragraphs from a recent number of *Uj Elore,* a Hungarian daily Communist paper of New York, will suffice. This paper, in an editorial printed in September 1922, shows the characteristic hope that out of the railroad and coal strikes, or any other similar strikes, may grow the means to the great end, the triumph of Communism through the general strike. In part this editorial says:

> The new factor of the American labor movement is the spiritual trend which fills with revolutionary solidarity the awakening masses. Soon there will appear, in every fight of the workers, that feeling of revolutionary solidarity which gives the masses participating in the fight a strong push, which makes them feel that they no longer fight only for temporary advantages, not only to preserve the attained results, but that they enter the fight on a wider basis, affecting the whole working class. The revolutionary aim steps to the foreground.
>
> The Communist self-consciousness of the workers has become a powerful weapon against capitalism which is already shocked by this strength, although the workers have not even used yet the weapon that has become hardened (as steel) by solidarity. What is this weapon?
>
> The thought of a *general strike* is this weapon which has become manifest among broad ranks in spite of all the soothing efforts of the trade

union pashas. The workers want to employ this weapon, they demand that it be employed . . . . The mass has issued the password that the terror of the government must be answered by a general strike . . . .

The masses grow more and more in favor of the revolutionary fight and with this they voluntarily accept Communist leadership. In trade unions the members know already that the bourgeoisie do not represent the interests of the workers and the court injunction has made even those sober who up to now supported the Gompers policy . . . .

The powerful weapon flashed up in the hands of the workers of America; the bourgeoisie is looking trembling toward the developments. In the strained situation the sober, earnest, and conscious words of the Communists have a commanding effect. It is up to the workers of America whether they will progress according to the revolutionary finger-post towards victory.

The cleverness of the editorial forces of the various Communist and other radical publications is frequently shown in hints of violence which leave in the readers' minds thoughts of possibilities that will lead to the desired end. Editorials which are almost "as gentle as a sucking dove" are more often than not wholly inimical to the government in spirit and are bound to leave inflammatory ideas in the minds of the readers. And often an apparently mild but insidiously terroristic editorial will conclude with a single paragraph breathing violence; as, for example, the following paragraph from a recent number of *Laisve,* a Lithuanian Communist daily published in Brooklyn:

Only when the workers manifest their solidarity and their clenched mass fist does the Government begin to reckon with them and speak about their constitutional rights — only then does the Government allow the proletariat a certain amount of concessions.

It is impossible to give more than a hint of the work being done by the Communist and other radical press of the United States. Every one of the upward of a hundred radical daily newspapers, not to mention the weeklies, monthlies, pamphlets, and books, is filled with matter breathing defiance to the established order of government in the United States and urging the workers to take the reins in their own hands, as was done in Russia, and establish the longed-for dictatorship.

In every city in the country there is a committee of the Communist party of America whose duties are to find ways of presenting their propaganda to non-Communists through the medium of what is called the "conservative" press. Unfortunately, the desire of most metropolitan daily papers to be fair and permit both sides of any question which is mentioned in their columns to be presented offers an excellent opportunity, of which the Communists are quick to take advantage, for the dissemination of Communist propaganda through newspapers which are distinctly loyal. Frequently American publications are imposed upon and print letters and signed articles which have been contributed under various guises and which in fact are merely clever designs of the Communists to establish a connection with a reputable publication for improper use in the future.

The columns of periodicals like *The Nation, The Freeman,* and *The New Republic* have been freely and widely opened for Communist propaganda to appeal to the so-called "intellectuals" who read these papers. This is not so serious, for the policy of these publications is plainly evident to anyone. They are classed as revolutionary and make no disclaimer of the charges that they are engaged, partially at least, in spreading the doctrines of the revolutionists. But when a publication like the official *Journal of the American Bankers' Association* falls into a trap laid for it, one must express surprise. If any organization in the country should be conservative it is that of the bankers. And when an issue of the official organ of that organization came from the press with an article by Ivan Narodny (alias Mueller, alias Ivan Ivanovitch, alias Jaan Siboul, alias Jaan Talue), a suspect during the war, there was reason for surprise. The article, to be sure, was an ostensible attack on the Soviet government in Russia, but it was planted for ulterior purposes after a considerable discussion and carefully laid plans by the Communists here, who had a quiet laugh at the ease with which they had effected an entrance to the bourgeois press. Narodny has served time for counterfeiting, has long been and admits that he is an active revolutionary, working from Russia, and has had a career of crime the details of which would fill a book.

All publications of the radical press of the United States are considered official organs by the Communist party, for all the official orders from Moscow are given to each publication in order that the instructions may reach all members of the party. As an example of this there appeared a proclamation signed by the Executive Committee of the Communist International, dated at Moscow July 22, 1922, calling upon "the workingmen and workingwomen of all countries" to keep up the fight for help for Russia. Referring to the demands of the sane countries of the world that private property be respected by the Soviet government before the question of recognition will be considered, this proclamation says:

> As regards the factories and mines . . . Soviet Russia has stated that she will never and on no account return them . . . . The Russian proletariat will not return them, because otherwise the rivers of blood by which it has saved the revolution will have been spilled in vain. The October revolution which gave the factories and the estates into the hands of the Russian leaders was the first step made by the international proletariat toward liberation from the capitalist yoke. No backward step will be taken, cost what it may.

The Communist and other radical papers not only have their own cartoonists, of whom Art Young is the most prolific and most effective, and their own poets

EDITOR CAPITALIST POLITICIAN MINISTER

This cartoon, illustrating the anti-Christian character of the revolutionary movement in the United States, was first published in Max Eastman's paper, *The Masses,* suppressed during the war and revived in the present *Liberator.* It was drawn by the radical cartoonist, Art Young and was captioned, "Having their Fling." Subsequently it was reproduced in the now defunct socialist and pro-Bolshevik paper, *The New York Call.*

and paragraphers, whose ability cannot be questioned, but they have their own press service in the Federated Press. This is in part a cooperative association of labor and radical papers. Its aim has been to collect and distribute all news pertaining to the labor and radical movements. It endeavored to get the sanction of the conservative labor organizations, but its radicalism was too well-known and in this the effort failed. The Communist party of America considers the Federated Press its own press service organization, and it is certain that several of the officials of the press service are active members of the Communist party. Upwards of 200 papers in the United States are affiliated with the Federated Press. Louis P. Lochner is the European director and acting business manager, and has an office in Berlin, where he is in close touch with the International Propaganda Bureau of the Communist International.

In order to facilitate the collection of funds for the Federated Press and through it the dissemination of radical propaganda, a Federated Press League was organized in Chicago on February 4, 1922. By this league membership in the Federated Press is stimulated, funds are collected frequently from parlor Bolshevik circles and wealthy people who believe they are giving to aid the "downtrodden" to express themselves and make themselves heard by the rest of humanity. A number of chain papers have been established from Boston to Los Angeles, and agents of the league, who are really working for the cause of the Communist party of America, are active in every city in the country. The officials of the league elected at the Chicago meeting were: Robert Morss Lovett, president; Mrs. Frances C. Lillie, vice president; George B. Hooker, vice president; E.C. Wentworth, treasurer; and Clark H. Getts, secretary.

It is evident that the Communist element is gaining full control of this news-gathering organization. Besides the Berlin office, an office has been established in Moscow; the Communist International uses this office for the purpose of sending out manifestos and strong propaganda to be published in this country. According to Robert M. Buck, chairman of the Executive Board, who is connected with the *New Majority,* a radical publication in Chicago, the central figures in the Federated Press are Jack Carney, editor of the radical *Voice of Labor*; Arne Swabeck, a Finn and editor of *Nytio,* who controlled 10 votes at the Chicago meeting; Editor Feinburg of *Solidarity*; William Z. Foster, head of the Trade Union Educational League and a delegate to the illegal convention at Bridgman; Carl Haessler, the college professor who spent two years in the penitentiary; Mabel Search of Milwaukee; Clark H. Getts, who has served a jail term; Carroll Binder, a college man; Louis P. Lochner, the European representative; and Maude McCreery, the woman agitator who was active in the establishment of chain papers throughout the country.*

---

*For the year 1923, Carl Haessler was managing editor, Tom Tippett business manager, and C.A. Moseley, editor. The executive board was composed of: Thomas R. Downie, chairman, *Labor News,* Galesburg, Ill.; Joseph Schlossberg, vice chairman, *Advance,* New York; E.B. Ault, *Union Record,* Seattle; R.D. Craemer, *Labor Review,* Minneapolis; Matti Tenhunen, *Tvomies,* Superior, Wis.; William Z. Foster, *Labor Herald,* Chicago; Arne Swabeck, *Nv Tid,* Chicago; J.A. Lochray, *Midwest Labor News,* Omaha; Albert F. Coyle, *Brotherhood of Locomotive Engineers' Journal,* Cleveland.

E.J. Costello was manager of the Federated Press until, because of a wrangle on the board, he was dismissed and Carl Haessler took his place. William Z. Foster, who among his numerous radical activities is a member of the board of trustees of the Garland Foundation, expected to turn over $100,000 from the Foundation to the Federated Press, and told a number of people that he was going to do so; but a row in the management of the organization upset these plans. Among the people to whom Foster made this statement were Mrs. Kate Crane Gartz, the Pasadena society parlor-Bolshevik, and Charlie Chaplin, the motion picture comedian. Foster also told them that the Garland Foundation could be depended upon whenever anyone got into trouble because of radical political opinions. Several of the organizers of the Communist party and its "legal" political branch, the Workers' party, among them William Thurston Brown of San Francisco, were promised regular monthly salaries by Foster, to be paid from the Garland Foundation.

A detailed account of how thoroughly the work of organization and especially of collecting money for the furtherance of the aim of the Communist party is done will prove interesting as well as illuminating. Bruce Rogers, a leading Communist of Seattle, went secretly to Los Angeles, arriving there on the night of March 24, 1922, to raise money for the Federated Press League and at the same time to spread Communist propaganda. These two objectives were specified in his instructions for the trip. A secret conference was held March 26 at which Rogers met William Thurston Brown, Ella Reeve Bloor, who was a delegate to the illegal convention at Bridgman, and Alfred Bush. Rogers explained the purpose of the trip and proposed that small groups of "thoroughly grounded Communists" who are members of craft unions travel from place to place and join the local unions during their short sojourns in industrial centers for the purpose of uniting the radical factions and starting Communist nuclei within the craft unions. He said that a group of printers and stereotypers had come to Seattle from Detroit and worked along those lines.

Those present at this conference endorsed the Rogers plan as he outlined it and decided to get in touch with San Francisco, Portland, Seattle, Salt Lake City, and Chicago for the purpose of inviting such groups of militant, foot-loose craft union men to go to Los Angeles and strengthen the local radical movement.

Rogers went to the Labor Temple in Los Angeles, but he later told friends that he had anything but a cordial reception there. He said the Federated Press had been laboring under a misapprehension in thinking that its news represented the viewpoint of the average American-born worker, who, he said, is as yet wrapped up in the capitalistic ideology. He made a short trip to San Diego, but returned in time to speak at a meeting of the open forum of the Socialist party. He was introduced as the representative of the Federated Press service and spoke on "The Origin of Newspapers and the Press Service." He afterwards told friends that he was very well satisfied with the way his Communist propaganda was received. His headquarters in Los Angeles was at the Van Winkle Hotel, 349 South Olive Street, which was kept by an Irishwoman, an old-timer in the radical movement, who has sheltered many Communists in her hostelry.

On the evening of April 6 a secret meeting was held at the home of a Mr. and Mrs. Kashub, at which were present Ella Reeve Bloor, Arthur Cotter, a Miss Moran, well-known among public school teachers because of her radicalism, Rogers, a Mrs. Mellentine, who is a member of the Severance Club of Los Angeles, and five others. There were no introductions and the meeting was shrouded in strictest secrecy. At this meeting further plans for the work of the Communist party were agreed upon, especially as to Rogers' work on the Pacific Coast. Rogers was scheduled to speak at the Modern School on the night of April 17, but cancelled the lecture because of the small attendance, for which he blamed lack of advertising. Mrs. Bloor was speaking the same night at a widely advertised meeting at the Shelley Club under the auspices of the Young People's Forum. This led to an arrangement with Emanuel Levin to establish a clearing-house for radical speakers so there would not again come about a conflict of dates.

Rogers worked his way into parlor-Bolshevik circles, using his connection with the Federated Press as an opening wedge. He was after big game, planning to raise enough money from wealthy radicals in Pasadena, Hollywood, and Los Angeles to establish a chain of papers in the Southwest to be controlled by the Federated Press. He was the guest of the Writers' Club in Hollywood, where he said he met a number of men with radical ideas who support the Federated Press. Mrs. Martha Kashub, Mrs. Gaylord Wilshire, and Countess Korzybska (Lady Edgerley) gave him valuable leads. On the night of April 12, he spoke at the Shelley Club about the necessity of building up a radical press service in the United States. Much of his lecture was taken from Upton Sinclair's *Brass Check*.

To some of his closest friends he told the real object of his trip to Los Angeles. He told them that the Federated Press, which was the only radical press service in the country, could not exist on the support it received from labor organizations for two reasons: first, it did not represent the viewpoint of the great mass of organized labor, being far too advanced and revolutionary for the conservative American-born working man; and second, no enterprise was ever financed by "passing the hat." He explained that he meant that the small contributions of organized labor were not sufficient to keep the Federated Press going.

Consequently, he said, the Federated Press representatives from Boston to the Pacific Coast had been instructed to go after the wealthy liberals and get as many life members for the Federated Press League at $1000 each as possible. "Do not offend the liberals, and do anything to please the parlor Reds," he said, is to be the watchword of the Federated Press. The interesting feature of this is that Rogers and many other representatives of the Federated Press are

Communists, and their propaganda and money-raising activities pave the way for later penetration on the part of the Communist party, whose open emissaries follow the leads and use the "sucker lists" they get from men like Rogers.

Rogers was greatly pleased with the result of his visit to San Diego, although it was brief. He reported that all the labor unions in San Diego had voted to support the Federated Press, and although in nearly every instance there was a motion to divide the money with Soviet Russia for famine relief, the trip proved a financial success. He said that support from the "highbrow" radicals was also forthcoming in a generous manner, and that the Templeton Johnsons, a very wealthy family of San Diego, were the only ones who had refused him when he had asked them for a $1000 donation, although formerly they had been among the chief supporters of the Federated Press. He mentioned as one who had given "very liberally" Lyman J. Gage, formerly president of the First National Bank of Chicago and Secretary of the Treasury under President McKinley and President [Theodore] Roosevelt. Of course Mr. Gage, who was then very old and had for years been a resident at Katherine Tingley's Theosophical Society colony on Point Loma, had no idea that his money was to be used to further the plans of a conspiracy directed at the overthrow by violence of the government he had once served. It simply shows the ease with which the Communists finance their work.

In addition to these wealthy people from whom he secured money, Rogers also told of finding a thriving colony of parlor Bolsheviki in San Diego who pledged their aid to the cause. In this connection he spoke of a certain Dr. Stone and a Dr. Ritter as among his "prospects." Rogers' trip to San Diego was not casual; he was ordered by the Central Executive Committee of the Communist party of America to go to that city during the convention there of the Congress of Social Workers, and to spread propaganda among the many radicals and semi-radicals in attendance.

Robert Morss Lovett, then president of the Federated Press League, wrote Rogers while he was in Los Angeles, urging him to canvass the movie colony in Hollywood, giving him the names of prominent actors who "helped us before and will do it again." Lovett has since denied having written this letter, but his name is signed to it and affidavits are in the possession of the proper authorities testifying to the facts as here stated. The letter, written from Chicago under date of April 29, 1922, reads:

> Dear Bruce: Mr. Getts and I just returned from Milwaukee and find your letter of the 15th in which you inclosed $500. A former letter also received while we were away inclosed $700, making a total of $1200 sent in to the office this month.
>
> Mr. Getts will answer your letters himself, but I wanted to take up with you the matter of canvassing the Movie Colony at Hollywood. First I want to tell you that I have personally written to about fifteen big producers and prominent actors at Hollywood, including Wm. C. DeMille, Allan Hollabar, Von Stroheim, Percival T. Gerson, Will Rogers, Charles Ray and

Charlie Chaplin. These men are with us. They helped us before and will do it again. Present the situation strong and don't let them off easy, for we need the money and need it badly. Work through the Severance Club and it will be easy for you.

I may join you in San Francisco next month, for we must put it over, and put it over by August, or we will be out of the office.

Good luck to you, Bruce. Please work hard. Your commission should be in Los Angeles by the 4th of May.

Warmly yours,
(Signed) Robert Morss Lovett

After raising many thousands of dollars from the wealthy supporters of radicalism in Los Angeles, Rogers went to Pasadena, where there is a large group of parlor Bolsheviki. On Sunday, June 11, Rogers met, at the home of a Mrs. Ellsworth in the fashionable Oak Knoll District, a number of wealthy radicals, including Mrs. Kate Crane Gartz, Mrs. Gaylord Wilshire, Mrs. Van Toll, Prince Hopkins, and others. He addressed them on behalf of the Federated Press, saying frankly that it was the only avenue through which the Communists, the Workers' party, and the Trade Union Educational League could reach the working class class and all those interested in the working class struggle. He said that the Federated Press was in dire need of funds and that he had been instructed to raise $25,000 in and around Los Angeles. After his address he talked privately with most of those present.

Rogers left Los Angeles for San Francisco June 15. The radical landlady at whose hotel he lived said that Rogers did more for the radical cause during his two months in Los Angeles than had ever been done before. She said that under the pretense of raising money for the Federated Press, he had collected more than $20,000 for the Communists. Part of the money, she said, will be turned over to the Federated Press, but it will be spent for the same purpose, for Rogers told her, she said, that the Federated Press is gradually growing into the one news-gathering agency which is firmly controlled by the Communists. Rogers collected money from the liberals, saying that the Federated Press was nothing more than an independent press service interested solely in getting the truth before the people; and from the labor unions, saying that it was about to become the official organ of the American Federation of Labor. The latter statement, however, drew forth a rebuke from Francis Drake, editor of the local American Federation of Labor organ, who said that the Federated Press was spreading Communist propaganda colored in the interests of disruptionists like William Z. Foster, Alexander Howatt, and Curley Grow.

CHAPTER FIVE

"Legal" Organizations

When the Communist party of America was officially declared to be an illegal organization in the United States, its avowed object being the overthrow by violence of the established government of this country and the inauguration of the Dictatorship of the Proletariat here, it immediately burrowed underground — and continued to function with even greater activity. But in order to carry on the propaganda for the soviet form of government in the United States, as it was under orders from Moscow to do, it became necessary to find some way of "legal expression" in order to reach the people of whom it hoped to make converts. There was no need to waste time, money, and energy in spreading Communist propaganda among Communists, but it was highly important that some means be found quickly to reach the hated bourgeoisie, to show them the beauties of Communism and to raise them to the high radical estate of Russia.

It was also necessary to have organizations to secure funds from the bourgeoisie to be expended in fighting the battle of the united front, for mass action against the present order of church, home, and state. For it has been from the outset, as established by the Russian Reds, the method of the Communists to extract money from the rich to finance their overthrow. This matter was the subject of much deliberation among the members of the inner circle of the Communist party underground, and experts were sent from Moscow to aid in the solution of this important problem. Finally, means were found, and today there are four chief organizations, classed as "legal," by which the fight against the United States government may be carried out and financed. There are also a number of subordinate bodies working to aid the chief "legal" branches, as well as non-Communist organizations, the activities of which directly lend aid to the work "in the open" of the Communists underground.

The legal organizations are definitely controlled by the Communist party of America, which in turn is controlled by the inner Soviet circle in Moscow. The programs for work by the legal organizations are drawn up by the Central Executive Committee of the Communist party and approved by Moscow before being put into operation by the various bodies whose activities are known to the public. It was partly for the purpose of effecting the contact between the legal bodies, the Communist party of America, and the directing head at Moscow that the illegal convention of the Communist party which was raided by Michigan state authorities was held in Bridgman, Michigan. The delegates to this convention, while influenced largely by the words and acts of the Central Executive Committee, were really the authorized representatives of the party to decide on the best means of putting into action the instructions from Moscow.

An example of the activities of the legal branches of the party is the dissemination of information regarding the interest taken by the Moscow Central Bureau of the Communist movement in the situation in the United States. Early in September 1922, the Central Executive Committee of the Communist party of America received from Moscow an appeal to the workers of England to aid the striking coal miners of the United States. The Central Executive Committee immediately set to work translating this document and the distribution of the translation was made throughout the countryside to the legal organizations in order that it might be made known to as many working men as possible. By this it was hoped to attract non-Communist workers to the ranks of the Communists, as the argument was used that the Moscow Government was fighting for the American working man and woman. This document, copies of which were sent to all Communist parties in the world, translated by the Central Executive Committee, reads as follows:

For The Aid Of The Striking Miners Of America
Workers of England:

It is now four months that the fierce struggle of the American miners with the Coal Barons is going on. For several months hundreds of thousands of workers without regard to language or race are defending themselves against the attacks of the American Financial Kings. An army of hired workers from the camp of the bourgeoisie, the establishment of martial law, a whole army of *provocateurs*, have been unable to break their unitedness and compel them to work for the exploiters for a further reduced pay.

Their heroic defense is beginning to bear fruits.

The coal reserves accumulated by the capitalists for this struggle are exhausted. American industry is becoming exhausted; the capitalists are facing the menace of a great defeat.

It is well known to the English capitalists that a defeat of the American exploiters will mean their own defeat and a strengthening of the English wage slaves. They have realized what constitutes their class interest and are coming to the assistance of American mine owners. They are loading and shipping to America a whole fleet with coal. Every steamer with coal arriving in a North American harbor strengthens the forces of the coal barons and nullifies the results which have been attained by the struggling workers.

There exists the danger that the struggle of our proletarian comrades, unexampled in its length and self-sacrifice, will become lost, thanks to the international union of capitalists.

This must be countered by the international unity of the workers.

English transport workers, harbor workers, miners! It is your turn now. You must understand that every loading of a ship with coal being sent to America is a blow in the back to the workers who are struggling there. You must understand that you are rendering support to the capitalists to the extent of your failure to interfere with the delivery of coal to America.

You must understand that the defeat of the American workers will inevitably react against you. The reduction of the wage scale and the increase of the working day in America will bring the same consequences in England.

If you present against the united front of the exploiters the united front of the exploited, then your aid will greatly increase the fighting strength of the American proletarians, and will help them to achieve victory. And you, equally with your American brothers, will reap the fruits of this victory.

This is why we call upon you to:

Hasten to the assistance of the American struggler!

Do not load coal for America!

Long live the unity of the English and American workers!

Long live the world social revolution!

Long live the Communist International!

(signed) Zinoviev
President of the Communist International

Accompanying this appeal by Zinoviev were instructions to the Central Executive Committee of the Communist party of America to promote agitation in an effort to arouse the striking miners to a point of armed insurrection. No opportunity is ever lost by the leaders of the world Communist movement to make of any trouble or disorder the spark to set off armed violence by which they hope to accomplish the overthrow of the government. These instructions, verbatim, are as follows:

The Central Committee of the Communist party of America must direct its particular attention to the progress of the strike of the miners of America.

Agitators and propagandists must be sent to the strike regions.

It is necessary to strive to arouse the striking coal miners to the point of armed insurrection. Let them blow up and flood the shafts. Shower the strike regions with proclamations and appeals. This arouses the revolutionary spirit of the workers and prepares them for the coming revolution of America.

(signed) Zinoviev
President of the Communist International

With this background it is possible to understand some of the work that is being done by the "legal" organizations through which the Communist party of

America is able to spread the propaganda looking toward the overthrow by violence of the government of the United States under orders from Moscow. It should also be borne in mind that these organizations frequently change their names in order to mystify the authorities and fool the public. First, probably, in importance among the various legal organizations is the Workers' party of America, ostensibly a political party of the laborers. The documents found at Bridgman demonstrate beyond the shadow of a doubt that the Communist party controls and directs every action of the Workers' party. By gathering the laborers of this country into a single political party and keeping them steeped in Communist propaganda, the leaders believe they can make converts of them.

The Workers' party of America was born December 24, 1921, at a convention called by the American Labor Alliance, secretly organized by the Communist party as a "cover." The convention call invited delegates from such organizations as the Finnish Socialist Federation, the Hungarian Federation, the Irish-American Labor Alliance; and the majority of the delegates to this convention were hand-picked by the Central Executive Committee of the Communist party of America. The delegates represented, besides those organizations just mentioned, the Italian Workers' Federation, the Jewish Workers' Federation, the Jewish Socialist Federation, and the Workers' Educational Association. They came from Colorado, Illinois, Kansas, Massachusetts, Michigan, Minnesota, Missouri, Montana, New Jersey, New York, Ohio, Pennsylvania, Virginia, and Wisconsin. There were 164 delegates and about 100 fraternal delegates. One represented the Industrial Workers of the World and two the African Blood Brotherhood.

J. Louis Engdahl, in opening the convention, said that it had been called for the purpose of establishing in this country a real revolutionary political party "to wage successful combat against and finally to achieve the overthrow of American capitalism." J.P. Cannon, at that time a member of the Central Executive Committee of the Cincinnati Communist party of America, told this first convention of the great victory that had been won by the workers in Russia, endeavored by inflammatory sentences to stir the delegates to revolutionary enthusiasm, and bitterly attacked capitalism. Caleb Harrison, one of the delegates to the Bridgman convention, was elected permanent chairman of the Workers' party meeting; Margaret Prevey, vice chairman; and Elmer T. Allison, J. Louis Engdahl, and W.W. Weinstone, another Bridgman delegate, secretaries.

Christmas Day was devoted to drafting the constitution of the Workers' party. Efforts were made by some of the ultra-radicals to call for immediate revolution, and much time was wasted on violent debates and virulent attacks upon the United States. But as the inner circles of the Communist party had prepared in advance the constitution, these debates were merely in order to give the rabid radicals an opportunity to work off their heat. The following day William F. Dunne, then of Montana and now of that State and New York, and candidate for governor of New York in the 1922 elections on the

Workers' party ticket, made an impassioned address on the activities of the I.W.W. in the West. The Sacco and Vanzetti case was also taken up and condemnation of the United States was voiced in resolutions adopted. The convention delegates then stood while the "Red Flag" was sung. The purpose of the Workers' party was described accurately in an editorial in *Uj Elore*, the Hungarian Communist paper:

> For the last two years the great mass of the American proletariat stood without a direct political leader. Persecution has forced the only revolutionary political organization, the Communist party, under the ground and it could continue its activity only as an illegal organization. As an illegal organization it could reach the mass only indirectly; therefore it could not exercise upon the mass such moral effect as is absolutely necessary in order to assert its leadership of the mass. The party itself never could have gained a bigger moral influence over the mass because with its organizations it never could step to the front rank of the mass. However, in spite of the most severe "legal" persecutions, the Communist work cannot stop; therefore, it is necessary to place a party at the head of the mass which, although revolutionary, cannot be persecuted. The Workers' party will fulfill this task.
>
> The Workers' party will meet the requirements of the American proletariat. It will be a powerful weapon for class struggle which cannot be knocked out of the hand of the proletariat with the slogan of "lawlessness." This party will take its stand at the head of every movement of the proletariat in order to lead it with revolutionary bravery and with Communist realism.
>
> The Workers' party will be based entirely upon the principles of the Third International. The organization of the Workers' party is the first step toward a big and strong revolutionary mass movement.
>
> The formation of this party proves, too, that, in spite of the persecutions on the part of the bourgeoisie, the proletariat can still find means with which to continue its attacks against the capitalistic order. There is now such persecution as to make it impossible for us to continue the fight. The working class looks with confidence into the future; it will be led by a political party which uses the well-tried tactics of the Third International, a political party which knows no compromise.

The Workers' party counts largely on support from the women voters. Great care was taken in effecting an organization which would reach all classes of working women, including, as the program states, "millions of workers' and farmers' wives isolated from the general field of the organized working class struggle," for it was deemed an absolute necessity to "win the women of the working class to the party's ideal" and to "unite them for and link them to the general proletarian struggle." Accordingly women's branches were started in various parts of the country with leaders whose duties included spreading propaganda, the substance of which, subversive of the constitution, is dictated through the Workers' party by the Central Executive Committee of the Communist party of America.

At the beginning of the railroad and coal strikes, when it was thought these troubles might lead to the longed-for General Strike which was to effect the violent overthrow of the government of the United States and the establishment of the Dictatorship of the Proletariat, it was quickly seen that the women's committees of the Workers' party could do some excellent agitational work among the families of the strikers. Accordingly, the National Women's Committee, which is a secret body, on April 1, 1922, adopted and set in motion a program for women's emergency work in the mining districts. A form set of resolutions was sent out to all women Communists in the districts to be adopted by the women's committees to be formed, and specific instructions were given the Communists, of which the following are portions:

> Before bringing this resolution to a vote, the members of the nuclei [that is, the inner circles of Communists] and the Number One women [that is, the women members of the illegal organizations of Communists] should do a thorough piece of agitational work to insure its enthusiastic acceptance.
>
> As soon as the vote is taken, a meeting of women should be held under the auspices of the union. A working committee should be appointed. *Number One women should see to it that they are on the committee.* The Chairman, however, should be the local woman who has the most experience and been most active in past strikes, irrespective of her being a member of Number One. This is important.
>
> Other working women in the locality, who are sympathetic, should by all means be encouraged to attend meetings and participate in the work.
>
> Number One women must not use this committee for propaganda *unconnected with the strike.* The efforts of Number One must be to create solidarity and morale. Plenty of opportunity for propaganda on issues directly related to the strike can be found.
>
> Number One women should suggest to the women's committees the forming of a literature committee with a view of publishing a leaflet for house-to-house distribution. The text of such a leaflet will be by the National Women's Committee. *This should be presented as the work of a local woman.* It may be modified or enlarged to fit local conditions.
>
> The National Women's Committee urgently recommends that this emergency project, unanimously passed upon, *shall remain secret and not sent out to the membership at large.*

Finally, the last paragraph of the "Principles and Aims of the Workers' Party" definitely and positively links this political organization with the Communist party. This document was found buried at Bridgman when the convention of the Communist party was raided, and the last paragraph reads as follows:

> The Workers' party declares itself in sympathy with the principles of the Communist International and enters the struggle against American capitalism, the most powerful of the national groups of capitalists, under the leadership of the Communist International. It rallies to the call, "Workers of the World Unite."

The whole work of the Workers' party is aimed at educating the working class and mass in Red Trade Union International ideas through active participation in the political life of the country. The subtlety of this method of preparation for future political action is cleverly conceived, and but for the fact that the connection between the Workers' party and the Moscow authorities is now known, the results of the methods employed would have been the source of much trouble in the future. This may yet result.

Next in importance, probably, in the legal organizations of the Communist party is William Z. Foster's Trade Union Educational League. This is aimed chiefly at the industrial life of the nation and is constantly at open warfare as a minority organization with the American Federation of Labor. Its militant and uncompromising attitude toward capital and its power within the American Federation of Labor show that it has large influence in that organization and is constantly making gains within the Federation membership. It was organized by Foster in 1920 and embraced at the outset the more radically inclined labor unions. Shortly after this organization was formed the Communist International promulgated the policy of "boring from within" the trade unions with a view to wrecking the trade union movement in this country. Foster was approached by the Communists and as a consequence he attended the Congress of the Communist International and the first congress of the Red Trade Union International, held at Moscow in July 1921.

Upon Foster's return from Moscow the Trade Union Educational League immediately became a propaganda agency for the Communist International and affiliated with the Red Trade Union International. Foster has repeatedly denied this, and has declared that no connection existed between his organization and the Communists. But, thanks to the Bridgman raid, absolute proof of his connection is now available. The *Labor Herald* is the official organ of the Trade Union Educational League. The principles and program of Foster's League were distributed widely throughout the country early in 1922 and the following sentences from it are significant:

> The Trade Union Educational League proposes to develop trade unions from their present antiquated and stagnant conditions into modern, powerful labor organizations capable of waging successful warfare against capital. To this end it is working to revamp and remodel from top to bottom their theories, tactics, structure and leadership. Instead of advocating the prevailing shameful and demoralizing nonsense about harmonizing the interests of capital and labor, it is firing the workers' imaginations and releasing their wonderful idealism and energy by propagating the inspiring goal of the abolition of capitalism and the establishment of a workers' republic.
>
> The Trade Union Educational League groups the militants in two ways: by localities and by industries. In all cities and towns general groups of militants of all trades are formed to carry on the work of education and reorganization in their respective localities. These local general groups, to

facilitate their work, divide themselves into industrial sections . . . . All the local general groups are kept in touch and cooperation with each other through a national corresponding secretary. Likewise all the local industrial educational groups are linked together nationally, industry by industry, through their respective corresponding secretaries. Every phase and stage of the trade union movement will have its branch of the life-giving educational organization.

The entire work of the Trade Union Educational League is based upon the following decisions of the Red Trade Union International:

1. — Workers' Control is the necessary school for the work of preparing the masses for the proletarian revolution.
2. — Workers' Control must be the war-cry for the workers of every capitalist country and must be utilized as a weapon to disclose financial and commercial secrets.
3. — Workers' Control must be largely used for the reconstruction of the outlaw trade unions and the industrial factions, the former being harmful for the workers' revolutionary movement.
4. — Workers' Control is distinct from capitalist schemes, and to the dictatorship of the capitalist class it opposes the dictatorship of the working class. In the various activities within the shops the so-called revolutionary nuclei perform the various functions promulgated by the Trade Union International.

Who is William Zebulon Foster, familiarly known as "Bill" Foster? The authorities have known that he was a "radical" for a long time, and he has been accused of being "Red," but there has not been much proof offered the public on the matter. Foster himself has denied repeatedly that he was anything but an honest working man, devoted to bettering the conditions of his fellow-workers. He has denied that he was a Communist, but at times has admitted that he was affiliated with the Communists. When he went to Moscow he attempted to make the trip in secret, but it became known, and after that he was a bit more frank about his sympathies with the Red movement.

Now it is possible to establish definitely that Foster is a Communist, a paid employee of the Communist party of America, and that the Trade Union Educational League, of which he was the founder and is the head, is a branch of the Communist party designed to "bore from within" the labor union branches of the American Federation of Labor and destroy that organization.

That Foster is not only a paid agent of the Moscow government but is also a paymaster is shown by the fact that when he returned from his secret trip to Russia, he brought with him, presumably to carry on Communist propaganda in this country, the sum of $40,000. On another occasion, in April 1923, the Trade Union Educational League, of which Foster is the organizer and head, received the sum of $90,000 from Moscow. In August 1922, Lozovsky attended the secret illegal convention of the Communist party of America at Bridgman, as a delegate from Moscow, and turned over to Foster for the use of the Trade Union Educational League the sum of $35,000, making a total of $165,000.* It is not to be inferred from this that this is all the money that the Moscow government or the Third International has sent to this country for the purpose of forcibly overthrowing this government, as undoubtedly many sums have been sent of which none but the immediate parties concerned have knowledge.

Foster has repeatedly denied that this League had any connection with the Communist party, but we have seen how he has discussed it openly in the inner councils of the party at their convention in Bridgman, Michigan. Among the documents left buried on the Bridgman farm August 22, 1922, when the convention was broken up by the raid of the authorities, were the question-naires, answered by the delegates in their own handwriting and turned over to the grounds committee for safe keeping.

Foster gave his age as 41, stated that he was born in the United States and was married — each in answer to questions submitted in mimeographed form. He said that he used English "in the main," but that he could speak German and French imperfectly. "When not in party employ," he said, his occupation was railroading. He said he once belonged to the Socialist party, and "has been active in the revolutionary movement" twenty-one years. His present position, he said, was the only office he had held, however, in the revolutionary movement. He had been "active in the Communist movement" one year and was at that time a paid employee of the Communist party of America, his office being given as "industrial director."

In response to the question, "How many times arrested?" he answered, "Many times in trade union work," but gave two months as his longest term of imprisonment. He said that he had never been deported and was not under indictment. This questionnaire having been filled out before the raid, his statement that he was not under indictment was true at that time. He stated that he was inclined to industrial work in the party, and that he had been a member of a labor union twenty-one years. It will be noted that his labor union experience coincides exactly with his time of activity in the revolutionary movement in his own opinion. He said he was still a member of the Railway Carmen's Union, and was formerly a member of the "Seamen, Street Carmen, I.W.W., etc.," and had held the offices of business agent, secretary and president in unions. He admitted that he had participated in scores of strikes in which he had "held a position of leadership." And he printed in capital letters, as if to emphasize his reply, that he had never belonged to the Army or Militia.

So much for Foster's own story of his life, as told by himself. In addition it may be said that he was born in Taunton, Massachusetts, October 25, 1881. From 1906 to 1911 he was a reporter on the *Socialist Call*, and when detailed to

---

*See testimony of A.W. Klieforth, Assistant Chief of the Eastern European Division of the State Department, before the Senate Committee investigating Communist propaganda in the United States, January 1924.

cover the activities of the I.W.W. he became so interested in the organization that he joined it. In 1911 he represented the I.W.W. at the Syndicalist Congress in Toulouse, France, and announced that he was a syndical-anarchist. He also attended the anarchist conference in Barcelona, Spain, on this trip and visited Germany before returning to America. Prior to this, his first trip to Europe, he took an active part in the free speech fight in Spokane, Washington, and was arrested and imprisoned for a short term for his participation.

At the Barcelona anarchist conference the policy of "boring from within" was stressed, and Foster immediately adopted it as his own, to be used in his future battles in America. When the Russian Revolution came and Lenin and Trotsky told of their plans for a great Dictatorship of the Proletariat to embrace the whole world, Foster evolved his scheme for "one big union." These two expressions have been great favorites of his – his pet slogans for years. The "boring from within" policy he has applied to the American Federation of Labor, planting men within the organization to alienate as many members as possible from the strictly labor features of the Federation and convert them to the idea of "one big union."

As a member of the I.W.W. and the American Federation of Labor, Foster was active in the strike of the Standard Steel Car Company, in Butler, Pennsylvania. He was general secretary of the Steel Strike Organizing Committee, principal organizer of the steel workers in Pittsburgh, and in 1912 was a member of the Home Colony of Anarchists in the State of Washington. He organized the Stock Yards Labor Council in July 1917, and endeavored to unite that body with the I.W.W. The following year he left Chicago for Pittsburgh to become secretary-treasurer of a special organizing committee of the American Federation of Labor in the Pittsburgh district. He represented the Electrical Workers at the conference to organize the Iron and Steel Workers, in Washington, in September 1919, and in January 1920 he promoted the railroad strike.

Foster is a believer in direct action, in force instead of the ballot to bring about changes in government, and in ownership of industries by Labor. He is secretary of the Syndicalist League of North America, a member of the National Committee of the American Civil Liberties Union, one of the trustees of the Garland Foundation, and a frequent contributor of extremist articles to the many radical papers in this country. He is the author of several books intended to incite the workers to violence against society.

Before 1910 Foster was working to form the greatest revolutionary movement the world has ever seen, and so the plans of Lenin and Trotsky fitted in exactly with his plans. The Russians had a better opportunity to put their revolutionary plans into effect, with the aid of Germany, but they found an able aide on this side of the water in Foster. By 1919 he was working to overthrow Gompers in the American Federation of Labor and completely to destroy that organization. In Chicago, when members of the I.W.W. were on trial he urged them not to attempt to fight the government openly, but to join the American Federation of Labor and "bore from within."

After becoming a leader of the I.W.W. and touring Europe as the representative of that organization, he became so pronounced in his stand for the overthrow of the government by force and so insistent about "boring from within" as a fixed policy of any organization that could be used to further his ambitious ends that the I.W.W. disagreed with him and he left that party. From the beginning his plans have been consistent, with the one aim of doing away with all organized government and giving Labor control of the world. His ideas were so radical that the I.W.W. paled by contrast, and even *Solidarity* refused to publish his articles. Little by little he has organized the radicals and Reds in all branches of industry, gathering them into the American Federation of Labor, until, through their influence and support, he has put himself into a position of importance rivaling that of Gompers.

In August 1920, Foster met with representatives of twenty-four internationals at Youngstown, Ohio, to vote for a proposed general strike of steel industry workers. The strike was carried by 98 per cent, chiefly through the efforts of Foster. He has always been interested in Negro activities and in 1919 he promised Lee Fort Whitman, the Negro radical, that he would aid him in bringing the Negroes into the steel workers' union. It is alleged that he was connected with a free speech campaign having to do with the Inter-Church World Movement in April 1920. In November of that year he left the staff of *The New Majority,* with which he had been identified for some time, and organized the Trade Union Educational League for the avowed purpose of hastening the evolution of labor from craft to industrial.

In December 1920, at a meeting of the Executive Board of the Meat Cutters' Union, held in New York City, he explained to the meat cutters how they could strike to force the surrender of all the capitalists and defeat the wage reduction and open-shop movement. He attended the first Congress of the Red Trade Union International, at Moscow, in June 1921 as a representative of the Amalgamated Textile Workers of America. Foster is now advocating on all occasions, as a preliminary to centralization of all power in the workers' hands, the amalgamation of all unions into the same craft. In April 1922, he stated in a speech in Chicago that if the workers received all they were entitled to it would mean the elimination of the employer class, and referred to the coming struggle between capital and labor as the most brutal war the world has ever known.

In advocacy of violence in the fight against capitalism Foster has written volumes. He was very much impressed with the French workers' struggles and the destruction of property accomplished by them in their strikes. It was during one of his visits to Europe that he had an opportunity of studying sabotage at first hand, and on his return to America he wrote:

Next to the partial strike, the most effective weapon used by the Syndicalists in their daily warfare on capitalism is sabotage.

Perhaps the most widely practised form of sabotage is the restriction by the workers of their output.

The most widely known form of sabotage is that known as "putting the machinery on strike." If he is a railroader, he cuts wires, puts cement in switches, signals, etc., runs locomotives into turntable pits and tries in every possible way to temporarily disorganize the delicately adjusted railroad system. If he is a machinist or factory worker, and hasn't ready access to the machinery, he will hire out as a scab and surreptitiously put emery dust in the bearings of the machinery or otherwise disable it. Oftentimes he takes time by the forelock, and when going on strike "puts the machinery on strike" with him, hiding, stealing or destroying some small indispensable machine part which is difficult to replace.

Another kind of sabotage widely practiced by Syndicalists is the tactics of either ruining or turning out inferior products. Thus, by causing their employers financial losses, they force them to grant their demands.

Sabotage is peculiarly a weapon of the rebel minority. Its successful application, unlike the strike, does not require the cooperation of all the workers interested. A few rebels can, undetected, sabotage and demoralize an industry and force the weak or timid majority to share its benefits. The Syndicalists are not concerned that the methods of sabotage may be "underhanded" or "unmanly." They are very successful and that is all they ask of them. (*Syndicalism*, pages 15, 16, 17 and 18.)

In advocating direct action as against political action, Foster wrote:

The superiority of direct action to political action in winning concessions from capitalism is clearly seen in a comparison of the achievements to date of the direct action and political action movements.

The chief cause for the greater success of the labor unions than the political party is found in the superior efficacy of direct action to political action. The former is a demonstration of real power, the latter merely an expression of public sentiment.

The campaign for "law and order" tactics that is continually carried on in the unions by various kinds of legalitarians and weaklings exerts a bad influence upon them. It must cease. (See *Syndicalism*, pages 20, 22, 23, 24, 25, 26, and 49.)

Regarding society in general and his utter disregard for it, Foster writes in *Syndicalism*, pages 27 and 28:

The Syndicalist takes no cognizance of society. He is interested only in the welfare of the working class and consistently defends it. He leaves the rag-bag mass of parasites that make up the non-working class part of society to look after their own interests. It is immaterial to him what becomes of them so long as the working class advances. He is not afraid of turning the wheels of progress backward, in thus constantly confining himself to the interests of the working class, as he knows that by freeing the working class entirely he will give social development the greatest stimulus it has ever known.

Later on, condemning patriotism, Foster writes:

The Syndicalist is a radical anti-patriot. He is a true internationalist, knowing no country. He opposes patriotism because it creates feelings of nationalism among the workers of the various countries and prevents cooperation between them, and also because of the militarism it inevitably breeds. (*Syndicalism*, page 29.)

All the doctrines expressed in the book, *Syndicalism*, Foster used in a book published later and called *Trade Unionism*. This latter book he distributed by the thousands of copies when he was lining up the forces for the great steel strike in 1919. In one place Foster, after having pictured the world with the workers in control, has written:

Under the new order as pictured above, Government, such as we know it, would gradually disappear. In an era of Science and Justice, this makeshift institution, having lost its usefulness, would shrivel and die.

Today a large branch of Government relates to war. The abolition of the profit system would render this useless. It would make impossible the fatal rivalry between the nations over markets, and thus destroy the very foundations of war. A friendly, spontaneous, international cooperation like that between the various states in the Union would supersede the present elaborate war departments.

Criminal courts, police, jails and the like would go also. Crime is due almost wholly to poverty. In a reign of plenty for all it would practically disappear. The few criminals remaining would be subjects for hospitals rather than jails. Likewise the civil courts, with their hordes of officials, would vanish. People would no longer have to wrangle over property rights.

The industries now in the hands of national, state and municipal governments would be given over completely into the care of the workers engaged in them. Unlike in our days of graft these workers would then have every reason to give the public the best possible service. The teachers would have full control over education, the doctors over sanitation, the postal workers over the transmission of mail, etc. This would certainly make for efficiency, for no other body would be so competent to control an industry as the workers directly employed in it. Surely no mere legislative assemblies could hope to be in possession of sufficient knowledge to even intelligently advise such groups of scientifically organized producers, much less control them.

With war, crime, class antagonisms and property squabbles obliterated, and the management of industry taken from its care, little or no excuse would exist for government. What few extraordinary occasions arose requiring legislative action to arrive at some sort of solution could be handled by the Trade Unions, which would still contrive to have many uses. (*Trade Unionism*, pages 24 and 25.)

As the Workers' party functions in politics and the Trade Union Educational League in industry, so the Friends of Soviet Russia is the "legal" financial branch of the Communist party of America. A member of the Central Executive Committee of the Communist party is known to have said that but for the funds collected by the Friends of Soviet Russia for the ostensible purpose of relief, the party would hardly be able to function in this country as a great portion of the relief money never leaves the United States but is used for propaganda. This organization was formed in 1921 by the Central Executive Committee of the Communist party for the purpose of securing funds for the relief of Soviet Russia and also "to expose and refute the lies which are constantly being circulated about her in the capitalist press and to present the real facts about Soviet Russia to the American people, and create a demand for the lifting of the blockade against her and the resumption of trade.

Article one of the constitution of the society provides that the funds collected shall be sent "to Russian Soviet authorities." The organization of this body was brought about by Caleb Harrison, one of the official delegates to the illegal Bridgman convention, and Dr. Jacob W. Hartman. The names of the first executive committee and advisory committee will prove its connection with the Communist party. The first-named committee comprised Allen S. Broms, Caleb Harrison, Dr. Hartman, Edgar Owens, Dr. William Mendelsohn, Dr. Leo S. Reichel, and Dr. J. Wilenkin. The advisory committee included Ella Reeve Bloor, William F. Dunne, William Z. Foster, Caleb Harrison, Robert Minor, and Rose Pastor Stokes, all of whom were delegates at Bridgman; and Elmer T. Allison, Dennis Batt, Allen S. Broms, Joseph P. Cannon, Jack Carney, Max Eastman, Ludwig Lore, Dr. Mendelsohn, Edgar Owens, Dr. Reichel, Mary Vorse, Hulet M. Wells, and Dr. Wilenkin.

The activities of this organization have spread rapidly throughout the United States and Canada. Branches have been established, propaganda spread by means of pamphlets, mass meetings and moving pictures. Affiliations with labor organizations, societies and associations have increased and new relief bodies have been organized. A subsidiary branch known as the American-Federated Russian Famine Relief Committee has been organized to purchase supplies with the money secured by the Friends of Soviet Russia. Speakers from radical unions, I.W.W. and Communist organizations are touring the country in the interests of this society. Among the organizations affiliated with the Friends of Soviet Russia are the following, all legal bodies:

Amalgamated Clothing Workers of America, American-Hungarian Workers' Federation, American-Lithuanian Workers' Literary Society, Chicago Federation of Labor, Czecho-Slovak Workmen's Council of America, Detroit Federation of Labor, Finnish Workingmen's Association, Lithuanian Relief Commission, Montreal Trades and Labor Council, National Croatian Society, New England Workers' Association, Russian-Ukrainian Workers' Educational Society, Seattle Central Labor Committee, Socialist Consumers' League, Society for Technical Aid to Soviet Russia, Tacoma Central Labor Council, Toronto Trades and Labor Council, the Workers' party, and World War Veterans.

The contribution list, a printed form used by the Friends of Soviet Russia at its inception, bore the interesting and illuminating legend, "Endorsed by the official representative of L.C.A.K. Martens," the official representative of the Moscow Communist Government who was obliged to leave the United States through fear of deportation, papers already having been issued.

The next legal branch in importance in the work of furthering the interests of the Communist party of America in the United States is perhaps the Young Workers' League, which is one of the pets of Robert Minor, the active Communist who was a delegate to the Bridgman convention. Minor's treachery during the war, which would have resulted in his execution but for the influence exercised in his behalf, is well known. The aim of this organization is to place the ideals of Communism before the youth of this country in a most subtle manner so that when they attain maturity they will be thorough Communists, ready for the work of moving toward the overthrow by violence of the Government under which they now live. This is an outgrowth of the Young People's Communist League and the Young People's Socialist League. It was recently reorganized for "legal" propaganda purposes by the Executive Committee of the Workers' party. The installation of the various circles is in charge of the national secretary, Oliver Carlson, alias E. Connolly, alias Edwards. The purpose of the League is to educate the young workers to understand their position in capitalist society, to show them the stupidity of trying to climb higher, and to map out a course of action for their emancipation.

Among the organizers are a number of well-known Reds, members of the Communist party of America. Mrs. Sadie Amter, Walter Bronstrup, D.E. Early, Max Kaminsky, and Mrs. Margaret Prevey are active in the organization. Something of the work of this organization was told in a previous chapter of this chronicle.

Associated with the Young Workers' League is a new organization, functioning as a legal branch, under the direct influence of the Communist party of America, and known as the Famine Scout Clubs. Not only is it easy to raise money for the Communists through the appeal of the children thus drawn into the movement, but it is also excellent training in Communism for them and a medium through which the radical propaganda can be circulated.

The Famine Scout Club movement was the brilliant thought of Rose Pastor Stokes, one of the delegates to the underground convention of the Communist party of America which was raided at Bridgman, Michigan, and an active Communist since the American beginning. The name selected would appeal to those interested in the excellent Boy Scout and Girl Scout organizations and at the same time it would offer an excellent beginning for planting the seeds of Communism in the minds of the young while raising money for Communist purposes. Mrs. Stokes traveled all over the country organizing these Famine Scout Clubs. The membership is not yet large, but enough young people have become interested to form another group of nuclei for radical propaganda. But

OFFICIAL ORGAN * JUNIOR SECTION * YOUNG WORKERS' LEAGUE OF AMERICA

Vol. 1. No. 3.   JANUARY, 1924   Price 5 cents

Why We Fight Against the Public Schools

THE capitalists have created two kinds of schools. One for their own children, private schools, where they are taught to rule over the workers, and the other, public schools, where they try to teach the children to be willing workers and silent slaves for those who are taught to be the rulers.

In the public schools, you, the children of the workers, are taught that this is the best government in the world. But you are never told that this government allows little children of 5 years of age to work under terrible conditions in mines, factories and fields in order to get a bite to eat. You are told that the organizations of the workers, like the unions and the communist parties, are wicked organizations that are unjust and unreasonable and bad all around. The child of the worker is taught to hate the working class and to support the capitalists. They tell you that they are giving you an education, but it is not true. They only teach you enough writing, reading

The World Belongs To Us!

and 'rithmetic to make you able to carry on work for the boss when you are old enough to be dragged into a factory or a mine.

In your religious training you are told that even if things are bad on this earth, everything will be wonderful when you die and go to Heaven, for there you will be in Paradise.

But we do not want to wait until we are all dead to go to a Paradise. That is all a lie. When you die, you are dead and that is all there is to it. We want our Paradise right here and now. We work hard and make all the beautiful things of life and we want to enjoy them now. And if we put up a good, strong fight for it, we can have our heaven on earth, where we shall live like human beings and not like beasts in a hole.

That is what the Junior Section is organized for We want to get all the children of the workers united into a strong organization. We want to fight, all of us together! The older men and women workers in the Workers Party; the young

---

A communist paper for little folks. *The Young Comrade*, official organ of the Junior Section, Young Workers' League of America.

membership is not one of the prime desires of Communists; the chief feature is to have as many nuclei as possible. For this reason clubs are organized with few members, through which appeals are made to the public to aid the famine sufferers in Russia. But the money collected goes to the Russian Red Cross, which, although associated in organization with the International Red Cross, is solely an organ of the Communist Soviet Government of Russia.

The American Committee for Russian Famine Relief was organized by Walter W. Liggett at the instigation of John G. Ohsol, a member of the Russian Red Cross, which is officially a part of the Soviet Government in Moscow, and former associate of L.C.A.K. Martens, Bolshevist "ambassador" to the United States. He desired to extend Russian relief work in order to reach elements in the United States who would not contribute to the avowedly sovietized Russian Red Cross Society. A contract was entered into between the Russian Red Cross Society, with Dr. David Dubrowsky, Ohsol and Dr. Michael Michailovsky* as parties of the first part, and the American Committee for Russian Famine Relief, with A.W. Ricker, Liggett and James H. McGill as parties of the second part. This contract was in essence an underwriting contract upon the part of the Russian Red Cross for the support of the American Committee for Russian Famine Relief.

This underwriting contract was not generally known and certainly the characters of the three Russians were unknown to the majority of persons lending their names to the support of the committee. The only public indication appearing in connection with the Russian Red Cross was that, on the letterhead of the American Committee, there was printed in small type this statement: "Distributing Through Russian Red Cross Under American Supervision."

The activities of the organization were first directed to holding public meetings for the purpose of raising funds for Russian relief work, but they quickly took on a political character, severely criticising the United States and praising Russia under the Communists. Isaac McBride, formerly a close associate of Martens and an active friend of Dubrowsky, early in 1922 addressed a meeting in Chicago which opened with cheers for Lenin, Trotsky and the Soviet government of Russia as well as for the Communist party of America. In Milwaukee a meeting developed into a political gathering for recognition of the Soviet government by this country. In Minneapolis a resolution was passed calling upon the United States government to establish at once trade relations with the present Russian government.

McBride stated: "We are going to milk the bourgeoisie of this country and they will help us to keep up the struggle against themselves." Mr. Ricker, one of the parties to the underwriting agreement, said that his sympathies and those of the committee were entirely with the Soviet regime. McBride also said that the Ameri-

---

*Dr. Michael Michailovsky is identified in the New York State Medical Directory as having an office at 18 East 41st Street, New York City. He graduated from some Russian University in medicine in 1897, is a member of the American Medical Association and the New York Academy of Medicine, and is listed as visiting dermatologist and urologist to the Sydenham Hospital.

can Committee was formed after it was realized that certain organizations, openly recognized as having Soviet leanings, could not perform the same work. He said:

> A number who were previously connected with the Advisory Council have been eliminated for fear that their presence might be looked upon with suspicion by the general public. One of those eliminated is Louis Post, former Assistant Secretary of Labor.

The activities of the Russian Red Cross in the United States first became apparent in 1921 when Dubrowsky, Michailovsky and Ohsol formed their committee for carrying on the work. Charles Recht, legal representative of the Soviet interests in this country, said that the Russian Red Cross was one of the two recognized Soviet relief organizations in New York in September 1921. The personnel of the committee of three Russians was the significant feature of the scheme to those who knew something of the inside of the Communist party's work here.

Dubrowsky had been a member of the staff of Martens and had been carried on the latter's payroll at $50 a week. After Martens' departure Dubrowsky was recognized in radical circles as the unofficial representative of the Soviet government. He was particularly active in connection with the Jewish Public Committee, and was the instigator of the plan to transmit to persons in Russia sums of money from their relatives in the United States. The significance of this scheme was noticed in view of the exchange value placed upon the ruble by Dubrowsky. When the exchange rate was not less than 4000 rubles to the American dollar, Dubrowsky was allowing but 250 rubles to the dollar, and charging ten dollars for transmission of money by cable and one dollar by mail. Dubrowsky's activities along this line were squelched by the Federal government.

Ohsol was first called to the attention of the public by Senator Watson of Indiana in 1919, when he was employed by the Federal Trade Commission. He was charged with being at that time a pronounced Socialist of the most virulent type. Ohsol was also a member of Martens' staff, looking after a large part of the latter's commercial work. He is a conspicuous Bolshevik propagandist. Michailovsky is a representative of the Commissariat of Public Health, an official unit of the Russian Socialist Federated Soviet Republic.

Strenuous efforts have been made to impress upon the American public that the Russian Red Cross is not affiliated with, or supervised by, the Russian Soviet Republic. This, however, is proved by an examination of the ordinances of the Soviet republic and the by-laws of the Russian Red Cross itself. On August 7, 1918, "the Soviet of the Commissaries of the People" issued an ordinance signed by Lenin as manager of the affairs of the people, and by the secretary of the Soviets, dealing with the Russian Red Cross Society, which says specifically, "The Russian Red Cross Society is under the high protection of the central institutions of the republic." This ordinance also orders the reorganization of the society to effect, among other things, the "immediate adoption of all possible measures for the purpose of attracting to the number of the members of the society the largest possible number of proletarian institutions, organizations and associations."

It was the Russian Red Cross workers in the famine districts of Russia, under the direction of the Soviet government, who gathered small children, suffering from hunger, into rooms decorated with the old symbols of the Russian religion, and commanded these starving children to pray to their ikons for food. When no food appeared in answer to their prayers they were told to pray to the Soviets for food. The children did so and the doors flew open as if in answer to their prayers and plentiful food appeared.

The bylaws of the Russian Red Cross Society, which were adopted at a general conference held in Moscow on November 20, 1921, contain the following statements:

> Paragraph 3 — The society shall co-operate with the military, naval and civil medico-sanitary institutions of the Russian Socialist Federated Soviet Republic, conforming their activities to the instructions of the latter.

In paragraph five of these bylaws appears the statement as to who may become members of the Russian Red Cross Society. It reads as follows:

> Proletarian organizations may become members of the society, for instance, Workers' Unions, factory and shop committees, medical aid societies and citizens enjoying active and passive suffrage, in accordance with the constitution of the Russian Socialist Federated Soviet Republic.

It will thus be seen that only citizens of the Russian Socialist Federated Soviet Republic may become members of the Russian Red Cross. The officials of the Russian Red Cross are well known Communists, including Litvinov, head of the foreign propaganda department of the Russian Soviet government. When Secretary Hoover officially warned the American public against contributing to these various Russian relief bodies, the Russian Red Cross and the Friends of Soviet Russia became very busy cleaning their books and records. The Russian Red Cross had issued a blank bearing the initials "R.S.F.S.R.," standing for Russian Socialist Federated Soviet Republic. These blanks were quickly destroyed in order that the connection of the organization with the Soviet government might not be disclosed. The same policy was followed by the Friends of Soviet Russia. In view of this it is interesting to note, in conclusion, the recent pronouncement of the executive committee of the Third International:

> We talk in two languages, that which we talk to the bourgeoisie we fool them with, that which we talk to the world proletariat is the truth. Our problem is the world revolution. We are going towards it. And everything is directed to this end.

CHAPTER SIX

Relief Drives; The Agrarian Program

Millions of American dollars have been poured into Russia, ostensibly for the relief of famine sufferers. It is now known that little of this money, except such as was sent through the channels of the American Relief Administration, the offical organization directed by Herbert Hoover, Secretary of Commerce in the Cabinet of President Harding, was used primarily to aid the famine sufferers. It went first to the Communist Soviet government in Moscow, where its disposition was determined. There was the Red Army to feed, clothe, and equip and the multitude of officials in Moscow to be cared for. It is known that occasionally some of the American-contributed funds went to famine relief, but it is also known that much of it never reached any famine sufferer.

One of the most pretentious "drives," which was intended to secure thirty million dollars for the Russian Communists, was that launched in 1922 by Captain Paxton Hibben, acting for the Russian Red Cross, an integral part of the Soviet government in Moscow. This "drive" was directly under the supervision of the Soviet regime. Captain Hibben is a Princeton graduate, received a Master's degree from Harvard, and studied law for a year at the same university. He is an ex-diplomat, ex-soldier, and a member of various clubs, and has connections which enable him to enter the homes of many loyal American citizens. His plea was based upon the suffering of the children of Russia, and appealed to the well-known generosity of Americans toward people in dire distress.*

*In view of these facts concerning the activities of Captain Hibben, it will not be amiss to record the following: Captain Hibben has for some time held a commission as Captain in the Army of the United States, Officers Reserve Corps, attached to the artillery of the Third Army Reserve Corps. Many representations as to his suitability for holding this commission have been made to the proper officials of the War Department, but apparently it was not possible to secure suitable action. In May 1923, Captain Hibben applied for promotion to a majority, and shortly thereafter, the Secretary of War appointed a board of three reserve officers to determine his fitness for retention or promotion. Captain Hibben appeared personally before this board on October 19, 1923, to testify "in regard to certain documents and papers in the possession of the War Department." The whole matter is still pending at this writing.

Captain Hibben came to New York from Moscow, where he had perfected his plans for this great relief drive with the Soviet authorities. The American people, Captain Hibben knew, could not close their ears to an appeal to save innocent children from starving. The American Relief Administration, which was, as has been said, the only organization through which relief could be sent directly to the famine areas without giving the Soviet authorities an opportunity to take as much as might be needed to keep the Red Army well-supplied and to satisfy the needs of numberless Soviet officials, was utterly ignored in Captain Hibben's scheme to raise funds and supplies to be distributed under the supervision of the Red Moscow authorities. Captain Hibben, besides being chairman of the American Committee for Relief of Russian Children, was secretary of the mission in America of the Russian Red Cross, which, as was shown in a previous chapter, is a part of the Soviet government in Moscow both by its own bylaws and by the laws of the Communist regime now in control of Russia.

Captain Hibben was employed by the Russian Red Cross in March 1922, taking the place of V.V. Chikoff as secretary of that organization. In a circular widely distributed by the Friends of Soviet Russia, with which he later became officially connected, Hibben is quoted in praise of the present government of Russia, saying that they "have fought the good fight." A part of this statement of Hibben's reads as follows:

> What I am interested in, and what we are all interested in, I take it, is those people over there who have fought the good fight; who have existed for four years in the face of an enemy world . . . . I don't want to see them lose that fight for lack of food of which you and I have plenty . . . and if millions of workers all over this country want to take up the job of feeding the starving of Russia, when the supplies of the American Relief Administration are exhausted, as workers, to help the workers of the only government of workers, by workers, for workers in the world, it is nobody's business to interfere.

This would indicate that Hibben suspected that the supplies furnished through the Friends of Soviet Russia and through the Russian Red Cross were going first to the Soviet authorities so that they might not "lose that fight for the lack of food," although what was left might find its way eventually to the famine sufferers. And he intimated in this statement that the American Relief Administration, under the direction of Secretary Hoover, was about to cease its actual work of feeding the real sufferers in the famine districts of Russia. Naturally, if the Hoover organization ceased functioning, there would be a better chance for the Soviet organization with which Hibben was connected to raise funds in this country.

On July 1, 1922, Hibben sailed for Berlin on the steamship *Homeric* to be present as a delegate from the Russian Red Cross in America to the International Convention of the International Workers' Famine Relief Committee, which was to open July 9 and which was convened at the initiative of the Supreme Central Executive Committee for Famine Relief. It was called by the foreign representative of this committee, Nicholas Krestinsky, former plenipotentiary representative of the Soviet government in Germany. Hibben arrived in Berlin too late for this convention. He did, however, have a number of talks with Chicherin and L.C.A.K. Martens, the Bolshevist "ambassador" to the United States whose activities in aid of the Communist party of America led to his departure. On July 19, Hibben left Berlin for Moscow, where he said he was to act as a representative of the Society of American Relief for the Children of Russia, of which he was a director, and where he achieved much publicity.

Hibben's work was fulsomely praised in the Moscow *Izvestia,* the Soviet official organ, of August 11, 1922, which printed an interview with him in which he said that the American Relief Administration would drop its work in Russia and then relief work would all have to be done through the Russian Red Cross. He also spoke of his relations with Dr. David H. Dubrowsky, whose activities here in behalf of the Communists have already been told. He mentioned the fact that there were in Moscow at that time four members of the national committee of the American Committee of Relief for Russian Children, Rev. John Haynes Holmes, Frank P. Walsh, Dr. M. Michailovsky, and John G. Ohsol. The records of Holmes, Michailovsky, and Ohsol in activities connected with the Communist regime have been told in previous chapters. Frank P. Walsh returned from Moscow by way of Montreal and immediately launched a campaign of bitter criticism of the United States government for its failure to recognize the present Russian government, and spread propaganda as to the wonderful progress made in that country under the Communist regime. He later became chief counsel for the Bridgman conspirators at an enormous fee. The *Izvestia* article says in part:

> In our interview with Captain Hibben he declared that Americans are very much interested in the welfare of Russian children, and that children who became orphans in consequence of the war and famine can count on thousands of friends in the United States who will help them through the American Committee of Relief for Russian Children, which is now under the charge of Mary Lena Wilson. The activities of the American Relief Administration developed to such a degree that many people forget the existence of other organizations in America and other countries which also carry on famine relief work in the Volga region.

Then, quoting Hibben, it says:

> The Russian Red Cross deserves all praise for its remarkable work done with the perfectly insignificant sum at its disposal, getting the public of foreign countries interested in the relief of Russian sufferers. The American Relief Administration will, sooner or later, stop activities in Russia and will leave the country. But the work of the Russian Red Cross, of course, will continue and try to cure the wounds of the Russian people caused by the famine and the blockade . . . . During the period October

1921 to June 1922, the Russian Red Cross in America shipped food supplies, clothing, and medicine worth $342,895 which were contributed in the United States and Canada. The collection of money and other kinds of distribution is still going on. I have just received a cablegram from Dr. Dubrowsky, who is head of the Russian Red Cross in America and is just back from a trip to Mexico; his cablegram says that Mexico shipped 10,000 sacks of corn and 5,000 sacks of rice and a shipment of medicine to the Russian Red Cross to be distributed among the starving. This shipment is the second one from Mexico as a result of Dr. Dubrowsky's efforts.

It will be interesting to note here by way of parenthesis that the Mexican officials had no illusions as to the disposition of these shipments. They were admittedly for the Red Army of Russia because, as E. Plutarcho Calles, premier in the Mexican cabinet, said, "We are working toward the same end," viz., the Dictatorship of the Proletariat, and Russia had the better opportunity because she did not have the United States hanging over her head like the Damoclean sword. These are almost, if not quite, the exact words of Calles to Dubrowsky. The reference to the Damoclean sword is Calles' picture to the Russian emissary.

Hibben's praise of the Russian Red Cross in America, of which he was at the time secretary, for "getting the public of foreign countries interested," has a double significance; for it is a part of the work of all agencies of the Soviet government, as officially prescribed, to disseminate Communist propaganda on all possible occasions. Hibben went on, in the *Izvestia* interview, to describe a new plan for subtle propaganda by means of "Red Cross" shops to be established in the United States to show how industrious the Russian people are under the Communist rule and at the same time to raise money for the Soviet relief movement. He is quoted as saying:

In the United States the Russian Red Cross intends to maintain its own existence quite independently and not to spend for administration a single kopek out of the amount collected for famine relief in Russia. Necessary means for the realization of this intention will be given by a long row of Red Cross shops in important cities of the United States in which home made articles will be sold for the benefit of the orphans, victims of war and famine in Russia. This enterprise will be not only a new source of funds for relief work but will give to Russian home industry a new market, for through these shops America will be given an opportunity to get acquainted with articles made under such circumstances. Right now I am dealing with the President of the Centroyuz (the Central Executive Committee of the Russian Soviet), Comrade Khinchuck, about methods to realize this plan in fact. *We are also anxious to arrange a trip of Russian dramatical actors to the United States, together with musicians and artists,* who will under the auspices of the Russian Red Cross help to collect means for the relief of Russia and *at the same time will prove to the American public the high standard of Russian art reached during a time of revolution.*

It is interesting to note that there are constantly offered for sale in this country, by the Friends of Soviet Russia, literature and supplies to raise money for Russian relief. On circulars the public is urged to "buy books, pamphlets, pictures, postals, leaflets, posters," and the order blank on which this appeal is made lists busts of Lenin for $3 and of Trotsky for $2; these are said to be replicas of the work of Claire Sheridan. Books like *Communism and Christianism,* by Bishop William Montgomery Brown, are also offered for sale in this appeal, as well as writings of John Reed, Albert Rhys Williams, and Isaac McBride. Communist magazines and Red buttons are on the same list.

Hibben's activities in behalf of Soviet Russia make it interesting to note that his experience has been vast and varied. His brilliance of mind has never been questioned. His scholarship while at college qualified him for Phi Beta Kappa, but he was not admitted. During the war his anti-British and pro-German sentiments made it seem advisable that he not be used for certain purposes in France. The authorities have documents showing that he was a paid propagandist for the Greek Royalists before the United States entered the war.

He has frequently referred slightingly to the United States government and criticized it severely for its stand in regard to Communist Russia, this at a time when that same Russian government was directly using every means at its command to effect the overthrow of the United States by armed rebellion. Hibben had a troublous career while he was in the diplomatic service of the United States, which covered practically seven years in Russia, Mexico, Colombia, Holland, Luxembourg, and Chile.

Hibben has stated that he was always "passionately French" in his sympathies, but that did not prevent him from challenging a French correspondent to a duel in Athens on one occasion early in the European war when a Frenchman made a scene in a hotel room where Hibben was entertaining a German correspondent and his wife at luncheon. The duel was fought with no injuries on either side. Hibben was a great admirer of John Reed, the brilliant Harvard anarchist, later a Communist, whose spectacular career was cut short by his death in Moscow. A year after Reed's death, Hibben was in Moscow, and in October 1921 he was photographed placing a wreath on Reed's grave. Reed's widow, Mrs. Louise Bryant, was later associated with Hibben in his pro-Russian work.

Through his connection with the Russian Red Cross, Hibben's plan received the endorsement of the Friends of Soviet Russia and the Workers' party, both "legal" Communist branches. It is interesting here to note that the latter organization was in desperate straits because of the raid at Bridgman in August 1922, when William F. Dunne, the party's candidate for the governorship of New York, was arrested with a number of other Workers' party men for attendance at the illegal convention. Official orders issued by C.E. Ruthenberg, executive secretary of the Workers' party of America, called for immediate and effective aid from all members of the party because "we are in the midst of a

Captain Paxton Hibben, Officers Reserve Corps, United States Army, attached to the artillery division of the Third Army Corps, and candidate for advancement to a majority, places a wreath on the grave of the American communist, John Reed who died in 1920 and is buried under the walls of the Kremlin. This photograph was taken about a year following Reed's death when Hibben visited Russia and gave his famous interview to *Izvestia* indicating how money was to be raised for the "starving children of Russia" on his return to America. Hibben denies that this photograph was taken in an officer's uniform of the United States Army.

great campaign of self-defense." He urged all foreign-born to become citizens, "not for patriotic reasons but in order to draw them into the political life of the United States." These official orders were sent out from the "national office" on September 14, and announced that a Labor Defense Council would be organized at once and that it was necessary to raise "tens of thousands of dollars." Frank P. Walsh was retained and conducted the defense of the Bridgman prisoners. Robert M. Buck, editor of *The New Majority,* official organ of the Chicago Federation of Labor, was chairman of the Labor Defense Council just referred to, and Sam T. Hammersmark, one of William Z. Foster's right-hand men, who had been active in the steel strike and the recent convention of the Trade Union Educational League, was secretary-treasurer of the newly formed organization. The appeal was addressed to "District Organizers, Federation Secretaries, Local Secretaries, District Executive Committees, Federation Executive Committees, and Local Executive Committees," and read:

Comrades: For your guidance the following statement of our policy and immediate plan of action has been formulated by the Central Executive Committee.

We are in the midst of a great campaign of self-defense by the working masses against the ruthless capitalist offensive and the Central Executive Committee instructs all party units to put the following into action.

1. Today our major campaign is to be directed against governmental authorities who are attacking us rather than against the yellow socialists and trade union bureaucrats. The immediate struggles of the workers are becoming more tense and taking on wider scope. We must develop to the highest point the resistance of the workers to the brutal attacks of governmental authorities on the fundamental rights of the workers. The situation necessitates our following a policy which will draw into the conflict the great mass of workers regardless of political differences.

2. We must energetically propagate the idea among the workers that the onslaught on the Communists and militants is a part of the attack launched against the working-class. Our activities in the strikes are the basis for this attack.

3. Our main slogans in this campaign should be "Workers, Fight For Unrestricted Right to Organize, Strike, and Picket. Defend These Rights by Means of All the Political and Industrial Power at Your Command." Our members must urge the workers to disobey the Strike Injunction and to carry on the strike in defiance of the injunction.

Our rallying cries are:

"Down with Government by Injunctions!"

"Down with the usurped power of the courts!"

"Down with the use of armed force against the workers!"

4. It is our task to organize the workers to demand and to attempt to take the rights of the much vaunted American democracy. The Communists and all militant workers are part of the working class, therefore the Communists and all militants must also have the unrestricted right of free speech, press, and assemblage.

5. We must fight energetically to secure for all the foreign-born

workers equal civil and economic rights. We must wage an intensive campaign for removing restrictions on citizenship and against the anti-alien laws. We must demand that the foreign-born workers have unrestricted right to work. We must work diligently for the development of the solidarity of the native and foreign-born workers. The party must make the following organization steps toward carrying out this program of agitation and action.

A. Our Federations should wage a vigorous campaign to have the foreign-born workers become citizens. Not for patriotic reasons but to draw them into the political life of the United states.

B. Our Federation should wage a vigorous campaign to have the foreign-born workers join the labor unions.

6. We must persistently propagate the idea in the unions and among the workers generally of independent political action by the workers and the need of a working-class political party.

> Fraternally yours,
> (signed) C.E. Ruthenberg
> Executive Secretary

That the raid of the Michigan authorities on the illegal, underground convention of the Communist party of America at Bridgman upset the plans of the Workers' party as well as those of the Communists was evident from another appeal, also sent out by Ruthenberg on September 14, 1922. It was difficult to conduct a political campaign when the party's candidates were under arrest for conspiracy to overthrow the government by armed force; and in this case the head of the principal ticket, that of New York State, was caught at Bridgman. William F. Dunne, candidate for governor of New York on the Workers' party ticket, could hardly appeal for any votes outside his traitorous party while in jail or out on bail facing such a charge. This second appeal was addressed "To All Branches, District Organizers and Federation Secretaries," and read as follows:

Comrades: The National Convention of the party, which was to have been held in Chicago, August 28th, will be held in New York City beginning on December 25th.

The immediate reason for the postponement of the convention was, as you know, the arrest of the executive secretary, a number of district organizers and other party workers as part of the campaign of terrorism which the capitalists are waging against the workers in connection with the great strike battles which have shaken the country during recent months.

The first decision was to postpone the National Convention for two weeks, in the hope that those suffering under the persecution of the ruling class could be quickly released and take their places in the ranks of the party.

The party, however, finds itself face to face with this situation:

During the next month or two we must mobilize all our forces for defense work. We must raise tens of thousands of dollars for bail so that all our comrades can be freed and carry on their party work during the period in which their cases are pending. Only six weeks remain before the

November elections. We must nominate candidates and carry on campaigns wherever possible.

The present industrial struggles will be over by December, the lessons of this struggle will be clear, and we will be able to base our new policies upon the developments which this struggle has brought to the American labor movement. The period from now on to December will be a period of preparation. The convention must and will be a greater demonstration of strength to our party. Details about the convention such as agents, delegations, finances, etc., will be forwarded later.

Let us take up immediate tasks of the party with enthusiasm and courage. Let us build more strongly than ever during the coming months, and make the December convention a demonstration of the power of our movement.

> Fraternally yours,
> (signed) C.E. Ruthenberg
> Executive Secretary

Details of the plans for the Labor Defense Council were also announced on the same date by Ruthenberg. This announcement stated that the Central Executive Committee of the Workers' party initiated this plan and would carry out the work, but city central committees and branches were instructed to organize local labor defense councils, to function under the national organization, and to invite other working class organizations to send delegates to the local councils. In order that it might appear to be a spontaneous movement of all workers, instead of a carefully engineered scheme of the Communistic Workers' party, the organizers were cautioned to send these invitations "in the name of the provisional committee as a provisional committee of the Labor Defense Council and NOT [capitals are Ruthenberg's] in the name of Workers' party." The instructions specified:

> The local Defense Council should at once begin a campaign of agitation and money raising. It should hold public meetings, send speakers to the unions, have resolutions introduced in the unions and in every way possible stir up the workers to the need of a united stand against the capitalist attack.

A part of the plans of the drive of Captain Hibben for funds and supplies was directed at the small farmers and farm workers, who are already being assiduously cultivated by the Communist party of America. Captain Hibben's idea was that the farmers had excellent crops but a poor market in 1922, and that, therefore, they would be ready to contribute out of their surplus products to feed the Russians. This appeal was started by the Communist-controlled Friends of Soviet Russia, and with the launching of the new drive by the Hibben organization the small farmers and their hired help were flooded with carefully prepared propaganda designed to appeal to their hearts for suffering humanity and at the same time convey to them unsound ideas concerning "capitalist" society.

The Communist party's agrarian program, which is now being put into effect throughout the United States and which is admittedly a program that will require time and patience to carry out to its fulfillment, is one of the most cleverly prepared and thought-out programs thus far produced. In its preparation is shown surprising appreciation of the psychology, conditions, and sympathies of the small farmer and farm hand. The program contains many pages of carefully prepared statistics, maps, and charts, showing "population distribution," "jobs of those engaged in agriculture," "farm wages and farm income," "farms and farm tenure," "comparison of East and West," "crops – production, distribution, consumption," "the agricultural press," "farmers' organizations in the United States," "the Negro farmer," "farm propaganda," etc.; maps showing yields, in millions of bushels, of corn, wheat, and oats; primary markets, export markets, cotton area; farm organization, and agrarian press circulation.

Following out the program of the Communist party of America, students whose duty is to become proficient as farm laborers primarily have been "planted" in various agricultural schools in the country. They are also supposed to inculcate as much of the Communist doctrine in their fellow students as may be done without creating trouble; but that is not their first duty as students. After having been prepared at the agricultural schools these students are sent to various parts of the country as county agents to seek employment as farm hands; this is easily found, owing to the shortage of farm labor in these days. Then their real work for the party begins. They are organizers and propagandists first, last, and all the time. They form nuclei wherever they are – two or three companions being enough at any one place. This movement, according to the plans of the Communists, will have the ground prepared by the time the great general strike comes, and the Communists themselves will be able to supply the necessary food for the fighters on the side of the proletariat.

Notes among the pages of the statistics contain such sentences as these:

> The concentration of industry in the Eastern half of the United States makes a comparison from an agrarian point of view important, because it seems to me the city proletariat will approach revolt more rapidly where concentrated and would, therefore, become more dependent upon the immediate farms than upon those at great distances . . . .
>
> True proletarian organizations among farm laborers are possible in a limited way only where large numbers of workers are employed together as they are during harvest in the wheat and fruit lands of the West. The "harvest stiff" migrates from farm to farm with numbers of his fellows specializing in only one farm operation. He comes from the city and drifts back to it for the winter. He is more nearly of the city. The farm laborer is an all-round farmer. His point of view is more like that of his employer; he is paid by the month, eats with the boss, and he is isolated from other workers. All these combined make wide-spread organizations among this strata of the agrarian population impracticable if not impossible under a system of capitalist agriculture.

The program opens with a division of the United States into sections in which the Communists are working. This portion of the program reads:

The American problem is not composite; it consists of several distinct problems. This is true because of the differences in historical backgrounds and developments which have followed separate courses, determined mainly by geographical conditions.

The United States should be divided into four geographical divisions . . . and each section studied separately. First, its reaction to the common capitalist pressure. Second, the particular policy and programs which will reach the individual farmers peculiar to that section — teach him that in resisting capitalist exploitation his interests join those of the city proletariat.

Studied from the point of view of the Proletarian Revolution the following chapters of statistical references will show that four geographical sections have a relative importance as agrarian units of the problem.

Least in importance is the West. It is the Siberia of America. This great area, thinly populated, thousands of miles from the great industrial centers of the country, is too remote to figure decisively in an Industrial Proletarian Revolution.

Next in importance comes the New England section. Agriculturally it is not self-supporting. It imports 75 per cent of its food supplies, but this section is important above the West as a unit in the agrarian problem because New England farms adjoin the great industrial section of the country.

The South ranks above the West and New England for two reasons: first, it is distinctly an agricultural community, whose markets are within easy reach of the great industrial centers; and second, because it involves race problems. Some of the state populations in this section are half Negroes. These descendants of the slaves and the poorer whites are competing for the crusts under the lash of the Landlord System.

This competition has sharpened the race antagonism between those members of the same exploited class, whether skilled or unskilled laborers or farmers.

This condition must be considered in the program for Southern farmers. It holds a menace to the proletarian revolution which will be seized by the bourgeoisie.

Above all the rest comes the great producing empire stretching from the middle Atlantic and including the Middle West, producing more food per man than any other country in the world. Here industry is concentrated. Here the city proletariat and agrarian are but a few hours apart. This section must be won over to the side of the city proletarian. All others are secondary to the vital importance of this section as a factor in the success of the proletarian revolution.

It is explained that the statistical material used in preparing this report containing the "agrarian program" has been compiled from the latest available sources, government, state, and corporation figures being used. After many pages of interesting statistics the report takes up the question of farm propaganda of different radical organizations, as follows:

The Non-Partisan League is an organization of farmers in the West North Central States. They have gained control of the State government of North Dakota and several State offices in other States; also congressional representatives from North Dakota.

Their propaganda teaches the farmer to "Fight the Capitalist" but is spoiled by holding the Non-Partisan League legislative program as the cure-all. The following is quoted from a summary of a history of the League which was issued recently by them:

"It is a typically American institution dedicated to the principle that the people should rule and that the ballot offers the remedy for economic and political wrongs."

As a matter of fact, the actions of the Non-Partisan League are more direct than their policies indicate. There is a Left and Right struggle within the League at present. Connections with the Left elements should be made and they should continue inside the organization. Some of their farm papers have a wide circulation; if controlled they could reach out into more important agricultural sections.

The I.W.W. has based its farm propaganda on the mistaken assumption that agrarian conditions in the wheat States are typical; that the migratory "harvest stiff" is the typical farm laborer.

In the most developed regions the same relations prevail upon the farms as are found in other industries . . . . The farm hand has become a migratory laborer, possessing all the characteristics of his industrial brother.

As the migratory workers specialize in only one farm operation, spend only a portion of their time on the farms and drift back to the cities in the winter, it seems obvious that they are not typical farm laborers.

The Socialist party farm propaganda was concerned principally in getting votes. Some of their leaflets were unscientific enough to use modern methods and machinery as a warning:

"Mr. Farmer: The great machine is invading your field of labor. The combine is coming your way. With it comes the big machine drawing thirty-two ploughs with its seeder and harrower, the steam harvester and thresher of the capitalists. With them are leagued the railroads and the mills. In a few more years the capitalists will have you hunting a job as a day laborer because you cannot compete with the corporation which combines capital, the land, the railroads, mills, elevators and farm machinery that does the work of forty horses and eighty men at the same time."

Combined farming should not be used as a bugbear; it is a desired end. Neither should the level farms of the Middle West where thirty gang-ploughs can be used be looked upon as typical. A thirty-gang outfit could hardly turn around in the average farm field. On the other hand, the "steam thresher of the capitalists" which they mention is universally used wherever cereals are grown; operated generally by a neighborhood farmer as a side line. Farm propaganda should at least be edited by farmers.

Particularly interesting in this report is an "outline of policy" which was adopted and is now being followed out by the agents and the Communist party under direction from the agrarian section of the party. It reads as follows:

1. Emphasize the necessity for work among the largest element of the agrarian mass — the small farmers.

2. Use the common interest in the struggle against capitalism which exists between the small farmer and the proletariat as a wedge to separate them as a class from the capitalist and petty capitalist elements.

3. Use the farm organizations of the small farmers as a field for propaganda, teaching them to strike rather than arbitrate.

4. Organize the agrarian proletariat wherever possible to further the work of preparation and separation of the agrarian elements.

5. Recognize the literal necessity for the city proletariat to give up some of its members to agrarian work.

I believe that proletarians in any occupation will react uniformly to a proletarian revolution. That is, they will support the interests of their class. Therefore, the agrarian proletariat can be expected to support the revolution of the city proletariat.

An agrarian policy must recognize, however, that conditions today prevent the organization of the true farm proletariat. Nothing short of revolution will bring them together as a class.

The policy must be directed to a preparation of the ground by propaganda to clarify the interests of the several strata within the agrarian population.

When the city proletariat overthrow the bourgeoisie, the agrarian population should begin a gradual process of reorganization; first, the true farm proletariat must be organized into Soviets; this will be strengthened by later addition of the more oppressed semi-proletarians: gradually the small farmers will begin to drift over until only those are left whose interests are directly opposed to the proletariat.

This process will be completed rapidly and without friction only if the agrarian policy during the pre-revolutionary stages is directed mainly to work among that element which makes up more than sixty per cent of the total farm population — the small farmer.

The proletarian and semi-proletarian elements are comparatively small. No practical agrarian policy can direct itself to these small unorganized elements as its dominant purpose. These elements will of necessity support the proletarian revolution.

On the contrary, a practical policy must be dominated by the purpose to guide the largest exploited elements of the agrarian — the small farmers. These are organized; and their organizations are formed to resist capitalist pressure. These farmers must be taught the direct issue betwen themselves as a class and the bourgeoisie.

While their interests are not entirely those of the proletarian class, in so far as they are the same they must be united with the proletarian.

From a revolutionary point of view it must be recognized that as a whole the farm population is generations behind. The overthrow of the bourgeoisie will bring the agrarians in one jump to the necessity of considering the reorganization of the very basis of their existence, that is, the small farm unit — a farm operated by the farm family and one farm laborer. The combination of these farm units is a development which will follow the revolution; will come, as it should, gradually as a result of the separation of the agrarian population according to their class interests. Wherever big farms exist the confiscation of these lands by the farm proletariat for the state must be the first step.

The organization of agriculture should be much more rapid in America than in any other country, because of the wide-spread knowledge of the advantages of modern machinery applied to the efficient unit of acres.

Communism cannot be preached to this small farmer element before the revolution; and only by demonstration after the revolution. But whatever unity of interest exists with the proletarian must be taught; and the use of economic weapons such as food strikes be advocated in their organizations as the only effective means to gain anything from the bourgeoisie.

This policy will be effective only when well-grounded Communists can be spared from the ranks of the city proletariat actually to live and work among the farmers.

The program now in effect called for a budget of $35,000. It included, as outlined in this report, the organization of a "legal Agrarian Bureau"; buying or establishing a farm weekly paper; training of county agents; an inventory of all radicals in the agrarian population; and regular conferences of agrarian leaders. In elaborating the subject of training of county agents, the report says:

> Believing that it is easier to make farmers than to make Communists, well-grounded young Communists who are physically strong and understand the situation they volunteer to enter should begin training at once. Training will consist of four months intensive practical work on special farms under the direction of the bureau. This will be followed by a winter's course in a scientific agricultural college. After this the county agent will be placed in an important agricultural section. He then becomes the outpost in three lines of work: distribution of propaganda, source of information, agrarian party organizer.

It was decided to start ten young men at once on this course of training. They must be self-supporting until they enter their scientific training in college, and $300 each was allotted for this college work. It is interesting to know that the "intensive practical work" is now being done on one farm in Connecticut, one in the South, and others in the Middle West.

CHAPTER SEVEN

American Civil Liberties Union

$\mathbf{A}$t the suggestion of Felix Frankfurter of Harvard, the American Civil Liberties Union decided to ask William Allen White to serve on the national committee of that organization. Frankfurter, William Z. Foster, who was seated as fraternal delegate to the unlawful Communist convention at Bridgman, Elizabeth Gurley Flynn, Crystal Eastman, Roger N. Baldwin, Morris Hillquit, Scott Nearing, and many other radicals, some of them Communists, are members of the national committee of this organization; and White's defiance of his friend, Governor Allen, in the 1922 coal strike troubles in Kansas was the recommendation for White's availability as a committeeman.

The American Civil Liberties Union is definitely linked with Communism through the system of interlocking directorates, so successfully used by the Communist party of America in penetrating into every possible organization with a view to getting control so that when the time comes for the great general strike which, they believe and hope, will lead to the overthrow of the United States government by violence, they will already have these bodies definitely aligned with them. The party has several members in the American Civil Liberties Union and the constant activities of that body are proving of great moral and financial benefit to the Communists.

Rose Pastor Stokes, who was a delegate to the illegal Bridgman convention, was one of those reported present (although she was not a member of the committee) at the meeting of the Executive Committee of the American Civil Liberties Union on August 28, 1922, at the Union's headquarters in New York. There the decision was reached, after discussion of White's desirability as a member of the National Committee, to elect him to the committee if, upon inquiry, it was learned that he would accept. Among the others at this meeting were Elizabeth Gurley Flynn and Robert Morss Lovett, then president of the Federated Press League, the connection of which with the Communist party has been shown in a previous chapter. Lovett wrote to the Communist leader, Bruce

Rogers, in Los Angeles, to canvass the motion picture colony, giving the names of several prominent movie people who "are with us," and who "helped us before and will do it again"; and to Norman M. Thomas, Walter Nelles, B.W. Huebsch, the well-known publisher, and Roger N. Baldwin, the "slacker" during the war who served a sentence in prison and who is one of the active heads of the organization.

At this same meeting of the Executive Committee it was also decided to arrange a meeting for Senator Borah on the amnesty question and to supply funds for the meeting. This is not the first time that Senator Borah's name has appeared in the minutes of the meetings of the American Civil Liberties Union, for he has asked this radical organization to prepare bills for him to introduce in the Senate of the United States. The minutes of a meeting of the Executive Committee on October 3, 1921, record that Senator Borah asked, through Albert DeSilver (among whose other activities was that of being treasurer of the I.W.W. Defense Fund), that the Union draft bills repealing Title 12 of the Espionage Act, under which the postal authorities still censored the mail. Included also were to be amendments to that section of the obscenity statute which would eliminate the words "tending to murder, arson, and assassination" under the "indecent" definition. The minutes of the following meeting, on October 10, show that DeSilver reported that the two bills had been prepared and forwarded to the Senator. In the minutes of the April 17, 1922 meeting, we read: "The material for Senator Borah has been submitted to him and it is expected he will make his speech to the Senate in a comparatively few days." On May 1 it was reported that Senator Borah was still contemplating his speech.

Complaint has frequently been made that the American Civil Liberties Union is never exercised about predicaments in which poor men who are not radicals may find themselves. Its interests and activities are always, without exception, in behalf of lawbreakers of the radical criminal class. A survey of the National Committee of this Union shows at once that practically the entire membership is made up of radicals of one stripe or another. The Union solicits funds from every class, exactly as do the Communists, to be devoted to the defense or other assistance of criminals, never to aid a man who steals a loaf of bread for himself or his hungry family or who commits a crime of this nature. Of course in soliciting funds from the public it does not always admit that the money is to be thus used; many people contribute with the hazy idea of uplifting the downtrodden. This Union busily sought aid for those of its own members and others who, caught in the Bridgman raid, were actually engaged in a criminal conspiracy against the United States government.

That the people who are directing the functions of the American Civil Liberties Union have been looked upon for some time not only as radicals but also in some cases as Bolsheviks is well known. Felix Frankfurter, one of the shining lights of the Union, as has been seen, once drew down upon himself a most scathing arraignment when he, as a counsel for President Wilson's Mediation Commission in the Mooney case, had the temerity to attempt to interest Theodore Roosevelt in the work he was doing. Ex-President Roosevelt's Americanism has never been questioned by friend or foe; his loyalty to Harvard, where Frankfurter has long been teaching, was famous among the students and alumni. He bluntly compared Frankfurter to Trotsky and found little difference.

Allusion is made here to Roosevelt's letter to Frankfurter, quoted in a previous chapter,* because of the former President's expression of opinion in regard to the I.W.W., the Mooney and Billings cases, and similar individuals and organizations; in the cases mentioned the American Civil Liberties Union was particularly active, in an effort to prevent the criminals from paying the penalties imposed by the courts of the country for the crimes committed. It was also exercised over the predicaments of Communists in various parts of the country who were sentenced under the anti-syndicalist laws of different states; and not infrequently we find in the minutes of their meetings a notation that appeal to the Supreme Court of the United States will be made in an effort to save the radicals convicted of conspiracy to overthrow by violence the government of the United States.

The activities of the Union, however, do not stop with trying to aid Communists and other radicals and criminals after they have been convicted of crimes. It also conducts political campaigns in various states in an effort to bring about the repeal of laws enacted to protect the government from conspiracies directed from Moscow, and it provides money for the Communists with which the anti-American fight may be conducted. The minutes of the Executive Committee meeting held May 8, 1922, show the following entry:

> An application from the National Defense Committee for a loan of $500 for ninety days was noted, and was referred to Mr. Baldwin to negotiate on his personal responsibility with the general approval of the Committee.

It is interesting to note that this National Defense Committee is wholly Communist, controlled from Moscow, one of the many "legal" organizations doing the work of the secret Communist party of America. Its membership is entirely of Communists, most if not all of whom were in attendance at the illegal, underground Communist convention at Bridgman. This committee was made up of Max Bedacht, J.E. Ferguson, L.E. Katterfield, Edgar Owens, and C.E. Ruthenberg. And this is the organization for which the American Civil Liberties Union authorized the negotiations of a loan "with the general approval" of the Executive Committee.

The chairman of the American Civil Liberties Union is Harry F. Ward, the preacher whose utterances on radicalism in the Methodist Textbook caused a scandal. He was formerly connected with the Boston School of Theology, is a teacher of Christian Ethics at Union Theological Seminary, and has been a

---

*See Chapter Three.

leading factor in the Interchurch World Movement and the Federated Council of Churches of Christ in America. His sympathy and cooperation with Socialists, the I.W.W., and radical and other anti-American movements have been notable. He was a pacifist during the war, and practically all of his associates in the organization have records as pacifists and defeatists in those troubled days; some of them were imprisoned for their refusal to fight when the United States was at war or for endeavoring to bring about the defeat of this country by actively aiding the enemy.

Ward's activities are best illustrated by citing a letter which was given out by the American Civil Liberties Union in April 1922, and which was addressed to Congressman Martin B. Madden, chairman of the House Appropriations Committee. In this, he attempted to influence Congressman Madden for the purpose of securing a cut in the appropriations intended for the use of that executive branch of the government which has most to do with the suppression of revolutionary radicalism, and of emphasizing the specious claim that at that time radicalism was on the wane. Ward's letter contained the following:

> Radical activities in the United States have greatly decreased since 1919 . . . . The underground propaganda . . . is obviously that conducted by the Communists in the United States. The fact that propaganda is underground is due entirely to the repressive measures directed against it . . . . The Soviet government is not responsible for this propaganda. It is a part of the international, revolutionary, working-class movement affiliated with one or another of the international bodies which express its programs and purposes.

As has been stated, the American Civil Liberties Union, a part of the open, legal machinery of the Communist party of America, and of which Ward is an official, is the central organization for the defense of radicals and Communists. Unquestionably, its files contain large quantities of information concerning the radical movement, since to gather such information is a part of its appointed function. In 1922, every independent investigating agency in the United States had arrived at an opinion quite the opposite of that expressed in this letter to Congressman Madden. The conclusion is forced that Ward's opinion was formulated as a result of a desire to cripple the defense mechanism of the government in its fight against revolution either by violence or by legislation, and to protect the activities of those who were his associates.

Ward's statement as to responsibility for Communist propaganda in this country sounds puerile in view of the recent controversy between Secretary of State Charles E. Hughes and Steklov (1923), the speech of Senator Lodge in the Senate (January 1924), or the Senatorial investigation into Moscow propaganda in the United States (1924). It stamps him as one whose assumed leadership is defective either in that he is unacquainted with the conditions which he assumes to know most about or in that he has a conscious objective in misinterpreting facts.

The American Civil Liberties Union owes its existence to the notorious

"Our government particularly in the arrest of the alleged communists in Michigan seems to take the position that it is a crime to be a communist: I cannot help but be reminded of the original communists who were the first converts to the Christian faith. If the Roman Government in the early days of Christianity had taken the same attitude, the entire Apostolic College would have been arrested, Saint Peter, Saint John and the rest of them. They would have been in the same position as Mr. Foster, Mr. Ruthenberg and the others are to-day. Fortunately the Imperial Government of Rome at that time was not so reactionary. As an American citizen and speaking for myself, I want to take my stand on the basic right for anybody in the United States to be a communist who wishes to be one."

11

The Jesus-Thinkers

By Michael Gold

JESUS suffered and died for something he believed good; he was not a verbose, tricky journalist, a successful parson, a cunning exploiter of labor, or even a politician, and for this we must respect him. For his age Jesus was undoubtedly an innocent and beautiful poetical voice of all that is best in the emotions of the animal Man; we can love him for that, as we love Shelley and Whitman. We have all of us his tender child-hunger in our veins, that makes us dream of a simple and gentle world, where there is no strife, where all is mild and fraternal, and where men are as little children. It is a beautiful weakness to try to live in that world now. It is a cowardice, too, and must be extirpated from one's soul with a terrible knife if one is to become a m... The spirit of Jesus, His legend in one's blood, le... fusion, ineffectiveness, and despair in the... Exactly as we must learn to break... fathers to become men, so we... Father of Jesus, and st... earth. Just as w... hood, so...

type of super-being, but he makes the typical Jesus-mistake of refusing to admit that there are obstacles in the path of such a world. There are governments, policemen, capitalists, politicians, armies, navies, gunmen, the state. To the Jesus-thinker these count for nothing. It is necessary only to be noble and to save other souls for nobility. It is not necessary to think out plans for meeting the opposition, for there is no opposition to nobility. It is not necessary to think about what might happen if millions of the poor suddenly rose against the rich; and the rich turned machine guns on them. It is not necessary to think about what to do with men who try to assassinate the leaders of a free and fraternal world, as they who sought to assassinate Lenin. The Jesus-thinkers care only for the nobility and purity of their own souls. They are ethical. But does a doctor dream of ethics when he is cutting some rotten flesh out of the side of a sick man? Does a drowning swimmer think of nobility and purity when he is caught by an undertow? He ...inks only of objective things, of the force of the waves. He ...aks of his own force. The doctor thinks scientifically when ...performing an operation. There is a science in human ...ry, too; that is what the Jesus-thinkers will never ad-...see. They mistake their own longings for the move-...f humanity. They are egotists, worried about their ...ls. They refuse to be objective. It is an ethical ...their eyes to acknowledge that the majority of man;

The Social Service Bulletin

Issued Every Month Except July and August by THE METHODIST FEDERATION FOR SOCIAL SERVICE
150 FIFTH AVENUE, NEW YORK CITY

EDITORS: HARRY F. WARD; WINIFRED L. CHAPPELL

The general policies of this publication are determined by the Executive Committee of the Federation for Social Service, subject to the approval by the General Council of the Federation who are responsible in the selection of topics and material to the public for its issuance, are determined by the Secretary and Associate Secretary

Entered as second-class matter January 21, 1919, at the Postoffice at New York, N. Y. under Act of August 24, 1912

Volume 13   JANUARY, 1923   No 5

THE COMMUNISTS IN THE UNITED STATES

The Michigan Communist Case.

The Facts. In August the Communist Party of the ... secret convention in the woods on Lake Mi... free speech and freedom of assembly. In from Chicago. Discovery on the third ... those offered except doctrines advocated by the hasty adjournment. Seventeen were ... no evidence ... States to suppress Communists have recently each, state and Chi... There is charged, ... United States ... Newbold, a Communist, was recently ... The issues. This is first attempt in ... ... arrested overt criminal act is ... other European countries. ... which is a commonplace of Communists. This ... afraid to listen to political discussion ... material found in Italy, Germany, France, and ... age, violence, or other unlawful reform. ... reports, personal correspondence. legislative bodies. In Great Britain, Walton ... criminal ... The doctrine v elected to Parliament. ... industrial or political reform. ... Criminal Syndicalism defined as "The doctrine Is the United States afraid to listen to ... who by word of mouth or writing advocates or teaches the duty, neces-European ... sity or property of such offences ... or ... printing, publishes any book, paper, document, or written culates, sells, distributes, or publicly displays ... advising or teaching ... such doctrine "or matter, in any form, containing or advocating ... word of mouth or writing, spread or advocate the openly, willfully and deliberately justifies ... exemplify ... organizes ... helps to organize or attempt to commit," such offences "with intent to ... assembles with ... society; or organizes ... group or assemblage propriety of the doctrine of Criminal Syndicalism; or voluntarily assembles with any doctrine of Criminal Syndicalism is guilty becomes a member of, or advocate the doctrines of the State Prison for not more than ten of persons formed to teach or advocate ... imprisonment in ... discretion of ... offenses "contrary" to the of a felony and punishable by ... than $5,000 or both at ... guilty of ... against the peace and dignity of years or by a fine of not more ... 76 men and women as ... The Indictment names ... in such case made and provided ... form of the statute ... the people of the State of Michigan.

Rev. Harry F. Ward of the American Civil Liberties Union expresses his opinion of the raid upon the Communist Convention at Bridgman in the Jan. 1923 issue of the *Social Service Bulletin* of the Methodist Federation for Social Service. A similar expression from Rev. Charles M. Lathrop, executive secretary of the Department of Social Service of the National Council of the Episcopal Church, says: "I want to make my stand on the basic right for anybody in the United States to be a communist who wishes to be one."

A page from Max Eastman's *Liberator*, Sept. 1922, showing title, "The Jesus-Thinkers" by Michael Gold. Among other things, Gold says: "The legend of Lenin is more beautiful to me than the legend of Jesus. * * * The Russian Bolsheviks will leave the world a better place than Jesus left it."

pacifist organizations of war-time fame, which were presumably financed by German agents in this country working desperately, and for a time successfully, to keep the United States from entering the war. To be sure, in its present form it has existed only since January 12, 1920, when it was formed as an outgrowth, and by the merging, of various organizations which were developed during the World War, dating from October 1914, and the members of which were pacifists, defeatists, German agents, radicals of many hues, Communists, I.W.W., and Socialists. Among the organizations included in the merger were such pacifist bodies as the American League to Limit Armaments, Emergency Peace Federation, First American Conference for Democracy and Terms of Peace, People's Freedom Union, People's Council of America, American Union Against Militarism, League for Amnesty for Political Prisoners, Civil Liberties Bureau, National Civil Liberties Bureau, American Neutral Conference Committee, and Legal First Aid Bureau.

Of these — and there were others of less importance but with equally impressive names designed to fool patriotic Americans and lend aid to the enemy — the Emergency Peace Federation was organized in Chicago in October 1914, by Rosika Schwimmer, an Austrian Jewess by birth, of Ford Peace Ship fame, who is now in the United States on a lecture tour, and Louis P. Lochner, a Socialist of German descent and sympathies, who is now the Berlin representative of the Federated Press, regarded by the Communist party as its official publicity organization. Two months later the American League to Limit Armaments was organized in New York by the same persons, for the purpose of combating militarism and the spreading of the militaristic spirit in the United States, obviously an effort to prevent this government from entering the war against Germany.

Associated with these pro-German agents in the organization of these anti-American bodies were: Jane Addams, Morris Hillquit (Hilkowicz), Rev. John Haynes Holmes, Hamilton Holt, David Starr Jordan, Mrs. Patrick Lawrence of England, Dr. Jacques Loeb, George W. Nasmyth, Elsie Parsons, George F. Peabody, Oswald G. Villard, Lillian D. Wald, Rabbi Stephen S. Wise, and L. Hollingsworth Wood.

The gradual evolution of the various anti-war and other subversive organizations into the American Civil Liberties Union brought quick results. Radicals of every stripe found a haven in this body, each where he could help his particular friends who were in trouble because of infractions of the laws of the country. Soon after the formation of the Union we find the names of Amos Pinchot, brother of Governor Gifford Pinchot of Pennsylvania, as vice chairman, and Scott Nearing and Max Eastman on the Executive Committee. And in the two years of its existence it has been used by all radicals to fight the existing government of the United States. The rallying cry of "free speech and free press" brought many well-intentioned people into its ranks and hundreds of others to place their names on the lists of contributors. The difference between free speech and the conspiracy to overthrow the government is not drawn by the leaders of the movement. Freedom to them means the license of treason and sedition. Zacharia Chaffee, colleague at Harvard of Felix Frankfurter, writes, preaches, and presumably teaches that there should be no law against anarchy or sedition.

The directors of the American Civil Liberties Union hold that citizenship papers should not be refused to an alien because of his radicalism, no matter of what degree. They profess to believe that no persons should be refused admission to the United States, especially radicals, and that aliens should not be deported for expressions of opinion or for membership in radical or even revolutionary organizations, even if they aim at the destruction of the government and social system of the United States.

The method to be employed in securing civil liberties by this Union, they contend, is through maintaining an aggressive policy. This can be effected by unions of organized labor, farmers, radical and liberal movements, free speech demonstrations (as they interpret free speech), and publicity through circulars and posters, but more particularly through personal influence with editors or subordinates on reputable newspapers, which is also their chief means of spreading subversive propaganda, and legal defense work. Thus the Union creates in the minds of Communists, anarchists, and all classes of radicals the idea that it is improper for anyone to interfere with their activities aimed at the destruction of American institutions.

The activities of this organization are extensive. It assists any radical movement through publications of high standing, in order to influence public sympathy toward the radical organizations; by furnishing attorneys for radical criminals, conscientious objectors, and radical or foreign spies; and it "bores from within" in churches, religious and labor organizations, women's clubs, schools and colleges, and the American Federation of Labor, in order to spread radical ideas. The Union maintains a staff of speakers, investigators, and lawyers who are working in all sections of the country. Lawyers are furnished on short notice wherever a radical criminal gets into trouble. A press clipping service is maintained which keeps the organization in close touch with every radical criminal or group of radical criminals in trouble, and immediate financial aid, publicity, and counsel are offered. Aiding in this service are some 800 cooperating lawyers and more than 1000 correspondents and investigators, representing 450 weekly labor, farmer, and liberal papers with 420 speakers and writers.

The American Civil Liberties Union was particularly active in aiding the Communists caught in the Bridgman raid. It was active in behalf of trouble-makers in connection with and prominently identified with the coal and railroad strikes, the Amalgamated Textile Workers' strike in Passaic, New Jersey, the National Committee for Organizing Iron and Steel Workers in Duquesne, Pennsylvania, and the Socialist party at Mount Vernon, New York; in fighting the New York State Supreme Court's rulings on free speech during 1920; and in the Sacco-Vanzetti defense in 1921. An office is maintained in Washington with the

Federated Press organization to handle matters requiring direct contact with the government. A special drive was engineered and directed by the Union, seeking amnesty for so-called "political" and industrial prisoners, people who had been duly convicted of crimes against the laws of the country. The organization established branch offices, and bodies were formed under other names. It maintains separate funds, such as an "amnesty fund" and an "I.W.W. Publicity Fund."

In addition to the regular services already furnished, an extra program was put forth to which special efforts were devoted. This program included: amnesty for 150 "political prisoners," of whom 103 were members of the I.W.W.; test meetings as a basis for getting laws before the courts on the question of free speech; a special campaign against the American Legion and the Ku Klux Klan; completing studies on injunctions and advising tactics for labor organizations; a campaign in schools and colleges for "academic freedom"; and further development of the National Bill Fund to reach all defendants in "civil liberty" cases. The policies of the organization are determined by the National Committee and the carrying out of them is left to the Executive Committee, which meets weekly. Rose Pastor Stokes, a delegate to the illegal Communist convention at Bridgman, is in close contact, and at times sits, with this Executive Committee.

The Harvard Liberal Club, the I.W.W., the World War Veterans, and many local "defense leagues" and "civil liberty" organizations are affiliated with the Union. The directors of the Union, who are members of the Executive Committee, are Roger N. Baldwin and Albert De Silver. Baldwin has stated, in setting forth the purposes and principles of the Union, that "the advocacy of murder, unaccompanied by any act, is within the legitimate scope of free speech." And in telling the position of the members of the organization, he says:

> All of them believe in the right of persons to advocate the overthrow of government by force and violence. We want, also, to look like patriots in everything we do. We want to get a lot of good flags, talk a good deal about the Constitution and what our forefathers wanted to make of this country, and to show that we are the fellows that really stand for the spirit of our institutions.

It should not be forgotten that Baldwin refused to fight for the United States during the war and was sentenced and served time for "slacking." The above was the advice given by Baldwin to Louis P. Lochner, representative of the Communistic Federated Press in Berlin, in reference to the methods to be employed in carrying out the propaganda of the People's Council, which was organized to imitate in this country the Workmen's and Soldiers' Councils of Soviet Russia. And it is evident that these people see no crime in the advocacy of crime alone, even when that crime reaches the stage of treason and sedition.

The following paragraphs from the 1920 Lusk Committee report concerning the American Civil Liberties Union will prove interesting at this point:

An examination, however, of the propaganda and agitation which has been carried on in favor of the forceful overthrow of this government shows that it does not consist of a mere expression of opinion, but invariably advocates measures for its effectuation. In other words, the representatives of revolutionary Socialists, Communists, Anarchists and other groups, state that by doing certain acts this government may be overthrown and in each instance the agitator urges his hearers or his readers to commit these acts. It is a well settled principle of law that any reasonable man is responsible for the logical and reasonable consequences of his acts and utterances.

While the Constitution of the State of New York guarantees the right of free speech it also contains the warning that the citizen may exercise it "being responsible for the abuse of that right." The effect of the activities of the American Civil Liberties Union is to create in the minds of the ill-informed people the impression that it is un-American to interfere with the activities of those who seek to destroy American institutions. They seek to influence legislators and executives to repeal or veto any act calculated to protect the state or the federal government from the attacks of agitators.

It is interesting to note that the anxiety of the American Civil Liberties Union is shown only where the abuse of free speech is called in question because of attacks upon property or government. The committee does not find anything in their literature which seeks to prevent a man from being punished because of libel or slander or because of licentious or immoral speech or writing. These writings or utterances are penalized under our institutions because they are deemed to be abuses of the right of free speech and that they will tend to destroy the reputation of an individual or they will tend to corrupt public morals. If the principles set forth in the "Statement of Civil Liberty" . . . were carried into effect, libel, slander, and immoral or lewd writings and speech could not be punished.

After some further analysis this report says:

> The American Civil Liberties Union, in the last analysis, is a supporter of all subversive movements, and its propaganda is detrimental to the interests of the state. It attempts not only to protect crime but to encourage attacks upon our institutions in every form.

The Union is closely identified with groups in practically every city in the country known as "parlor Bolsheviki." Speakers are furnished for these dilettante radicals, whose influence would amount to little but for the fact that they can be counted upon for financial contributions to any movement that promises them a thrill. It has been said that many idle men and women become identified with this parlor Bolshevik movement through emotionalism and because it gives them something to think about. Whatever the reason, the Communists and the Civil Liberties Union agitators make use of these groups for financial aid and as means of spreading propaganda.

Just at present the Workers' party of America is receiving the attention of the

American Civil Liberties Union, and through that organization the aid of the parlor Bolsheviki. The Workers' party being the "legal expression" in politics of the Communist party of America, and its standard-bearer in New York, William F. Dunne, being charged with criminal conspiracy for his participation in the illegal Communist convention in Bridgman, the party is having a hard row to hoe. Among other attempted activities at this time is an appeal for funds from any source.

The Workers' party, as a branch of the Communist party, has access to the "sucker lists" of people who have contributed to the finances of the party in various cities, and besides has "sucker lists" of its own which are shared with the Communists. The most remarkable feature of these lists is the number of names of prominent people upon them. For instance, the list for Philadelphia, which the Workers' party has for use on the ground that the people have contributed to the funds of the Workers' party (and of course the information is dutifully passed on to the Communists), contains approximately two hundred names, almost all of them well-known people. The name of Mrs. Gifford Pinchot, wife of the Governor of Pennsylvania, is the seventh name on the list, which also contains the names of at least six members of the well-known and wealthy Biddle family. It is not intended even to insinuate that these people knew that they were contributing, if they did contribute, to the finances of an organization the chief aim of which was the overthrow by violence of the United States government; they have undoubtedly contributed frequently to causes which they were told were for the uplift of the downtrodden or the bettering of the conditions of the working class. Thousands of Americans in other cities have, by contributing to similar funds, placed their names on similar lists.

W.W. Weinstone, executive secretary of the Workers' party of America in New York, was in hiding for some months after the Bridgman convention was raided, and this had embarrassed the party, especially with Dunne, the leader, in jail or out on bond. However, Weinstone, who is a known Communist, still sent out orders for the campaign from his hiding-place. The party had difficulties in obtaining signatures to get the candidates on the ballot, as the membership, dismayed by the publicity attending the connection of the party with the illegal Communist party, was unwilling to furnish the signatures to the petitions. They were therefore compelled to pay men to do this work and, by order of E. Lindgren, who was held by the State of New York for extradition to Michigan charged with having participated in the illegal Bridgman Communist convention, were asking members for funds to get the paid solicitors busy. That is where the "sucker lists" proved their worth. The apprehension felt by Weinstone in his hiding-place was indicated by the following letter which he sent out under date of September 25, 1922:

> To All Branches of the Workers' Party Local, Greater New York.
> Dear Comrades: Our party organization, for obvious reasons, has thus far failed to function effectively in the campaign. So far as getting signatures on the petitions is concerned we have fallen down miserably.

This means that if we depend upon our party membership to get sufficient signatures to place our candidates on the ballot, our party will not be on the ballot. If we do not get on the ballot, it will be a great blow to us.

We must under all circumstances get a place on the ballot for our party. [The italics are Weinstone's.] And since we shall not be on the ballot, if we depend upon the party membership, we are compelled to pay people who will get signatures for us.

A few thousand dollars is necessary immediately. We must raise that money at all costs. The City Central Committee passed a motion to the effect that every branch must contribute a sum of money for the campaign equal to fifty cents per member. If a branch has thirty members it must send in to the Local Office, $15; if it has forty members it must give $20, etc., etc.

Comrades — this matter cannot be delayed.

Hurry Comrades — by October 6th the Local must raise one thousand dollars for the campaign. Send in the money immediately.

Let us get on the ballot and begin a real campaign.

> Fraternally,
> (signed) W.W. Weinstone
> Executive Secretary

P.S. — Branch Organizers. The leaflets for the Ratification Meeting of Sept. 29th are ready. *Come down and get them. Get some comrades to distribute them.*

The Communist International at Moscow had originally planned to have the Communist party of America make every effort to secure the election to Congress and to other offices of persons friendly toward Soviet Russia, and for this purpose promised to give the organization in this country a quarter of a million dollars for a campaign fund. But the inaction of candidates in whom they had placed confidence, and the casual activities of others, made the Moscow Reds, plotting on the internal politics of the United States and with an organ to carry out their plots, lose confidence, and they decided to withhold this fund at least until "the goods have been delivered."

Information reached the Communists of America that Moscow officials were particularly indignant at the action of Senator France of Maryland in introducing legislation to have the United States transfer six steamers to Poland, and that the Moscow people said this action showed that Russia could not depend upon such friends. When the Communist International was informed of this state of affairs, it abandoned its original plan and instructed the party here to exert all its efforts to using the elections for propaganda purposes. The Communist International, however, did appropriate $30,000 for the conduct of the election campaign by the Communist party through the Workers' party of America.

CHAPTER EIGHT

The Industrial Program

The plan elaborated by the Communists for the purpose of gaining a foothold among the workingmen of various industries includes the formation of a series of "nuclei" or groups, each consisting of ten members with a leader, which are pledged to the support of the revolutionary program. Only the leader knows the members of his own group or nucleus, and a limited number of other leaders. By this method it was hoped that by gradual extension of the numbers of nuclei through propaganda, further insinuations of revolutionary thought would result, until finally a sufficient minority would be under control to influence the passive thought and actions of the majority. For it must be remembered that the ultimate influences behind the world revolutionary movement are, by a developed instinct, specialists in minority rule.

There are but few groups of workingmen in the United States, either generally speaking or in a single industry, that do not contain the germs of Communism in the form of nuclei. In many places the work of propaganda is being carried on more and more openly with little organized opposition, either from the workmen or the individual employers, where in previous years attempts of this sort were regarded as illegal and carried out in an underground manner. Dissatisfaction of any sort is a productive fertilizer for the growth of the seed of Communistic propaganda. Planted in the form of nuclei, Communists under direct orders of the party leaders take especial advantage of strikes to carry ignorant passions to open violence and to win adherents to their cause.

There are but few strikes of any magnitude in which this dire influence is not felt. It was especially evident in the New England textile strike of 1922, and later in the coal and railroad strikes of the same year. The history of these attempts to utilize a big strike for the production of disorder is best illustrated by a short account of the coal strike. Whatever may be said about the ultimate causes of the 1922 coal strike, and certainly the actions of the United Mine Workers and its officials were not above criticism, Communist leaders saw therein an opportunity to further their program. Agents were sent into the Pennsylvania field, and very soon here and there nuclei were organized. Through their leaders the nuclei were put into touch with those groups which had been in existence for a longer period. Most if not all of the members were enrolled in the United Mine Workers, and through their locals naturally exerted a good deal of influence on the policies of the union as a whole, bearing in mind that a well-directed, secretly organized minority can always control to a greater or lesser extent the policies of a presumably democratic organization.

The gradual amalgamation of union and non-union workers in each line of industry into a single organization, first in cities, then in states, and then in the entire country, is the first general step, which is now being taken. Then will come, according to the schedule prepared by Moscow and American Communists, the amalgamation of all workers of all industries, first in cities, then in states, and then in the entire country. When this is accomplished the stage will be set for the great general strike, if it cannot be developed from a local disturbance before that time. The Communists plan this as the first general direct move toward the overthrow of the government by force of arms.

Many more steps have been taken toward this goal than the general public realizes. Communists attended, as members of the Maintenance of Way Union of the railroad group, the convention of that body in Detroit on the 5th of October, 1922, and showed their victorious hand when for the first time they were able to force a resolution through calling for the amalgamation of all rail workers. William Z. Foster, out of jail under bond for his participation in the illegal Communist party convention at Bridgman, was active at this meeting of the Maintenance of Way Union. An Associated Press dispatch from Detroit, under date of October 5, tells the story:

> The Maintenance of Way Union, in convention here, went on record today as favoring a union of the chief railroad workers' organizations as a step toward more concerted action in matters relating to labor. A resolution instructing officers of the brotherhoods to "prepare for the amalgamation of the unions" was adopted after several hours of heated debate in which friends of President E.F. Grable charged that the proposal was put forward by "a radical group."
>
> One speaker declared that it was evident that "representatives of Soviet Russia or the Industrial Workers of the World are secretly sitting in the convention hall." The affairs of the convention, this speaker said, apparently were temporarily in the hands of William Z. Foster, "who is known wherever labor is organized as an ultra-radical."
>
> Foster attended one of the sessions on Tuesday without credentials and has since been barred from the floor.

This is the fight that all American workers, in unions or out, are fighting in their own ranks. Unfortunately, before they or the American people appreciated the seriousness of the situation or understood the designs the Communist regime in Moscow, through the Communist party of America, had on the United States government and its institutions, the Communists had succeeded in planting many members in the different industries, in the unions, and among the non-union workers, and had such a foothold that they could not be eliminated. The sane, loyal American members of the Maintenance of Way Union have just discovered the extent to which their organization is dominated by the Communists.

Besides the active Communists "planted" in the labor organizations or converted to Communism by the missionaries thus included in the membership, there are a number of active "legal" bodies aiding in this work of aligning all labor for the united front "preparatory to the General Strike." Among these are the Society of Technical Aid to Soviet Russia, the Workers' party of America, and the Friends of Soviet Russia, which are the most important. When it is understood that these organizations are in fact one and the same as the Communist party of America, it is easily seen that this is an important means of agitation which is legally utilized under the innocent guise of technical, famine, or some other kind of relief for Russia. In a recent report by the Central Bureau of the Society for Technical Aid to Soviet Russia, sent to the Communist authorities in Moscow, it is shown that the influence of this organization is rapidly expanding throughout the United States and Canada. A branch has also been established in Panama.

In this report it is stated that the Society for Technical Aid to Soviet Russia had collected, in 1922, $620,000 in this country for its work in behalf of the Communist movement here and in Russia. In fact, because of the comparative poverty of the rest of the world, the United States is very largely financing the ruling group in Russia, whose only American policy is the destruction by force of the government of the United States. Of the $620,000 collected here on behalf of this seemingly excellent charitable movement, $10,000 passed immediately into the coffers of the Communist party of America. The rest was variously expended, a considerable sum going in gold to the Communist circle in Moscow. The balance is variously used in buying tools for Russia and promoting industries in that country, and in financing and spreading propaganda in this country. This sum was collected in less than six months, and sustains the hope of the Communists that more than $1,000,000 a year can be counted on from this source alone in the United States.

As an example of the thoroughness with which the work of the Communists in industries is done, correspondence in April 1922 between James P. Cannon, national chairman of the Workers' party of America, and T.R. Sullivan of St. Louis, one of the delegates to the Bridgman convention of the Communist party, may be cited. This correspondence referred to the work of the Communists in the southern Illinois coal fields, the scene of the Herrin massacre. Under date of April 17 Cannon wrote to "Dear Comrade Bob," asking for "a little report on the activities you are carrying on in the coal fields, stating just what is being done, and whether the work is being turned into account for organization purposes of the W.P." (Workers' party). Sullivan is also requested to "write something for the *Worker* about the Workers' party activities in this strike in your district."

To this letter from the leader of one Communist organization, Sullivan, as a Communist leader, replied on April 22, in a letter which throws no little light on the miners' strike, and shows something of the strength of the Communists in the ranks of the coal miners. This letter reads:

> Dear Comrade: In compliance with your request for a little report on the work being done in the Illinois coal fields, I would say that to date as a result of meetings which I had in southern Illinois, together with consultations with other comrades active in the mine workers, the following program has been formulated and adopted and is now in progress of being put into effect by means of the organization of caucuses inside of many local unions. The program is first, that all members of the Workers' party shall give their fullest and heartiest support to the aggressive carrying on of the miners' strike. Second, that we stand for no split or dual unions and are pledged to give our individual support to fighting any such tendency in the mine workers' organization. Third, that we stand solidly for the basis for state agreement and will fight uncompromisingly any move for separate state agreements. Fourth, that we support in every way possible the demand for a special national convention to reinstate Alex Howatt and the Kansas miners.
>
> We are carrying on a systematic organized campaign, for the purpose of carrying this program into effect, throughout the Southern Illinois coal fields, active work is being done along these lines in Zeigler, Christopher, Herrin, Valler, Johnston City, Collinsville, Bellville, W. Frankfort, Weaver, O'Fallon, Sesser, Royalton, Buckner, Benton, Staunton, Livingston, Maryville and other towns in Southern Illinois Coal Fields.
>
> Our plan is to carry on this work of organizing these Left Wing caucuses and to circulate especially among those in these caucuses our party literature. This to be followed up with personal talks and where possible with mass meetings. This work, I believe is most fundamental and in a short time will result in our securing large numbers of the most intelligent and aggressive members of the United Mine Workers into the ranks of the Workers' party.
>
> Needless to say, some of the work which we are doing in the way of building a machine inside the United Mine Workers cannot be given publicity without bringing down upon our, as yet, incomplete organization the attacks of the powerful reactionary machine. I can say, however, that we have good reason to believe that by next winter we will have a very strong position in the U.M.W. of A., District 12. We are off with a splendid start on this work and there is going to be no let up until we have thoroughly entrenched ourselves.

This correspondence is but a sample of what is going on daily throughout the United States between men whose work is to lay the foundation for the overthrow of the United States government. It was selected solely because of its part in the recent coal strike, and shows from their own records what the Communists did to bring about the massacre at Herrin.

Among the documents abandoned at Bridgman, Michigan, when the Communist convention was raided by the Michigan authorities and the delegates fled or were arrested, were copies of two reports to Moscow on the work done by the organization in industry in the United States. These reports cover the entire country, show the part taken by the Communists in the agitation, ostensibly in behalf of Sacco and Vanzetti, but more importantly to serve as a medium for creating unrest and hostility toward the government, and prove the statements frequently made that the Communists are working inside the labor unions toward the end of overthrowing the United States government by force. Erasures in the copies of these reports indicate that an effort was made to prevent the public from learning by any chance that Foster's Trade Union Educational League and the United Labor Council were controlled by the Communists.

The first of these reports reads:

The periodic reports received from our comrades show great activity in the industrial field. Our comrades have taken leading parts in constructive movements; at all times placing the labor movement as a whole above sects, party policies or theories. We are well represented at the United Mine Workers' Convention and the Railroad Telegraphers' Convention, doing our share of the preliminary spade work which must be done before broader fighting organizations can be developed.

We have organized the [Trade Union] Educational League, which has already established a Bureau of Railroad Workers and which is preparing to enter other industries, particularly among the steel, packing and building trades workers. As a step toward the unification of independent unions we have made the [United Labor] Council of New York and vicinity a live body and organized the United Labor Council of America, which initiated a convention of all independent unions to be held in New York in the first week of January, when a permanent federation will be formed. Under our leadership the United Labor Council, in conjunction with the American Labor Alliance, Workers' League, and other organizations cooperated with defense organizations, agitating the cases of Sacco and Vanzetti. Our comrades in unions throughout the country have led the movements for the introduction of the shop delegate system, affiliation with the Red Trade International, Relief of Soviet Russia, Defense of Communists and other class conscious workers and have done much to make the unions face the problem of unemployment as a class issue. In Chicago we have made the *Voice of Labor* an industrial organ. Everywhere we support the labor press, urging unions to stand with the Federated Press.

New York
Active in the United Hat and Cap Makers' campaign to revive the Needle Trades Workers' Alliance for all unions in the industry, numbering 400,000 workers. Opposition by President Schlesinger of the I.L.G.W.U. Active in cloakmakers' strike.

Active in Locals 22 and 25 where we faced expulsion by the machine.

Propaganda to turn the I.W.W. toward the Red Trade International and at the same time seeking to overcome sterile dualism.

Initiating amalgamation of five shoe workers' unions, in conjunction with our comrades in the United Labor Council.

Practically control knit goods workers' union.

Active among Foodstuff Workers, Public Service Organizations and Office Workers.

Important contacts with ex-soldiers.

After a long period of hard work we have gained some success in directing union activity through the Unemployment Council.

International Ladies' Garment Workers' Union, nineteen members in four locals. Industry not well organized. "Open Shop" quite extensive in dressmaking line.

Arranged a conference in Needle Trades for reviving Needle Trades' Alliance.

Chicago

Amalgamated Clothing Workers, seventy members in eleven locals. Industry 100 percent organized. Many skilled workers unemployed. One local of 12,000 being won over to shop delegates system. Opposed bosses' scheme to turn over plant management to workers as a means of strengthening speeding up shop benefit system. Faced expulsion for opposition to machine. Verblen expelled without fair trial. In some locals the officials refused to hold meetings from May to August. Under pressure from us they finally resigned and our comrades took their places.

Railroad workers, 50 members in four locals, 70 percent unemployed. Dual unions inactive. One Big Union dead. We have commenced our Trade Union Educational League Railroad Bureau here as the only means of dealing with so large an industry.

Similarly in the Building Trades, where we have forty-two members in thirteen locals in six trades. We lead the rank and file movement against the Landis award, and are using the R. & F. committees to make for united action of crafts and scattered locals. Very strong in five carpenters' locals.

We have foreign language comrades in ten steel plants and are faced with a great educational problem, the same as among the railroad workers already referred to, and among the stockyard workers, where we also have the problem of dualism to contend with.

Among the printers we are working with some success for a closer affiliation of trades.

Among the machinists we successfully resisted a split when there was a move to take a faction over to the Amalgamated Metal Workers.

At the Illinois State Federation of Labor Convention (October 17-22, 1921), we led successful fights for resolutions endorsing Friends of Soviet Russia, planning support of Mooney, Debs, Larkin, Gitlow and other class war prisoners, planning action for a shorter day and union relief work for unemployed, recognition for Soviet government of Russia, planning united action by all crafts in building trades to oppose Landis award.

Boston and New England

As far back as July we led movement to unite a score of shoe workers' unions, including some scab unions. The job promises to be successful. Also planning shop delegate system.

Baltimore

International Ladies' Garment Workers, twenty-five members in Ladies' Waist Makers' Union. Active in strike committees. Twenty-three members in Cloak Makers' Local.

Amalgamated Clothing Workers, eight members.

Also members in Painters, Butchers and Bakers, Journeyman Tailors, American Tobacco Workers, United Cloth Hat and Cap Workers, German Barbers, Jewish Barbers and I.W.W. locals.

Campaign among independent unions to send delegates to convention called by United Labor Council.

Cleveland, Toledo

Active Unemployment Council.

Active in United Mine Workers, International Ladies' Garment Workers, Painters, Carpenters, Bricklayers, Needle Trades, Food Stuff Workers, Electricians, Pattern Makers, Machinists, Moulders.

Detroit

Active in International Association of Machinists, I.W.W., Journeyman Tailors, Amalgamated Metal Workers, Carpenters' Union, Painters.

St. Louis

Active in United Mine Workers, Building Trades, Rank and File Committee.

California

Building Trades, San Francisco and District. Forced Building Trades Council to support general strike made necessary by open shop drive. Founded Rank and File Committees in building and other trades. Led one of the greatest fights ever made by organized labor, although open shop won. Opposed dualism which sprang up following defeat and as a reaction against bureaucratic betrayals.

Seattle

Formed committee of 100 from Central Labor Council in order to prevent use of Seattle *Union Record* for furthering financial schemes of the labor leaders.

The committee of 100 leads a real anti-capitalist movement among organized workers, and has working captains in the following trades: machinists, boilermakers, shipwrights, building laborers, office employees, foundry employees, iron molders, painters, dyers, cleaners, pressers, blacksmiths, building service employees, auto drivers, lady barbers, metal polishers, auto mechanics, city fire fighters, ship-yard riggers and fasteners, news writers, union waiters, bakers and confection workers, barbers, carpenters, sign painters, laundry workers, Typographical Union, tailors, musicians, bakery sales girls' local.

Buffalo
Bridge construction workers, needle trades.

Pittsburgh
Difficulty in making entry into steel workers.

Minneapolis, St. Paul, Duluth
Minneapolis — Railroads, 6 members; machine shops, 2 members; building trades, 3 members.
St. Paul — Packing houses, 2; railroad shops, 4; machine shops, 2; garment industries, 2.
Duluth — Some in iron ore and logging.

This report to Moscow could not fail to give the Red ringleaders there a comprehensive idea of the extent to which the work has been moving forward in the United States. It is evident that the preliminary work of "planting" representatives of the Communist party membership in the trades and industries has been thorough. It must be borne in mind that the establishment of these "nuclei" is for a definite purpose; to spread propaganda by word of mouth looking to the organization of Communist groups in every industry, and gradually to get control of the workers in these industries. Once that is accomplished it will be easy, they believe, to make active Communists of all the workers, then to seize the industries, and when the general strike comes, to turn all these workers against the government in armed insurrection.

In the second report found at Bridgman, which does not go so much into detail as to membership in various industries, it is shown that forty per cent of the active Communists are members of unions and are working as instructed to advance the cause of Communism. The remaining sixty per cent are working among non-union workers. Difficulties are encountered because of the fact that some of their members cannot speak English. This report also gives some of their plans for the future. It reads:

> In judging the accomplishment of the party in the labor union field there must be taken into consideration not only the period of amalgamation and controversy which seriously interfered with the carrying on of this work, but also the fact that at least 60 per cent of our members are not members of labor unions. That from the 40 per cent who are members of labor unions, about one-third belong to unions outside of the American Federation of Labor, and that even of those who do belong to labor unions, there are a considerable number who cannot be used to carry our message to the workers in their various respective organizations due to the difficulties of language.
>
> The results so far show that it has been especially difficult to get the foreign comrades to participate in this form of activity even in cases where methods were used to make it specially suitable for them to take part in nuclei work.
>
> Those at present active in nuclei work are primarily English, Jewish,

and German, and here and there Finnish comrades. From the other nationalities there are very few who participate in this work.

In addition to the foregoing tremendous difficulties, there must also be taken into account the general state of affairs in this country where the bulk of the revolutionists are not within the labor unions, but are outside, either not organized and unwilling to join the existing labor unions, or organized in dual "model" unions.

We have, therefore, a situation where the bulk of the revolutionary element in this country, Communists, sympathizers, anarchists and Socialists, are not part of the organized labor movement. As a result of this fact, the influence of the few thousand revolutionists who are organized in the Communist party of America is very limited. To this may be added the fact that in many industries labor organizations have hardly taken root, and in others there exist certain conditions which make it impossible to organize the workers without making gigantic efforts with a big apparatus and an enormous treasury behind it. Many of our members are in these industries, working as laborers, which generally makes them ineligible to membership in the American Federation of Labor.

The only feasible method suitable to the situation in the party was the establishment of the machinery for industrial work which at the beginning would function along the lines of the party. Later attempts were made to centralize the already established party nuclei along trade lines so as to coordinate the work in the various labor unions.

The coordination of this work has been made extremely difficult through the underground [illegal] organization, and many opportunities have been lost through lack of connections or through the impossibility of reaching the comrades in proper time with the proper advice.

Taking all these difficulties into consideration, the work accomplished so far bespeaks the correctness of the policy pursued by the party and the tremendous possibilities for the party by concentrating further upon this part of the party activities.

The progress made in the various districts, as reported by the district industrial organizers, the reports not being very complete, are as follows:

District I (Boston headquarters). Nuclei in needle trades, cigar makers, building trades, shoe workers, textile workers and railroad shop crafts.

The nuclei lack centralization and have been largely organized by the individual efforts of comrades in those unions. The industrial department in the district has not been functioning. The total number of those organized in these trades does not exceed one hundred.

The conditions in the other eleven districts into which the United States is divided by the Communist party are then similarly analyzed, and the report continues:

At best the prospects of our influencing the labor movement are mainly in the predominantly Jewish organizations like the International Ladies' Garment Workers, Amalgamated Clothing Workers, Hat, Cap and Millinery Workers, etc.

There is a splendid chance for our propaganda, and a strong

revolutionary element, and there are strong nuclei among the textile workers; also the United Mine Workers.

Among the shoe workers there are great possibilities for our work. Also among the automobile workers. There is also a good possibility for strongly entrenching ourselves in the machinist organizations and we have some good working groups in that organization. The prospects, however, of obtaining decisive influence in that organization are remote.

Our activities in the I.W.W. have led to their liquidation in a number of Eastern cities.

In the building trades we have strong groups in Chicago, New York, San Francisco and also other large centers. The more radical elements, especially among the painters and paper hangers, as well as the carpenters, are joining us in our work.

In the independent unions we have been especially successful among the Amalgamated Food Workers, the Metal Workers, Textile Workers, and Automobile Workers.

Our exact influence, however, in the I.W.W. and the independent unions, cannot be definitely known for lack of reports.

The Workers' party of America in September 1922 sent an appeal to all members, announcing the designation of October 1922 as a "red month," in which active recruiting must be done for the party. This party boasted of being the only revolutionary political party existing legally in the United States, and in this drive for membership let down the bars so that it would be less difficult for radicals to qualify for membership. The appeal showed very clearly the real nature and plans of the organization, which is permitted to function openly and legally, and to have candidates for office on the ballot in New York State. The appeal was sent to all radical papers with instructions to print it on October 1. The appeal to the second district, New York, read in part as follows:

Proletarians of all countries — unite!

Join the ranks of the Workers' Party of America!

Manifesto of the District Committee of the Second District Russian Federation Workers' Party of America.

The District Committee, Second District, Russian Federation, Workers' Party of America, which includes the States of New York, New Jersey, and Connecticut, has designated October as a red month, a month of recruiting new members. The District Committee Appeals to all conscious workers of the Russian Colony to become acquainted with the program of the Workers' Party and join its ranks. The Workers' Party of America is the only revolutionary party existing legally in the United States. It numbers in its ranks the most forward, conscious element of the working class, distinguished by self-denial and preparedness for battle.

During the month of October every conscious worker or group of same can, without unnecessary difficulties or formalities, join our ranks. We call to ourselves only those who are ready to sacrifice themselves in the interests of the working class.

Join then the ranks of the Workers' Party! Strengthen and help that party, which will lead the working class of America to complete liberation

Bishop William M. Brown of Galion, Ohio, member of the House of Bishops of the Protestant Episcopal Church, resigned as Fifth Bishop of Arkansas to become a self-styled "Episcopus in partibus Bolshevikium et Infidelium." The cover of his book, "Communism and Christianism." Checks given by Bishop Brown to C. E. Ruthenberg, executive secretary of the Communist Party of America and to Joseph Lang, alias Joseph Pogány the Hungarian Revolutionist who is now the party "boss" sent from Moscow.

from the capitalist yoke, and the establishment of a Workers' Republic in the form of a Soviet Government.

For more detailed information apply to I. Yanishevskaya, 208 East Twelfth St., New York City.

The name and address given were those of the secretary of the Russian Federation of the Workers' party. He was also an employee of the All-Russian Jewish Relief Committee, "Idgeskom."

In an official bulletin issued by the Central Executive Committee of the Communist party of America shortly before the Bridgman convention, the following instructions were given to all members, showing conclusively that the entire industrial movement is controlled by the secret, illegal, directing branch of the party. All members were cautioned to read the bulletin carefully and to see to it that the instructions were carried out to the letter at once. After stating that the party had launched on enlarged work, it had this to say under the head of "Industrial Activities":

> The proper conduct of this line of activities is dependent upon the alertness and understanding of our forces, and must be controlled and guided by No. 1 [illegal]. The same principle applies here as was laid down before, that all decisions as to policies and fundamental principles, as well as tactics, are to be decided upon by No. 1 before being carried out in No. 2 [legal].
>
> We must organize nuclei of members of No. 2, and work as a unit within these nuclei, and become a live factor in all these activities; but at all times keep our own forces intact. We must endeavor to create left wing militant groups within the labor organizations, in which we must also become the leading factor.
>
> The majority of our members must be on all important committees. All organizers must be chosen from our ranks, such as Sub-District Industrial Organizers, organizers for industrial, trades and local unions.
>
> All nuclei connections of No. One must be kept separately through the various units, and be held in readiness to be called at any time by the organizers.
>
> All reports to the lower units connecting No. One with these activities must be given verbally, and not appear in writing or in print.
>
> In cases where new nuclei of No. Two are organized and a member of No. One cannot be placed as organizer, a member of No. One must be assigned to keep all connections of his membership; his connection in turn must be recorded with the District Industrial Organizer.

With knowledge of the methods and plans of the Communists it is easy to see the parts they have played in the strikes in industry that marked the year 1922. It has already been shown that they played leading parts in the railroad and coal strikes, and it is known that they were particularly active in the textile strikes in New England. Agents were sent from various parts of the country to each of the New England cities where the strikes were declared, reporting regularly to the higher officials of the Communist party, and were directed in their work by the Central Executive Committee of the party. The American Federation of Labor fell into a simple trap set for it by the Communists, either knowingly or in childlike innocence, when it pledged $2000 a week to support the strikers.

Typical of these agents was one Joseph Kowalski, a Pole and an alien. Kowalski had been deported a short time after the sailing of the *Buford* for participation in Communist enterprises and giving vent to seditious utterances. In December 1921 he returned to America under a false passport, and quickly came in contact with leaders of the Communist party in this country. Kowalski was active in both the New England textile and coal strikes, making frequent trips from New York, where he made his headquarters, to centers in New England and Pennsylvania. It is a matter of record that between the beginning of the coal strike and his arrest in August, Kowalski himself organized over 2000 striking miners in nuclei of ten members each, and through them violence was promoted and the policies of the unions and their members influenced. Kowalski was only one of many such agents.

Kowalski's arrest led to his proper identification and a clue to his activities while abroad. It was established that at least part of the time, he had been an influential and highly placed member of the Cheka, the Commission for the Suppression of Counter-Revolution of the Russian Soviet Government, and as such had been responsible for the continued detention in jail of seven American citizens. He was convicted of violation of the Deportation Act and sentenced to Atlanta Penitentiary for one year and to be again deported.

As an example of the cleverness with which the Communists work, the textile strikes are illuminating. It was pretended that intense rivalry existed between the Amalgamated Textile Workers and the United Textile Workers. Both were conducting strikes on similar lines, but they contended that they were not only in no way connected but were actually hostile to each other. Undoubtedly many of the rank and file of the organizations believed this. But the leaders knew the fact that both were controlled absolutely by the Red Trade Union International, a Communist organization of Moscow with active agents in this country.

This organization has the same principles as all Communist bodies, aiming at the taking over by the workers of all industries and the establishment of the Dictatorship of the Proletariat after all organized government has been overthrown by force of arms. Naturally, only the leaders of the "rival" textile organizations knew of the relationship between the two, as this and the overlordship of the Red Trade Union International were kept a profound secret.

CHAPTER NINE

The Stage And The Movies

The Communist party of America was quick to see the excellence of the stage and the screen as mediums through which Communist propaganda could be fed to the public without contravention of the laws. As soon as the report of this phase of extending radicalism to the general public was explained to the high Communist authorities in Moscow, a plan was agreed upon to enlist the movies and the stage for this purpose, and Moscow stood ready to spend whatever money was necessary to further such a movement. Charles Recht, the highest Soviet representative of Communist Russia in America today, took up with Will H. Hays, as head of the motion picture industry in the United States, the matter of producing radical films to cost $8,000,000, the money to be furnished from Moscow. It is impossible to say exactly how much of this $8,000,000 was raised in the United States and sent to Moscow, but it is safe to say that three-quarters of the amount came from the pockets of citizens of this country, and the chief purpose for which it was solicited was the destruction by force of this government. Publicity attending this proposal resulted in the failure of the scheme to flood the United States with propaganda films; the Recht scheme fell through.

Unfortunately for the loyal American members of the labor unions of this country, the Communists have linked labor with Communism in the film service that is supplied to motion picture houses throughout the country. In addition to this general service, a special class of films is being used at union and non-union workers' meetings, picnics, and other gatherings. These pictures are especially designed to create dissatisfaction among the workers by showing exaggerated pictures of life among the rich and the contrast of life among the very poor. In urging the use of these pictures the Communists point out that messages may be conveyed to the public by means of the screen which would not be permitted by law to be spoken from a public platform.

Many prominent "movie favorites," men and women, as well as stars of the legitimate stage, are involved, knowingly or unknowingly, in this plan to sow the seeds of Communism through entertainment for the public. Isadora Duncan, the dancer, who expressed vitriolic indignation because it was suggested, when they were held for brief investigation at Ellis Island, that she or her new Russian husband might be tainted with Communism, is quoted far and wide in Communist newspapers and magazines, published in many languages, in her expression of favor for the Russian Communistic regime. It can be found in big, black type in these Communist publications, as follows:

> The martyrdom which Russia is suffering will be as fruitful for posterity as the martyrdom of the Nazarene.

She has never denied having made the statement, as far as is known; she has preached Red Communism in this country, and she numbers among her intimate friends many Communists both in America and in Europe. Yet she was indignant when the suggestion was made that she or her husband might be a Communist.

In this connection it is interesting to note that all artists — actors, singers, dancers, and the like — coming to the United States from Russia are obliged to secure permission from the Soviet authorities before they are permitted to leave Russia. This applies to all, including the Moscow Art Theatre Company, whether of Russian origin or of any other nationality. This permission is granted only if the artists agree in writing to three conditions which are included in the contract that enables them to leave Russia. These three conditions are:

1. The artists agree not to conduct propaganda while in the United States against the Soviet regime. Special preference is shown those who agree to conduct propaganda for the Soviets.

2. They agree to deduct from their earnings, for the benefit of the Soviet State, twenty-five or thirty-three percent of their earnings while in this country. (There are evidently two forms of contract.)

3. They agree to return to Russia at the expiration of their leave.

In order to justify these demands and in order that certain artists will not be alarmed at thus signing away their receipts to the Soviets, the Soviet government has appointed a "special committee" which supervises the trips and instructions to the artists. This committee consists of reliable members of the Communist party, but for the purpose of distracting the attention of the capitalist nations from the committee, all official papers are signed by Krassin. It is believed that the money thus collected goes to the International Propaganda Bureau in Berlin, which regularly sends funds to the Communist party of America to aid it in its fight against the government of the United States. It may be stated authoritatively, at any rate, that a goodly portion of this money, collected from lovers of opera, the stage, and dancing in the United States, is used for propaganda of the Communist movement. The artists are "remitted" the amount of their "taxes," according to the contract, if they disseminate Communist propaganda in the United States.

Some of the artists coming from Russia are opposed to the Communists, but they are not allowed to leave the country at all unless they agree to the terms set forth above. In order to control them and divert their attention from the real purpose of their trip, and to conceal from them the use of the money they contribute to the Communist coffers, the "special committee" hides behind the name of the Central Famine Relief Committee. The supervision of such artists and money is turned over to innocent-appearing Soviet organizations in various countries, such as, for instance, the Russian Red Cross in the United States. Incidentally, it should be mentioned here that, according to official statements by Soviet authorities, the danger of famine in Russia is past; crops have been excellent, and there is no starvation due to famine. In fact grain is now being exported to Central European countries. This authoritative information should be sufficient answer to the hysterical pleas to the American public to "Save Starving Russia."

The connection between the tours of Russian actors and artists and the Soviet ring in Moscow is shown in the certificate furnished the Russian Red Cross representative by the Communist authorities, which reads as follows:

> R.S.F.S.R. (Russian Socialist Federated Soviet Republic) Central Famine Relief Committee. Special committee for the Organization of Artists' Tours and Art Exhibits, of the People's Commissariat for Education.
>
> Dated at Moscow,_____ , 192__, No.__ .
>
> The Special Committee for foreign artistic tours and art exhibits hereby certifies that the Representative of the Russian Red Cross in America is granted the right to be an Agent of the Special Committee for arranging in America appearances of Russian artists and for the organizing of art exhibits.
>
> The Representative of the Russian Red Cross in America is authorized to conduct, in the name of the Special Committee, negotiations with impresarios regarding the conditions under which artists will appear and will conclude in its name, contracts with the impresario-promoters with the sanction of the Special Committee in each particular case, in accordance with instructions given to the Russian Red Cross. The Representative of the Russian Red Cross is obliged to render to Russian artists aid in the judicial defense of their interests in the event of a violation of the contract on the part of the impresario.
>
> (signed) B. Krassin
> Acting Chairman of the Special Committee

Early in the movement the Communist ring in Moscow awoke to the fact that the American people were profligate with money spent on foreign theatrical and operatic talent. It took but a short time for them to begin the organization of companies to be sent on tour in the United States in order to get some more of that easy money for Moscow. It has already been noted that a part of the plan of Captain Paxton Hibben as set forth in an interview in the Moscow *Izvestia,* official organ for the Communists in the Soviet regime in Russia, involved arranging "a trip of Russian actors to the United States, together with musicians and artists who will under the auspices of the Russian Red Cross [which is controlled by the Red government of Russia] help to collect means for the relief of Russia and at the same time will prove to the American public the high standard of Russian art reached during a time of revolution."

The spoken word, however, and even singing and dancing, do not carry Communistic propaganda as far or as adroitly as do the films, which accounts for the fact that the Communists are devoting more attention to the films than to the legitimate stage. To be sure, the stage brings in a steady, reliable income which the Moscow ring greatly needs, and so this feature of the work is continued. Every "artist" sent over from Russia under contract with the Soviet government allots a definite portion of earnings to the government as specified in the contracts. And the people of the United States who patronize these performers may be assured that they are seeing the best there is in Russia; for there is abundant and reliable evidence that instead of a "high standard of Russian art reached during a time of revolution," the stage and all the arts in Russia have fallen into the lowest state of degradation reached in any country in modern times. With the theatres patronized exclusively by the peasants and workers the stage has been brought down to a new low level. The drama is now almost entirely lewd and suggestive beyond anything ever seen in any country before.

Inasmuch as some controversy has arisen over the documented facts stated above concerning the relations between the Soviet government and the Moscow Art Theatre, other evidence which clearly substantiates these official statements is presented in the following. During the winter of 1921-1922, Mr. Morris Gest successfully initiated "Russian" dramatic propaganda in this country by presenting the Chauve-Souris at the Century Theatre in New York. On August 28, 1922, most of the New York morning papers carried announcements to the effect that Morris Gest and F. Ray Comstock were bringing "Europe's foremost theatrical organization, the Moscow Art Theatre," for a limited engagement to begin in January 1923. These articles comprised about a column and a half each in the *New York Times* and the *Herald,* and were identical in language and of a style easily recognized as written by a press-agent. In the course of a lurid description of the histrionic abilities of the Moscow Art Theatre group, the press-agent release said (italics added for emphasis):

> *Permission of the Soviet government has been obtained for the American tour under unusual circumstances.* The company has a leave of absence from Moscow for seven months from next January. But under the conditions of this leave of absence it must return to its home stage in time to celebrate the silver jubilee of its founding in the early autumn of 1923. [As a matter of fact this troupe is still in the United States (January 1924).]

The culmination of the negotiations in Mr. Gest's invitation and the Moscow Art Theatre's acceptance marks the completion of one of the most intricate, prolonged and costly parleys in the annals of the contemporary theatre. Ever since last February, when Mr. Gest made the first overtures to Moscow, the cables have been kept busy. Thousands of words have passed in both directions, and in June, Nikolai Rumiantseff, business manager of the theatre, arrived in New York to conduct negotiations in person.

The Moscow Art Theatre evidently started for America promptly. Cyril Brown, special correspondent of the *New York Times* at Berlin, cabled his paper, under date of September 2, the following:

> The Moscow Art Theatre Argonauts will sail on their own ship from Soviet Russia on September 10 with the intent to tour America and display Russian art, *under a pledge to refrain from all Bolshevistic propaganda or any other political activity,* under the management of Morris Gest. The Soviet government has placed a special ship at the Art Theatre's disposal for transportation of scenery, properties, and personnel from Petrograd to Stettin, Germany.
>
> *The Soviet was forced to tender shipping* because the railroad service is such that special trains could not be spared to transport the Art Theatre with its elaborate bags and baggage.
>
> Water transportation for the troupe from Petrograd to Danzig costs 333,000,000 Soviet rubles.
>
> *It took a lot of red tape before the Soviet government gave permission* for the Art Theatre's journey to America . . . .

The advance guard of the Moscow Art Theatre landed in New York on the last day of 1922, according to the *New York Times* of the following morning. The party included Sergei Berthenson, designated as the manager. A release by the American Defense Society, comprising the substance of the documentary evidence above given, had some days previously been broadcasted to the American press, and it had caused vigorous denials and protestations of disbelief on the part of many interested persons notwithstanding its authoritative character. Upon landing, a reporter asked Berthenson:

> "It is said that 33 per cent of the profits from the American tour will go to the Soviet government."
>
> "That is not true," said Mr. Berthenson. *"The proceeds of the first five performances will go to the Russian Relief Association,* which is like the American organization now working in Russia. It will be devoted to feeding and clothing destitute Russian people and especially the children. We do not pay any state tax to the government nor have we consulted the Soviet in any way before coming to the United States."

The players themselves landed January 4, 1923. In the large party at the dock to greet the new arrivals were Sergei Rachmaninoff, the pianist, and Boris

Anisfeld, "who has done many of the scenic settings at the Metropolitan Opera House." When Constantin Stanislavsky, "one of the two founders of the famous cooperative organization," was told that their entrance to this country had been protested by the American Defense Society on the ground that support of the Moscow Art Theatre would contribute either directly or indirectly to the support of Communist propaganda in this country, he said through an interpreter, shaking his head: "It is not so. We have no connection with the Soviet government."

The next reel in this "Russian" theatrical scenario is given by the *New York World*, September 15, 1922. The article follows a "double head" and is itself "double leaded," thereby placing the information it contains in the important or "must" class. The caption reads: "Kahn Backs Russian Art Theatres Here. Metropolitan Opera Chairman Also Helped Bring Balieff's Chauve-Souris To America." The body of the article follows:

> Otto H. Kahn, Chairman of the Board of Directors of the Metropolitan Opera Company and liberal patron of the arts with many millions, is the silent figure, sometimes called "angel," back of the Russian Art Theatre movements in America, the *World* learned from authoritative sources yesterday. Mr. Kahn, when questioned as to his cooperation with Morris Gest of Comstock-Gest, admitted he was instrumental in the New York presentation of Balieff's Chauve-Souris and that he was sponsoring the coming visit of the Moscow Theatre Company to America.
>
> The financier, one of the best known patrons of the arts, did not go into figures regarding his support of Mr. Gest, but was enthusiastic in his praise of the producer who brought to this country new and striking organizations . . . .

The same issue of the *World* contained a special dispatch from London in which it is stated:

> Feodor Chaliapin, famous Russian baritone-bass, who sails for New York October 25th, and who is to fulfil a contract with the Metropolitan Opera Company, today said he is to receive 30 per cent more than Caruso ever got from the Metropolitan for the same number of performances. His contract is for a minimum of fifteen appearances.
>
> Chaliapin told *The World* representative he intended to go into the movies while in America and would play the leading part in a novel scenario in which he is collaborating with Maxim Gorky.

The *World*, in comment following the dispatch, places Chaliapin's salary at $4,000 for each appearance at the Metropolitan.

The busy Mr. Gest then returns from Europe again in a gray topper and will neither confirm nor deny cabled reports to the effect that he would bring to America Lady Diana Manners or Eleonora Duse. He did say, however, according to the *Times* of August 16, 1923, that "he had now got his parents with seven brothers and sisters living in Berlin, after spending four years in getting them safely out of Odessa. They will remain in the German capital, he added, until his mother's health has been completely restored. Then he will bring his family to America."

Meanwhile, it is announced from Moscow through the medium of the *Times,* June 29, 1923, that "the ex-Imperial ballet of Petrograd will give a season in New York next winter, with full cast of two hundred artists from the Petrograd schools and a selection of its unparalleled costumes and decorations. Ivan Vassilivich Ekskosovich, Director of the State Theatre, Petrograd, informed the *New York Times* today that authorization had just been received for an American tour, which, unlike the Art Theatre, will be unpreceded by performances in Europe."

After reciting the difficulties which beset the company during the trying days of the revolution when "bullets flew in streets outside, though stage and dressing rooms were in arctic cold through lack of fuel," yet nothing daunted, these Russian stage-folk of the Petrograd State Theatre "carried on its business as usual," the story continues: *"Now there has been formed a mixed company with the State to run the Petrograd State Theatre in Russia and abroad."* (Italics added.)

The Labor Film Service was the name of an organization, as usual using "labor" as a medium of appeal, formed for the express purpose of presenting radical films for exhibition before American audiences. The field director of this organization was, from the start, J.D. Cannon of Seattle, Washington, a radical leader who had been active in iron and steel workers' strikes, and an official of the Mine, Mill and Smelters' organization. Cannon carefully canvassed the United States, selling stock in the Labor Film Service at $10 a share, chiefly to members of labor unions, with the argument that he was going to present films to counteract the capitalist films being shown which placed labor in a false and undignified position. He made no secret of presenting radical films, although to the union members he did not admit that he was working for Communism. He announced that the pictures presented by his company would be propaganda in behalf of radicals and labor unions, motion pictures describing what he called the terrible conditions existing among the working classes in the United States. The pictures were designed to stir up antagonism and hatred between workmen and their employers.

One of the first pictures presented was *The Contrast,* by John W. Slaton, a well-known radical of Pittsburgh. One of the pictures in this masterpiece portrayed a child taking food from a garbage can beside a dog belonging to some rich person, and was entitled: "To be seen in any great city – it costs $10 a day to feed this dog." The advertising matter concerning this picture proclaimed:

> The girl in this picture will be seen coming around a street corner, seeking something to eat from a garbage can, acting as though she feared

detection. Then a maid will be seen carefully leading the pedigreed dog into an elegantly furnished dining-room to partake of a tempting chicken dinner, but already surfeited it declines to eat.

Cannon harped on his desire to present the "truth" to the public through the medium of these pictures, and *The Contrast* may be cited as an example of his idea of the truth. It was also advertised that the following suggestive questions would be shown on the screen in connection with this picture:

> There were no labor unions in Egypt during many centuries. Why did that nation lose her civilization two thousand years ago?
> There have been no strikes in China for six thousand years. Does that account for her long death-like sleep and submerged millions?
> In view of these facts, what would happen in America if the labor movement would be crushed?
> If it is dangerous, therefore wrong, for labor to organize and strike, is it not equally wrong for capital to organize and raise prices?
> If wage workers should not organize solidly, why should lawyers, doctors, business men and ministers organize?

Another graphic bit of screen advertising shown during the progress of the picture reads:

> The next scene will be thought-compelling. It will show a worker's dining-room table with empty dishes. The wife enters from kitchen, babe in arms, little girl clinging to mother's skirts, and she will say: "Mamma, I am hungry." The mother will bid them all to sit at the table and wait for papa, with whose coming she expects food. He enters, but is empty-handed. When the mother sees this her head bows, tears start, the babe is pressed tightly to her breast. The father throws his coat aside, looks at the empty table and hungry family, reads the splendid extract from the Declaration of Independence, folds his arms and shakes his head.

The American Federation of Labor made a report on Cannon in 1921 in which it was pointed out that he had been a member of the Western Federation of Miners, and when he came East he was appointed organizer for the Metalliferous Miners, of which Charles Moyer was the head. The report continued:

> Just previous to his arrival the late John Mitchell was having a series of conferences with the mine owners for the purpose of getting recognition of the union when Cannon began making speeches advocating action along the lines of the Western Federation of Miners, with the result that the mine owners backed up on the Mitchell proposition and not only refused recognition, but decided to give any organization that might be formed a fight.
> In the territory of which Mr. Cannon was in charge, comprising the

States of New York and New Jersey, there were more than 40,000 men engaged in this industry. He has been very active in all radical movements; has talked syndicalism and approved Sovietism. He has taken sides with secessionists against the legitimate trade union organization, and has been very close to Morris Hillquit and Sydney Hillman and groups of similar stripe. He is now selling stock for the Labor Film Service Company, an organization in which Hillquit is interested.

In one of his letters sent to the labor unions throughout the country, Cannon stated that his company had secured another picture, *The Jungle,* based upon Upton Sinclair's novel, which he said had been made five years before. "It was produced," he wrote, "before the evil influence now so evident in the moving picture world got such a hold on industry. We are going to revise the picture and bring it up to date." This process, it developed, was to make the scenes depicted by Sinclair appear to be true pictures of today. An attempt was made to publish a *Labor Film Magazine* in connection with this company, but the New York police authorities refused to grant it a permit. It was plainly evident that a part of the work proposed was to take moving pictures of any situation reflecting against the government in its treatment of workers in the enforcement of law and order, and to display them at radical meetings for the purpose of inciting class feeling. Another of Cannon's letters, this one addressed to a radical in Oakland, California, contained the following informative paragraph:

> Our enterprise bears the endorsement of such prominent leaders as Norman Thomas, Rabbi Judah L. Magnes, Scott Nearing, Louis Waldman, I.M. Sackin, etc. We also have endorsement of the Central Federated Union, United Hebrew Trades, Italian Chamber of Commerce and other labor organizations.

Robert C. Deming, director of the Connecticut Board of Education, came into possession of some literature of the Labor Film Service as far back as 1920, and in referring to it made use of the expression that "Lenin and Trotsky are not short of agents in this country." It is also known that a motion picture producer, Guy Hedlund, of Hadlyme, Connecticut, had at that time been approached with an offer to go to Germany for the purpose of developing film publicity. This offer, it is understood, was refused, as it was evident that this propaganda was intended to aid the radicals.

The film, *The Contrast,* was probably the most successful picture presented by this company. It was shown, sometimes publicly and at other times secretly, in practically every important city in the country. Its connection with the Moscow Communists was plainly demonstrated, although not for public information, at a meeting of the Chicago Federation of the Friends of Soviet Russia, a Communist branch organization, at 220 West Oak Street, on March 2, 1922. At that time a representative of the Labor Film Company was present soliciting business for this film for use by the Friends of Soviet Russia. Moritz J.

Loeb, of the Friends of Soviet Russia, took occasion to state that not only was this body a relief organization, but its members were really friends of Soviet Russia and used their influence to promote the efforts of that regime to secure recognition. He said specifically that the real function of the Friends of Soviet Russia was to bring pressure on the capitalist governments, especially the United States, in order to force them to recognize Soviet Russia officially.

Loeb, who was then secretary of the Chicago organization of the Friends of Soviet Russia, said that the film could be used for propaganda purposes and shown in regular motion picture houses, and that through this propaganda many sympathizers could be reached who would not be willing to sit through, or even attend, a lecture on the subject. The representative of the Labor Film Service assured those in attendance at this meeting that the film had been made in a most radical manner, showing things that a speaker could not give utterance to on a public platform.

The Cooperative League of America, the American branch of an international organization which has in its membership a number of Communists and radicals of other hues, officially endorsed the Labor Film Service and urged all persons interested in the cooperative or trade union movements to patronize it. It is interesting to note that labor union officials, Communists, and "parlor Bolsheviks" were also interested in this organization.

The Communists are never asleep on matters that can be turned to their advantage. When *Orphans of the Storm,* one of D.W. Griffith's great plays, was produced, the Communists discovered that it might be utilized as excellent propaganda for their cause. Accordingly the word was sent out for all Communists to "press-agent the film as much as possible," and this was done. This is not meant to reflect, even by inference, that Mr. Griffith was interested in aiding the Communists, but the Communists believed that he was aiding them and appreciated it.

The attitude of the Communists is best explained by indicating the "atmosphere" of the plot as shown by one of the captions. This read: "Danton, the Lincoln of the French Revolution!" The film was afterwards suppressed in France.

The early success, much of it under cover, of the Labor Film Service Company (although after a year or more it proved a failure) resulted in other efforts to enter the radical film field. In California the Mission Pictures Corporation was organized and a Mrs. Clews, prominently identified with the Teachers' Council movement in Los Angeles, approached a number of the wealthy radicals of that city and Pasadena asking support for this company, which had been recently formed, and the first picture from which was *Science of God.* This company at that time was preparing to start work on another radical picture to be called *Robinson Crusoe, a Social Pioneer.*

Bruce Rogers, a notorious West Coast Communist, who was in Southern California collecting funds for the Communist party of America and the

Federated Press League, sold a film scenario to Lasky. The real author of this scenario, it was said, was in Alaska, but Rogers disposed of the picture and enjoyed the proceeds.

In the Communist files are found mentions of Charlie Chaplin, Will Rogers, Norma Talmadge, Lila Lee, Allan Hollabar, Charles Ray, Percival T. Gerson, Rob Wagner, Eric von Stroheim, Joseph Schenck, William C. De Mille and others connected with the motion picture industry. Some of them are known to be in hearty sympathy with Communism and to be close friends of Communists, to whose cause they have contributed largely.

When William Z. Foster, the salaried industrial director of the Communist party of America, was in Los Angeles shortly before the party convention at Bridgman, Michigan, which he attended as a delegate, he was the guest of honor at a reception given by Charlie Chaplin, the film comedian, at which were present many radical members of the "movie" colony at Hollywood and a number of parlor Bolsheviks. Among them were William C. De Mille and Rob Wagner. On this occasion Chaplin is said to have told Foster that neither he nor any of the stars associated with him had any use for Will Hays. "We are against any kind of censorship," the comedian said, "particularly Presbyterian censorship."

At this reception the great importance of motion pictures with their educational and propagandist appeal for the cause of the labor movement was openly discussed and several instances were cited of the introduction of radical ideas into motion pictures and onto the legitimate stage. Mrs. Kate Crane Gartz, a wealthy Pasadena society woman who has many friends among the radicals, told those present at the reception that she had recently been approached by a scenario writer named Hocheimer, and asked for a large sum of money to put radical Communist propaganda into scenarios "to do the greatest possible good to the cause." Mrs. Gartz was one of those who gave Comrade Plotkin, an organizer for the Garment Workers' Union in the East, letters of introduction to Charlie Chaplin appealing for funds to aid the strikers, when Plotkin was sent by the Communists to agitate among the railroad strikers in Southern California.

As an instance of radical propaganda finding its way onto the legitimate stage, the Communists call attention to *The Fool,* which was tried out at the Majestic Theatre in Los Angeles, preparatory to placing it on Broadway. Richard Bennett took the principal role: that of a minister of the Gospel who undertakes to settle a strike, forces the company to accept the strikers' terms, resulting in the loss of millions to the company, and does a number of impossible things in defiance of the present social system. The character of "the Fool" is said to have traits of Jesus Christ as well as of Dostoevsky's "Idiot." Since Hauptmann's *Die Weber,* the drama depicting the revolt of striking weavers in Silesia, it is said that no stronger radical labor propaganda has been produced for the stage. One of the most effective scenes in *The Fool,* it is reported, is one showing a Polish labor agitator in a fiery soapbox speech against the ten-hour day and for better working conditions and higher wages.

Foster, who is one of the trustees of the Garland Foundation, told Charlie Chaplin and Mrs. Gartz on his visit to Los Angeles that the Garland fund could be depended upon to be used in aiding any of the radicals who got into trouble with the authorities. But Foster was especially prolific with promises to the effect that there would be many uses for the funds promised by the eccentric New England Harvard youth. He said the Federated Press was to get $100,000 and a number of Communist workers on the Coast were promised salaries.

Bruce Rogers was the money-getter for the Communists, to whom Robert Morss Lovett, Harvard '92, as president of the Federated Press League, wrote urging him to see and collect money from William C. De Mille, Allan Hollabar, Dr. Percival T. Gerson, Will Rogers, Charles Ray, Charlie Chaplin and Eric von Stroheim whose pro-Germanism made him a prominent figure during the war. Lovett said in this letter, which was quoted in an earlier chapter, that he had written these men, that "they helped us before and will do it again." It may be of interest to "movie fans" to know that William C. De Mille married a daughter of Henry George and has been very active in single-tax movements.

It has been known for a long time that Charlie Chaplin has been interested in radical movements and a heavy contributor to radical funds; much of this money found its way into Communist channels. Chaplin, Lila Lee, a Famous-Players star, and Raymond Griffith, playwright, motion picture producer, and actor, were among the guests of Mrs. Gartz and Prince Hopkins at the now famous dinner given in honor of Upton Sinclair, when there was a gathering of radicals of every known hue, on April 5, 1922. Among the speakers on this momentous occasion was the redoubtable Chaplin, who told with great gusto of his pride in having given District Attorney Woolwine of Los Angeles what he called "a good lesson regarding the real meaning of syndicalist ideas." Chaplin said that he had visited Woolwine in his office and discussed with him the subject of criminal syndicalism. He asked Woolwine to show him one of "those terrible, cut-throat, murderous I.W.W.'s," whereupon one of the I.W.W. prisoners was brought from the jail for his edification. Chaplin said that he and the district attorney questioned the prisoner and "were much impressed by the intelligence and enthusiasm of the clean-cut young radical."

It was in August 1922 that Charles Recht, the New York lawyer who defended Ludwig C.A.K. Martens and succeeded him as head of the Soviet Russian government representation in this country, conducted negotiations, as was stated earlier in this chapter, with Will Hays, as head of the motion picture industry in the United States, regarding the order Recht received from the Moscow government to purchase films to cost $8,000,000. These films were to be made in the United States and to be entirely for propaganda purposes. They were to be anti-Christian, anti-capitalistic, and to show the great advantage of Communism over the present state of affairs in the rest of the world.

Recht sailed for Europe early in September 1922, with an appointment to meet Norma Talmadge, the film star, and her husband, Joseph Schenck, a motion picture producer, on September 25, at the Hotel Breslin in Berlin. From there they were to go to Moscow to conclude the negotiations for an extensive picture propaganda campaign. Schenck and his wife, it is understood, failed to get to Moscow because they could not get satisfactory guarantees for their personal safety. Will Hays may not have had the slightest idea of what Recht was deliberately aiming at during the negotiations the two had, and when the proposal was publicly exposed the deal fell through.

The Friends of Soviet Russia undertook some time ago a nationwide motion picture campaign to aid in obtaining American gold for the Soviet government to handle under the guise of relief funds. These pictures were taken in Russia and were manifestly propaganda films. Censors in various parts of the country so cut the films, however, that they were at last reduced to nothing but lantern slides. Automobiles were furnished to take exhibitors of these slides from one city to another in order to get as extensive publicity for the propaganda as possible.

Early in 1922 a number of prominent New York people allowed their names to be used as patrons and patronesses of a "Russian Fair and Costume Ball" given by the American Committee for Relief of Russian Children, under the impression that they were really lending aid to famine sufferers. They did not know that their efforts were being made to aid in the perpetuation, through the force of the Red Army, of the present regime in Russia before any thought would be given to the starving children. The names of some of the most prominent writers, artists, and some society women misled by plausible appearances were sandwiched in with the names of Scott Nearing, Charlie Chaplin, and Constance and Norma Talmadge.

In connection with the efforts to disseminate Communist propaganda by means of public amusement should be mentioned renewed activity on the part of the Communists to capture the youth of the world for Communism. In a circular "about the session of the Bureau of the Communist Youth International," marked "strictly confidential," found in the mass of documents captured by the Michigan state authorities when they raided the illegal Communist convention at Bridgman, the Executive Committee of the Communist Youth International in Moscow gave specific instructions that the Communists of all the countries of the globe must make a special drive to get at the young children who are gathered in such organizations as the Catholic youth unions, the Y.M.C.A. organizations, and the Boy Scouts. This document was in German.

In passing, it should be mentioned that the Bridgman raid was the greatest blow sustained by the Communist party of America, and therefore by all radicals, in the history of the United States. The Michigan authorities caught seventeen of these men actually conspiring to overthrow the United States government by force, found the records of every delegate to the convention, the financial statements of the party, "sucker lists" of many cities, written instructions to the Communists from the directing circle in Moscow, of which

Lenin and Trotsky are the active principals, and almost countless documents which prove the conspiracy and the guilt of every person in attendance.

The document pertaining to capturing the youth of the world for Communism confesses that these organizations of youngsters constitute the "greatest obstacle to the development of Communist youth organizations," and so should serve to keep loyal citizens of all countries firmly behind such bodies. One part of this circular says:

> There are four big groups of such unions [referring to organizations which "count big masses of young workers among their members" and which must be combatted "with great energy"]:
> 1. The Catholic youth unions (mainly in Latin countries and their colonies).
> 2. The Protestant youth unions (. . . in Central Europe and Scandinavia).
> 3. The Young Men's Christian Association (in the Anglo-Saxon countries).
> 4. The Boy Scouts.

The full text of this circular, intended as a guide book or handbook to be used by those bent on debauching the youth of the world with Communism, runs to upward of 10,000 words. With the strict confidence enjoined by the Communist organization issuing it broken by the offĭcials bent upon the enforcement of the law, this document now constitutes a challenge to loyal parents and Americans of maturity to lend aid and support to every move that strengthens these organizations of youth whose influence among young workers is so great that the world-wide Communist organization fears them and must outline a campaign of battle to alienate them from ideas of religion and patriotism.

CHAPTER TEN

Army, Navy, And The Government

In the conspiracy to overthrow the government of the United States by "armed insurrection," the Communist party of America, coached specifically by the Communist International of Moscow, aims first to undermine the military force of this country, including Army, Navy, and local police organizations. The handling of the local situations is left to the Communists of the various cities, but the question of the Army and Navy is squarely before the national organization. The illegal Bridgman convention was to have considered this feature of the Communist work, but as the conspirators were rudely interrupted by the Michigan authorities they did not get to this part of the convention program. However, certain documents found by the authorities after the raid show plainly what the plans were.

It should be mentioned here that the celebrated Boston police strike, before the Communist party of America was organized, was a part of the Communist movement in this country. It was engineered by the Left Wing of the Socialists, which had seceded from the Socialist party and was awaiting the coming of organized Communism to the United States. These Left Wing Socialists, who later joined the Communist party, boasted of their success in precipitating the police strike, and they were officially credited with this manifestation of their strength both at Moscow and by the Communist party of America, when the question of amalgamation came up. The incident has been cited more than once by the Communists as evidence of the ease with which the police can be handled when the great general strike comes which is to result in the overthrow of the government.

Two distinct lines of attack, based upon the success of the Communist organization in Russia when the Russian government was overthrown, are being used in the Army and Navy of the United States. These lines of attack were dictated by the Moscow officials to be put in practice in the United States. The orders, issued from Moscow, are on record. They are subtle, as are all the methods of the Communists when subtlety is necessary, but the plans

161

and the working out of the program are known to the high officials in the Army and Navy departments of the government.

First, all ideas of pacifism are to be encouraged. This includes the use of civil organizations devoted to pacifism, disarmament, "no more war" days, and any movement which will tend to reduce the military forces in size and ability. In all such organizations the Communists are interested and in many of them they appear as members, sometimes under the guise of reputable citizens, in others openly as revolutionary workers. This is aided by propaganda, printed and circulated by word of mouth by Communists within the ranks of the Army and Navy, full of references to the "horrors" and "cruelty" of war, with many citations, some real and others imaginary, of hardships suffered by soldiers. The life led by the officers is always pictured as one of ease and luxury, while the ranks are driven to a dog's life by these officers, so falsely painted.

The second method is more difficult and more subtle, involving the enlistment of men in the Army and Navy for the creation of nuclei of Communism. Great care is used in selecting the men for these important posts for the dissemination of disloyal and treasonous ideas and theories, since the work must be handled with the greatest finesse. The duty of these men is to make converts to the cause of Communism within the ranks of the soldiers and sailors, so that when the great occasion comes the men will revolt by companies, battalions, and regiments, as they did in Russia. The example of Russia is always cited as an example of what may be accomplished if the preliminary work is well done by the men to whom it has been entrusted.

The Secretaries of War and Navy in the cabinet of the President of the United States are aware of the efforts which are being made by the Communists to undermine the fighting forces of the nation and to make them ready either to turn their weapons on their officers or to disintegrate in the face of danger. Both of these tactics were employed by the Communists in destroying the Russian army and navy as weapons of the government, and with that experience in mind, and kept ever in the thoughts of whoever can be found to listen, the Communists are patiently but persistently working within the forces of the United States. Secretary of War John W. Weeks, in 1922, after pointing out that army training has always been conducted with a view to "teaching loyalty, love of country, and a spirit of sacrifice," said:

> The War Department has been aware that the Communist program has stressed the breeding of disloyalty among the Army and Navy personnel as well as among citizens at large. Though all opposition to the military establishment is not occasioned by such influences, undoubtedly many loyal Americans have lent their support to movements inspired by radical organizers.

In view of the situation in the Near East at present, it is interesting to note that secret instructions were sent out early in 1922 by the Bureau of Western

European Secretariat of Propaganda under instructions of the Third Communist International. The United States is subordinate to this Western European bureau, and the instructions were received by the Communist party to be used here, substituting the United States for England or France where the names of those countries were used. These secret instructions were largely devoted to work in the Army and Navy establishments of all "capitalist" countries, because although Russia has a well-trained, well-equipped, well-clothed and well-fed Red Army of approximately a million men, the Communist parties of other countries "possess but a trifling number of weapons," so read the instructions, and "one must come to the conclusion that the military organization of the Communist International lacks the forces which it could lead to a decisive battle with capitalism, without which, of course, it is impossible to obtain a victory over capital, and the World-Wide Soviet Republic." The secret instructions continue:

Such a condition of affairs has long since prompted the necessity of devoting attention to the army and navy of the capitalistic States, and by increased and intense work utilizing the experience of the de-composition of the Russian White Guard Army, to attain such a condition of affairs that in the ranks of the capitalistic armies there would be Red sections *which would de-compose the Army as a whole and turn their bayonets against the capitalistic class.* This was considered by both the Second and Third Congress of the Communist International in compiling the thesis on propaganda and work, but unfortunately the work in this respect gave absolutely no results. This must not stop the active Communist forces from continuing the work commenced in this region. But to the contrary, particularly now, the phantom of impending capitalistic wars is hovering before the world and the armies and navies of the capitalistic States, manned by compulsory, obligatory, or voluntary enlistment, are almost entirely consisting of the most anti-militaristic youths inclined to adopt the Communistic idea.

The work and organization in this section must be placed at the head of all the future work of the Communist International and its members, and all its strength and means must be devoted to it.

The principal attention in the first place must be devoted to the personnel of the Navy, where the soil is particularly fertile for active Communist propaganda and work, particularly in the English and French navies. It is necessary to work under the following general conditions:

1. All sailors, by the manner and nature of their lives, are devoid of nationalist ideology, and they, as a matter of fact, are internationalists.

2. The conditions of service of sailors on submarines, cruisers, and in general on ships which make distant trips are extremely difficult; they enjoy very little rest, their maintenance is very unsatisfactory, and the service is very dangerous to life.

3. The war did not bring to sailors the moral satisfaction and peace which they were expecting, but to the contrary, it is bringing on the coming monstrous war on the seas.

In the final summary one should not forget that sailors are least of all subject to subordination and are very much inclined to insubordination and disorders. In this respect the example of the Great October Revolution [Bolshevist], where an honorable part was played by the Kronstadt and Baltic fleets, and the German Revolution, where the principal participants were sailors, are convincing facts. On the basis of all this the Bureau and the Russian branches of the Communist parties must strive to create in all the principal ports special nuclei of organizers and agitators who must strive with all their efforts to get into contact with the personnel of naval vessels, to organize among them nuclei with their own people in them, and *to distribute energetically special literature.* The nuclei on the ships must maintain a permanent contact in accordance with the movements of the ships with the port organizations of the Communist party and the latter must regularly maintain the contact among themselves and inform one another of the movement of ships, countersigns and conditions of entry. The port nuclei must not limit themselves to the establishment of contact and the transmittal of literature, but must strive also to the bringing together of the crews of ships and the proletarian population of the ports and to the generalizing of their ideology, remembering always that the fishermen principally are the source for the supplying of the personnel of the fleet and that their influence can reflect very much on the attitude of the sailors now and particularly during possible mobilizations. Simultaneously the work already commenced in the occupied territory (on the Rhine, Upper Silesia and Constantinople) among the territorial armies of the Entente must continue to grow and to spread into the detachments already in England, France, etc., proper.

At the present moment it must bear in mind the youths which are entering the Army on the latest drafts, among whom there is a *particularly favorable soil for Communist agitation and the propaganda of pacifist ideas.* In this respect it is necessary to give the French, German and English parties full initiative in the sense of determining the tactics and program of agitation obligating them to conform their work to local conditions. With this it is necessary to point out that their agitators should strive to utilize as often as possible the thousand and one little details of the daily life of the soldier in order to *undermine his obedience to the officers, the bourgeois discipline and his duties in defending the bourgeois peace.* Along with this there must be conducted on a broad scale *an increased propaganda of pacifist ideas, ideas of disarmament,* and to prove that it is only for their own benefit that the capitalists and bourgeoisie create big armies and are preparing for their own game new conflicts of peoples when they wish to live in peace.

The general slogan: *Only if the proletariat be master in every country will the cause for new conflicts disappear.*

This secret document was signed by Zinoviev, chairman of the Central Committee of the Third International; Katayama, the Japanese Communist who was in charge of the propaganda section in Moscow; and Arngold, the secretary. It was dated in Moscow in December 1921, and the official copy reached the United States by courier early in 1922. The Communist party of America, obedient to the "iron discipline" of the Third International of Moscow, became active along the lines laid out in the secret instructions. The results were soon apparent to the officers of the Army and Navy and in course of time the higher officers of both military establishments recognized the symptoms. Then it was that Secretary Weeks made the statement quoted above, and Secretary of the Navy Denby issued the following orders to the entire service:

1. My attention has been called to the fact that *there is a sinister propaganda by societies having their origin in foreign countries to undermine the morale of the Navy and to insinuate into its personnel elements of disloyalty and disorder.*

2. I have the most profound confidence in the loyalty and devotion of commissioned and enlisted men of the United States naval forces. I have no fear that men in any considerable number may at any time, anywhere, be seduced from their allegiance to their country's flag. It is not, therefore, through any thought or suggestion that the United States Navy is in the slightest danger from this propaganda that I issue this warning.

3. I fear only that some few of our men may be induced innocently at first, when on shore, to join societies having for their purpose the advancement of ideas contrary to our form of government, or which may result in lawlessness. There are, of course, in a personnel as large as that of the Navy, some discontented men, and in the hearts of discontented men false doctrines find ready acceptance.

4. I am trying by this warning to save a few individuals who might otherwise affiliate themselves with societies teaching those things which cannot be tolerated in an organization sworn to uphold the constitution of the United States and to obey all lawful orders. Should there be any such men in the Navy today, it is almost certain that if they do not disentangle themselves from affiliation with such organizations, they will ultimately be detected.

5. I am trying to lessen the number of prisoners in naval prisons. I could not hope to show leniency, however, to any man who, in combination or alone, in violation of his oath, committed acts of disloyalty to his country.

6. Because I have been one of you I know that all men have their periods of unhappiness — of imagined ill-treatment, homesickness and discontent. Such periods come to civilians as well as to men in the naval service. They are a part of life. We must not let them lead us into such folly as desertion or resistance to lawful authority nor particularly into revolt by word or deed against a form of government that has proven in the main a government of liberty and justice.

7. The world is full of false thought today. I would save that service of which our country is so proud, and of which I happen to be at the moment the head, from the hurtful influence of improper theories of government, or false dreams of a better State to be created by anarchy and violence. I would go far to save any one man from the consequences of misdeeds, whether such consequences take the form of physical punishment or only of the deep remorse which must ever follow him through life. So I appeal to the officers and men of the service to be ever alert in guarding themselves ashore and afloat from the preaching of sovietism, communism and anarchy.

(signed) Edwin Denby
Secretary of the Navy

It was only three months after the secret instructions from Moscow quoted above arrived in the United States, brought by Dr. Leo S. Reichel, member of the Communist party and of the Central Bureau of the Society for Technical Aid to Soviet Russia, and therefore a courier to be trusted with so important a document, that Secretary Denby found it necessary to issue his warning, and Secretary Weeks to issue his statement regarding radicalism in the Army. It is easy to read between the lines that these instructions had been put into action promptly by the Communists and that the effect had already been felt in the Navy. Loyal Navy officials have been particularly watchful since the captain of an American ship in Pacific waters adopted the Soviet idea of permitting the crew to decide what port to make for a holiday ashore. That occurred but a few years ago and the captain was quickly relieved of his responsibilities at that post.

Military authorities are loath to speak of sudden dismissals from the service in recent months of men who were acting as Communist agents in the ranks of the Army and Navy. It was thought best to dismiss them without "making a noise about it" instead of court-martialing the men and sentencing them to prison, which would have furnished material for the Communists in stirring up other soldiers and sailors to resentment and rebellion.

By skilfully used propaganda and personal intercourse the Communists succeeded in planting the seeds of Communism in the minds of many of the American soldiers who saw service in Russia during the war, and on the German frontier and in Germany after the armistice. Officers were shocked at the Communistic ideas inculcated in the minds of troops who had served in such situations, on their return to the United States. It is not believed possible that all such seeds have been exterminated, but much has been done toward wiping out the evil in both branches of the military establishment. All of which has made the Communists more determined to push their work with greater vigor.

Whenever police or soldiers are called out on strike duty the Communists become very active in trying to alienate them from their duty. Clever talkers are sent into the strike district to talk with soldiers and police whenever possible; "under cover" men they are sometimes called, for they do not let it be known that they are connected with the Communist party or any radical movement. They present their arguments, skilfully prepared, solely with the view of making the soldiers forget their duty or sympathize with the law violators to such an extent that they will be remiss in their duty, and thus morale is undermined. These carefully selected men never appear among the strikers, never address strike meetings, and to all appearances they are not particularly interested in the strike except from a humanitarian point of view.

Another group of Communist workers is also on duty at all strikes where soldiers are sent to keep the peace. This second group devotes itself to keeping the strikers agitated by speeches and by circulars and posters distributed among the strikers. They address secret or open meetings of the strikers, urging them to stand firm in their hostility toward the employers and in general adding fuel to

Stop Riot and Murder!

Workers, men and women!

The Communist Party speak˭ ˭o ˭˭ a very serious issue.

Our party has arran˭ ˭˭ to demand
the immediate withd˭ ˭˭˭˭
is starving the ˭˭
establishm˭

No. 418 (File)
This Communist leaflet was issued April 20, 1921

THEN AND NOW

APRIL 6, 1917—APRIL 6, 1921

Four years ago, on April 6th, 1917, the United ˭
the World War. The declara˭ ˭on of war was ma˭
Wilson, who was returned ˭ ˭on the pro˭
˭atic political machin˭ ˭ld k˭
mess. Congress
˭ound to
˭rum˭
˭˭

The Tulsa Massacre!

By the time this leaflet is in your hands all the horrible details of the
mass murder of the helpless Negro population of Tulsa, Oklahoma will be
known to the entire world.

There are no words vivid enough to describe the action of the well
dressed armed mob of business men who, with automobiles and airplanes,
surrounded the Negro quarter in Tulsa on June 1st, setting fire to their
homes, destroying ten city blocks and rendering homeless more than ten
thousand Negro workers; ruthlessly slaying men, women and children; kill-
ing over 90 and wounding more than 200.

There is only one appeal to organized force. The only language that the
rages—that is the appeal that will stop these fiendish and bloody out-
bloodthirsty capitalist of America can understand is the language of
ORGANIZED POWER. Only by reprisals—by answering force with force
—will the business mobs and their White Guards, the Klu Klux Klan etc.,
be restrained from continuing their brutal and cowardly assaults upon the
Negro and working class population of this ˭˭try.
If there is any red l˭˭

˭working class of America
˭s, who are the victims of
˭murders the workers re-

˭America, must come to
˭ns are darker˭hued than
˭White, we, the workers,
˭S—which uses its GOV-

˭is country. Almost all
˭age workers, whom we
˭pidly being reduced to
˭se than chattel slavery
˭y idly and permit the
˭s of our fellows? The
˭hing but the beginning
˭tire working class of
˭ Negro wage
˭ men

SOLDIERS!   SOLDIERS!

Do not shoot your brothers, the railway and mine strikers!

They are not your enemies! They are fighting in order
to obtain a scrap of bread for their families. They are useful
citizens; workers who have produced millions of dollars' worth
of wealth for the war profiteers. Many of them fought on
Flanders' Field. They are now trying ˭ ˭ollect some of that
democracy and freedom they are pr˭ ˭ ˭the same as
thousands of ex-service men are fig ˭us that
war profiteers are opposing becaus˭ ˭˭˭to
disgorge some of the loot stolen
country.

Soldiers! Whether you ar˭
militias of the various states.
You did not enlist to engage i˭
strikebreakers and scab herd˭
help the profiteers take the˭
the helpless women and chil˭

'Remember this, the wo˭

Soon you may be in ˭
to be crushed by armed

Perhaps, even now.
your father ˭r your br˭
Would you˭ ˭nt them
existence?

It is not treaso˭
workers!

Central

A FAIR TRIAL?

A Record of the Prejudice and
Dominated the Legal P˭˭ and
Press i˭˭

Ce˭

Tr˭

INDUSTRIAL COMMUNISM ˭ ˭ I.W.W.

PRICE 5 CENTS

Leaflets distributed by the Central Executive Committee of the Communist
party of America. Labor disturbances or conflicts of any kind always bring out
similar circulars suited to the occasion. In the center, an appeal to the members of
the militia on guard over property during the coal strike in Pennsylvania.

the fire by class hatred. A third group devotes itself entirely to the soldiers, placing in their hands appeals printed by the Communists urging them not to oppose the strikers. One such appeal reads:

Soldiers! Soldiers!
Do not shoot your brothers, the railway and mine workers!
They are not your enemies! Today they are fighting in order to obtain a scrap of bread for their families. They are useful citizens; workers who have produced millions of dollars' worth of wealth for the war profiteers. Many of them fought on Flanders' Field. They are now trying to collect some of that democracy and freedom they were promised, just the same as thousands of ex-service men are fighting for the bonus that war profiteers are opposing because it would compel them to disgorge some of the loot stolen from the workers of this country.
Soldiers! Whether you are in the United States Army or the militias of the various States, do not shoot at the strikers! You did not enlist to engage in the infamous occupation of strike-breakers and scab herders. Refuse to do it! Do not help the profiteers take the last crumb from the mouths of the helpless women and children of the working class.
Remember this, the workers are never your enemies!
Soon you may be in their ranks and you would not want to be crushed by armed force!
Perhaps even now, in some other part of the country, your father or your brother may be in the ranks of the strikers! Would you want them to be murdered because they ask a mere existence?
It is not treason to refuse to become an assassin of the workers!
Central Executive Committee of the Communist party of America,

(signed) J. Davis
Executive Secretary

In *Truth,* a Communist paper, of August 4, 1922, is found an article written with the approval of the Central Committee of the Communist party of America, devoted to the need of constantly stirring up trouble and in efforts to make everyone dissatisfied with the existing state of affairs. In this article appears the following sentence: "In soldiers' organizations the bonus issue may be injected to alienate them from the government." While the bonus question was before Congress the Communists prepared to use the issue for its own ends, whichever way the question was decided. If it were passed by Congress the Communists were prepared to launch an attack on the granting of a bonus on the grounds that it was a move by capitalism to add more taxes to the poor working man; if defeated it was to be used to show that capitalism was refusing the soldier "his just reward."

In another Communist paper is an editorial declaring that the desertions from the United States Army were at the rate of "one every forty minutes." This editorial says: "The deserters are to be congratulated. It would have been better still if they had shown the same intelligence before they ever entered the army, but perhaps it is just as well that they learned their lesson by bitter experience. They know now what jackasses they were. They will not be caught in the trap again."

Among former soldiers, men who served in the Army during the European War and have since been demobilized, the Communists are working hard, with many agents. The American Legion as a whole has loyally withstood the efforts to win it over to the cause of Communism, and the organization is unalterably aligned against Communism. But it is true that secretly the Communists have many representatives in the ranks of this loyal organization, and the fight will have to be kept up continually to prevent increases. Knowing that the effort to subvert the Legion is well-nigh hopeless, the Communists have devoted their attention more particularly to the World War Veterans, an organization which is Communistic in principles and which is openly supported by the Communist party. Indeed, among the documents seized at Bridgman were official reports of the World War Veterans which showed a close working arrangement between the two bodies. It is generally accepted that the World War Veterans organization is one of the "legal" expressions of the Communist party.

The *Soldier-Worker* of Butte, Montana, official organ of the World War Veterans of Montana, is as Communistic as the official organs of the Communist party of America and boasts of its connection with Communist movements. It prints with pride a letter of commendation from the Secretary of the "International of Former Combatants" in France. It supports all amnesty and pacifist movements, attacks capital in every issue, and is a part of a national group of similar papers backing the World War Veterans and the Workers' party of America, preaching the same doctrine. As an example of the kind of information conveyed in these papers, to the exclusion of news of opposite character, three short items from a single issue are presented herewith:

A report from Helsingfors stated the French battleship *Curacao,* which was the flagship of the English Baltic Fleet, with a base at Helsingfors, has returned home, after a minor explosion which produced some damage. Our correspondent, however, learns that there is a report in Finnish military circles to the effect that the cause for sending the *Curacao* home was not an explosion but a mutiny among the crew on board, who refused to operate against the fleet of the Russian Workers' Republic of Kronstadt. As the mutiny threatened to spread to other ships, the battleship was sent home.

* * *

Reports from Tilsit are that the crew of the French squadron at Libau raised the Red flag. The crews of the warships demanded of their officers to be returned to France immediately. The French vessels were immediately sent home and an English squadron steamed in to occupy their positions at the port of Libau.

* * *

According to a Soviet wireless message, mentioned in *Avanti* of May 4, General d'Anselme admitted in a conversation with representatives of the Odessa Soviet that the Bolshevik propaganda had "demoralized" 60 per cent of his soldiers.

Not content with using every possible effort to demoralize the Army and Navy of the United States, the Communists have been recruiting for a Red Army of America. Regular recruiting officers are sent out with literature, enlistment blanks and programs for the purpose of enrolling men to fight in the Red army in this country. This work, naturally, has to be kept entirely secret, and because of that fact practically nothing has been printed or known publicly of this part of the movement. It is impossible to say how far this illegal movement has gone. But it is known that the Communists have discussed a certain location in an Eastern state as a suitable site for the gathering and hiding of arms and ammunition to have ready when the time comes for the armed insurrection.

While the American troops were occupying portions of Germany after the armistice, they were flooded with propaganda from Communist parties of Europe intended to incite them to insurrection and to plant the seed of Communism to be brought back to the Army in the United States. One such bit of propaganda, which was furnished by a former soldier who brought it back with him from Europe, signed by the "Communist party of Germany," reads as follows:

American soldiers, do you know why you are here?

Thousands of miles across the sea are your homes, your friends, your job and your future life. Your family is waiting for your return, your mother or your wife, or maybe your sweetheart is anxiously waiting to become your wife.

Why can't you go back now?

Why did you come here in the first place?

Your motive was an honest one, an honorable one. You came to Europe to risk your life for democracy, to destroy the beast of militarism and make this world a better place to live in. You fought bravely and you won. Perhaps the German working people could not have made their revolution and thrown off the Kaiser if you had not delivered such deadly blows at the Kaiser's military machine. You never had anything against the German people — only against the military clique. We know that and appreciate it.

You have accomplished your object. Now you are lying about camp and waiting. You want to go home.

You are not here to help us complete our revolution, but to prevent it. Your Government and all of the Allied governments are supporting the same scoundrels who helped the Kaiser throughout the war — the Ebert-Scheidemann Government. The real German revolutionists, the working class, are fighting against the Ebert-Scheidemann Government, because the Ebert-Scheidemann Government helped the Kaiser and will always fight against the right.

Yet your Government is recognizing them and dealing with them, and doing everything it can against the real German revolutionaries, the Spartacus people, as they are called, who have always fought against the Kaiser and have rotted in the Kaiser's prisons and been shot by the Kaiser's firing squads during the war.

Your officers won't let you talk to the people around you for fear that you may learn the facts about the revolution.

They make you drill five to six hours a day for fear that if you have time to think you may figure out for yourself why you are here.

You are being kept in Europe to prevent the rule of the working people.

You know that the working people always get the bad end of it from the capitalists. Some of the American boys who have been demobilized have gone back home to ask for their jobs again. The bosses are welcoming the men as "heroes" and then giving them back their old jobs — but paying them starvation wages, around a dollar and a half a day. The longer they keep you here, the better able they will be to cheat you out of a job or cheat you on low pay when you get back.

You came to Europe for democracy, but you are being kept here for the big bankers of Wall Street and of Paris and London and Berlin. You are being kept here to prevent the German revolution from overthrowing the junkers and bankers who supported the Kaiser, and you may be kept here to shoot down French working men who rebel for real liberty, and you may be sent to England to fight there some more years as strike-breakers against the English working people who are now trying to get the liberty they fought so long and bravely for. Or, you may be sent to Ireland to shoot to death the new Irish Republic.

You came for democracy, but you are not being kept here for it.

As a part of the drive conducted by the Communist party of America against Army and Navy recruiting for the military establishments, the party circulated a letter said to have been written by a prisoner in the Atlanta penitentiary to Eugene V. Debs, after his release. The name of the writer is not given and it is not known why he is in prison, although the circular says that "it is from a man who served a term of years in the Navy and has been rewarded for his patriotism by a long prison sentence." The circular also states that "it is a fine bourgeois reformation they get at this walled-in inferno." After quoting the letter in full the circular adds two paragraphs intended to check enlistments. They read:

This man who served the best years of his life in the United States Navy and is now in pentitentiary warns young men not to be deceived by the fraudulent and alluring advertisements posted on city billboards and to steer clear of the Navy if they do not wish to enter deliberately upon a period of slavery under tyrannical rules after having signed away their rights as citizens, including the right to make a complaint.

The warning voice of the imprisoned marine whose eyes are now opened and who would save other young men from sharing in his lamentable experience is well worthy of serious consideration.

The letter from the prisoner, which it is boasted was smuggled illegally out of the prison, is full of the complaints frequently heard in Army posts and among enlisted men in the Navy who have been punished for infractions of regulations. It recites punishments for offenses which are known to everyone who knows anything about military discipline and the necessity for it. It contains no charge of anything except what is caused by chafing under discipline and resentment at punishment for violating the rules. One paragraph, however, says: "The struggle of the oppressed will be won in time and then your name shall be a household word to the new generation."

The Communists have planted their agents in government circles, in departments in Washington, in bureaus in other cities, with the intention of organizing nuclei of Communism wherever possible and of securing information as to what the government is doing. One of the pledges exacted of Communists, in accordance with regulations adopted by the party in convention, is that no Communist shall accept a government position "except under Civil Service." At first it was ruled that no Communist should work for the government under any circumstances, but this was modified when the leaders sought to obtain information on government activities from loyal employees. The safeguard of Civil Service regulations, they believe, will protect Communists in government employ, because if any attempt is made to dismiss them they can raise the cry of "free speech" and have sufficient fanatical support in Congress to save them their jobs.

It is safe to say that not a department in Washington is entirely free from Communists. These men have been "planted" deliberately and spreading of propaganda is a part of their duty to the Communist party. In some of the departments there have been several known Communists at various times who were protected by their superiors in their positions. The most notorious example of high government officials protecting radicals and encouraging them by word and deed was when Louis F. Post was Assistant Secretary of Labor. Post's radical activities won strong approval from the Communist party officially.

The Communist idea of government and the theory upon which the Communists demand the destruction of the government of the United States are brought out in the Thesis on the Relations of Number One and Number Two (the illegal and the legal branches of the Communist party) adopted at the convention at Bridgman before it was raided by the Michigan authorities. This thesis, which when adopted becomes a part of the regulations of the party, and which was adopted just before the raid, reads like a textbook, as follows:

> 1. Government is force organized by one class to keep another in subjection. When the subject class becomes conscious of the oppression under which it labors it organizes to overthrow the class in power. This struggle, of necessity, develops into a struggle of force against force — of the armed force of the oppressed class against the armed force of the class in power — the Government.
>
> 2. This being an accepted phenomenon based on historical fact, it is the task of the Communists to prepare and organize the working class for this struggle against the master class, the capitalists, and against their organized Army force, the Government.

3. The great mass of the working class can be consciously organized for this task. Weighed with the burden of false education, prejudice and terrorism of the master class and the Government, they cannot be formed into organizations, consciously under the control of the Communists.

4. It is the function of the Communists therefore, as a most conscious, militant, revolutionary section of the working class, to organize themselves into a party and by means of this party prepare the rest of the working class for the struggle against the capitalist system and the Government.

5. The nature of the struggle — the overthrow of one class by another — makes it impossible, as history has shown, for a party with this program to carry on its most essential work in the open. The conflict with the Government is so open and so frequent that the revolutionary organization working openly would be disrupted and ground to pieces by the superior force of the State. The Communists, therefore, are compelled to function as an underground party — the Communist party.

6. Work in the underground limits activities, is very cumbersome and does not suffice for the overthrow of the capitalist system. The Communist party is obliged to penetrate all existing working class and semi-working class organizations to reach the masses, using these organizations as tools and auxiliaries of the Communist party. One of these organs is the open political party, consisting of revolutionary workers, not all of whom are real Communists. The program of this party, by its very nature, is restricted, in that it must adapt itself to the laws of the country.

7. This Labor party can by no means replace the real Communist party. On the contrary, the underground party must be built ever stronger and firmer. It must guide and control the Labor party, through the influence of its membership, through its official organs and all other means of propaganda at its disposal.

8. To perform its function as the directing and controlling body the Communist party must be made up only of the best, the most advanced, the most trusted, tried and intelligent section of the working class. It must exercise a rigid discipline, removing from its ranks all who merely comprehend the principles of Communism but fail to carry on the work of the party. Not understanding alone, but activity, willingness to sacrifice and to do every kind of dangerous work must determine membership in the Communist party.

9. The tasks of the Communist party and all the organizations that it creates must be clearly defined, in order that all may serve their purpose without conflict and waste or duplication of effort. The specific functions of each party may vary at different stages of the development of the class struggle. At the present preparatory period undoubtedly a large part of the work can be done in many parts of the country openly, leaving for the underground party functions which, though limited in quantity, nevertheless are of extreme importance, without which no real Communist movement can be conceived of.

10. The main task of the Communist party is to organize unrestricted Communist education and propaganda, thus insuring that the full Communist message is made clear at all times. The Communist party must carry on all such work as cannot be done openly; it must build and support the Labor party and other open organizations and direct their activities.

11. The Communist party must at least once a month issue its organs, dealing theoretically and analytically with all the problems of the class struggle and of the party. It shall give direction to and formulate the slogans for the work of all its open organizations. The attitude of the Communist party to its open organizations and especially the Labor party shall be a favorable and encouraging one. It must, however, always point out the deficiencies in the activities of the Labor party. The Communist party shall devise ways and means of reaching the membership of the Labor party with its illegal organ in order to further their education. The Communist party must also issue all such literature as cannot be published legally.

12. The Communist party must issue leaflets dealing with the struggles of the workers in a realistic manner, so that the masses will perceive that the Communist party understands the struggle, but it is unable to work openly because of the nature of its organization.

13. The Communist party must constantly make recruits to its ranks from the membership of the Labor party, labor unions, and other working class organizations. It is one of the main tasks of the Communist party to develop and strengthen its organization.

14. The groups of the Communist party must meet regularly at least once a month.

15. The Communist party is the section of the Communist International in this country and is the only body capable of stating the official position of the Communist International.

16. The task of the Labor party is to participate directly in the everyday struggles of the workers, endeavoring to develop the struggles for immediate needs into revolutionary mass struggles. It must conduct open propaganda and education, participate in the elections, issue papers and leaflets on the basis of immediate demands, bringing the masses more and more to the Communist position. As far as possible all editors of the Labor party organs must be members of the Communist party.

17. Through the Labor party membership the Communist party permeates all existing working class organizations acting as nuclei within the organization. In the labor unions the Labor party must form a left wing acting as nucleus and taking the leadership in it.

18. The Communist party shall endeavor to establish the same discipline, wage scale and regulations for all officials of the Labor party and its open organization as prevail in the Communist party. It must always be remembered that the real revolutionary party — the American section of the Communist International — is the Communist party of America, and that the Labor party is but an instrument which it uses the better to carry out the work among the masses. Only through membership in the American section of the Communist International — the Communist party of America — can the American workers become members of the Communist International.

19. As organs of the Communist party the Labor party and other open organizations must be under its direction and control. The discipline of the Communist party is supreme for Communist party members. The convention of the Communist party must be held prior to the conventions of the Labor party and determine all policies for the party and all its open organizations. It is the duty of the committees and of the membership to carry

out these policies in the Labor party and all other organizations. In order that the work of the Communist party and Labor party may be conducted properly and the Communist party at the same time be safeguarded from the clutches of the Government, the Executive Committee elected at the convention of the Communist party shall divide into two parts, the major part becoming the Number One Department and devoting itself to the carrying out in the Communist party of the policies laid down by the convention and the Executive Committee, the minor part becoming the Number Two Department and devoting itself to carrying out in the Labor party the policies laid down by the convention and the Executive Committee.

20. This policy of division of work shall be followed in all subordinate committees of the Communist party.

21. The functions of organizers of the Communist party and Labor party being different, and the safety of the organization making it imperative, the organizers of the Communist party shall, as a rule, not be organizers of the Labor party.

22. The Communists must seek to control all committees in the Labor party. By better understanding of principles and more active participation in the Labor work, they must win over the membership of the Labor party to the real Communist position.

23. Members of the Communist party must work as a nucleus in the Labor party. Although all the policies are laid down in the Communist party, the activities of the Communists in the Labor party evolving out of these policies must be left to the understanding, better organization and generalship of the members of the Communist party.

24. Communist party members act as a caucus in the Labor party nuclei in the labor unions. Decisions on all important matters must be made in caucus meetings.

25. As the situation becomes more revolutionary, the Labor party, gaining the support of the masses, will become more revolutionary in form, character and activity. In such a situation, the Labor party shall formally amalgamate with the Communist party and assume its name.

26. The underground Communist party, remaining as an organization within the open party, must continue to be the directing and controlling body. It remains intact and must continually be strengthened. There must be a periodical purging of its ranks and the discipline made more rigid. New blood from the open party and other open organizations must be introduced into the underground organizations.

27. Even though the Communist party shall have come above ground and act as the section of the Communist International, the underground organization remains as the directing organ of the open Communist party. All important policies must first be taken up by the underground organization and its decisions put through in the open party. The underground must continually be reinforced, since even when fighting in the open, the activities of the open party will depend on the vigor, understanding, strategy and generalship of the underground organization. The open party being a mass party cannot have the discipline and understanding of an underground organization and will respond to calls to action only in proportion as the underground membership is disciplined and exerts influence. This status will continue up to and through the revolution and to the establishment of the Dictatorship of the Proletariat.

The thesis on tactics adopted by the Third International sets forth, among other things, that:

> The new international labor organization is established for the purpose of organizing united action of the world proletariat, aspiring toward the same goal: the overthrow of capitalism, the establishment of the Dictatorship of the Proletariat, and of an international Soviet republic, for the complete elimination of classes and the realization of Socialism, the first step toward the communist commonwealth.

Commenting on this, the Communist party of America has officially stated that:

> This definition of the aims of the Communist International laid down in the statutes, distinctly defines all the questions of tactics to be solved . . . . The world revolution, i.e., the decay of capitalism and the concentration of the revolutionary energy of the proletariat, its organization into aggressive, victorious power, will require a prolonged period of revolutionary struggle . . . . The Communists declared, while the war was raging, that the period of imperialism was making for an epoch of social revolution, i.e., of a long series of civil wars in a number of capitalistic countries, and of wars between the capitalist states on one side and proletarian states and exploited colonial peoples on the other side.

Bearing these statements in mind, with particular emphasis on the plans of the Communist International through the Communist party of America, it is interesting to read a statement in *Truth,* which speaks officially for the party, in its issue of August 4, 1922:

> Mere talk, regardless of its eloquence or volume, will not expose the capitalists to the working class. The Communists must put forward concrete proposals. *Tangible, immediate demands in line with the workers' interest must be made on the Government.* Our activity in Congress is subsidiary to and dependent upon the mass struggle on the outside. The bourgeoisie will do their best to kill all our propositions. They will refuse even to consider the workers' problems. This will materially aid us in exposing the capitalist. This will help us to give a political character to the whole struggle . . . . When we make these definite demands on Government, when we put forward our immediate legislative demands, we do so not with the idea of solving the insolvable — the contradictions of capitalism — but in order to rally the masses around practical concrete plans of combat which will further draw them into the struggle against the state and expose its character.

Early in September 1922, a delegation of the Communist party of America sailed for Europe and established itself. It then discussed with the Russian Communist leader plans for an intensive campaign among Congressmen of the United States for the immediate recognition of the Soviet government of Russia by this country. One of the American Communist leaders stated that certain

Senators are already in line for this drive and are continually working toward securing such recognition. He said that *these Senators are in constant communication with Communist leaders here and directly with the Commissariat for Foreign Affairs in Moscow. He declared that the Moscow government had determined to spend several millions of dollars on propaganda for recognition by the United States if it could be assured of success as a result of this expenditure.*

The general plan to be adopted, thus, was discussed in Moscow with American citizens sitting in the conference. These Americans have already announced to the Communists that they must devote their attention to certain people "during elections both National and State."

This delegation sailed in September 1922. In the latter part of August of that year Communist representatives had gone to Washington and had held conferences with members of the Congress of the United States.

CHAPTER ELEVEN

The Labor Defense Council;
Women's Clubs

The now historic Bridgman raid — the spectacular capture by the authorities of the State of Michigan of a group of Communists with a mass of incriminating documents, Communists who had met in the woods in annual secret, illegal convention to further the plans of the Communist party of America, under the direction of Lenin, Trotsky, *et al.*, for the overthrow by violence of the government of the United States and the destruction of the American concept of home and church — had a galvanic effect upon the ring of arch-conspirators in Moscow. It was immediately suspected that someone, on one side or the other of the factional fight within the party, had been guilty of divulging secrets and revealing the fact of the illegal meeting to the authorities as a move to defeat the rival faction. This factional fight had been almost entirely settled before the Bridgman convention met, and one of the reports at the convention dealt with this feature of the situation in the United States. Some delay in the carrying out of the destructive program of the party in this country had been caused by this division in the organization.

Immediately upon receipt of information regarding the raid and the consequent breaking up of the convention before its work had been accomplished, Moscow started a courier post haste to the United States bearing with him peremptory orders from the Executive Committee of the Communist International to both factions in the American party to unite at once. The minority faction was ordered to submit without further delay to the will of the majority; and the majority was ordered to admit the minority without prejudice. Both factions were reminded of the "iron discipline" clause in the regulations of conduct and membership in the Communist organization. Expulsion from the party and from the entire Communist movement was the penalty for any individual who refused to obey this command to unite.

The courier by whom these orders were dispatched reached the United States late in September 1922, and on October 1 representatives of the majority and minority factions were called into secret conference in New York to hear the orders from headquarters. There was nothing to do, for expulsion from the Communist party and the world-wide organization left no place for such radicals to make their bed. They could not join the anarchists, socialists, or any other radical organization. Certainly they could not become conservatives of any stripe. They were branded with Communism, and if this brand were erased it would leave a scar by which they could always be recognized as "traitors" to Communism. And the records of millions slain without trial, by arbitrary dicta, in Russia tell the whole tale of the "traitor" to Communism.

This party division having been healed, the organization immediately turned its united attention to the needs of those arrested in the Bridgman raid. Through the energetic efforts of the American Civil Liberties Union, whose radical activities have been noted in another chapter, some of the prisoners had been released on bond, but others still languished in the Michigan jail, awaiting trial. Money was most urgently needed to get these men out of jail, and to prepare for the defense of the Communists, when they came to trial. It was then reported that Frank P. Walsh, just returned from Moscow, was to be the chief attorney for the defense. The engagement of defense attorneys cost money, real money, and it is safe to say that they would not be satisfied with contingent fees. It was common report in Communist circles in New York that Walsh insisted upon a fee of $50,000 for his services: one fourth to be paid at once, one fourth before the trial opened, and the remaining $25,000 before the first case went to the jury.

Numerous conferences were held by the leaders of the Communists as to how these funds were to be raised. Moscow could be counted upon for certain amounts, but Moscow has been a bit wary of sending back to the United States much of the money it goes to such pains to collect here unless it is shown that it is absolutely necessary to make such expenditure. William Z. Foster, one of the delegates at Bridgman; Roger N. Baldwin, draft dodger, of the American Civil Liberties Union; Eugene V. Debs, now out of jail after being pardoned for his anti-American activities during the war; Elizabeth Gurley Flynn, the active woman radical, of the Workers' Defense Union; and others were concerned in these conferences.

For several weeks the conferences went on, committees were named in all parts of the country, and plans were matured for establishing all the connections possible to present a "united front" of "labor" in defending these men accused of conspiracy. One interesting phase was the way the American Federation of Labor was "hooked" into the plan. On October 7, 1922, William Z. Foster was in New York, working on the plan of the Labor Defense Council. It was suggested to him by a fellow Communist that it would be possible to get the endorsement of from six to ten organizations which were members of the American Federation of Labor; these endorsements could be sent to other member organizations; and when a sufficient number had been obtained all the endorsements could be printed in circular form and sent broadcast until the entire Federation could be said to have joined in the Labor Defense Council. This plan was adopted and worked like a charm.

The work of national organization was begun early in September while a number of the Bridgman prisoners were still in jail, unable to secure the bonds necessary for their release. By this time it had been agreed that inasmuch as the Communist party of America, which is an illegal and underground organization, could not direct the fight to aid the Bridgman prisoners, the Workers' party of America, as a legal organization of the Communists, should assume the leadership. This was particularly fitting because William F. Dunne, the party candidate for the governorship of New York, was one of those arrested at Bridgman as a delegate to the Communists convention. This, of course, established the immediate connection between the Communist party and the Labor Defense Council, for the Workers' party is not allowed to take any steps on any matter without having the approval of the Central Executive Committee of the Communist party. Accordingly, on September 24th, C.E. Ruthenberg, a Communist and a delegate to the Bridgman convention, who was secretary of the Workers' party, sent out an official order to "To All Party Branches, District Organizers and Federation Secretaries," which read in part as follows:

The Central Executive Committee of the party has decided that the party must take the initiative in bringing into existence an organization which will unite the workers in the defense struggle.

For this purpose the Labor Defense Council will be organized.

The Labor Defense Council will be a delegated body which will include representatives of the Trade Unions, the Trade Union Educational League [William Z. Foster's Communist organization within the trade union movement of the United States and so recognized by the Soviet Government of Russia], the Workers' party, the Socialist party, the Farmer-Labor party, the Socialist-Labor party, the I.W.W., the Proletarian party, the United Toilers, liberal organizations and workers' social, relief and cooperative organizations.

The purpose of the Labor Defense Council will be:

To conduct the defense of the victims of the Michigan raids and those arrested in connection with the Michigan case in other parts of the country and to defend other similar cases arising out of the present attack upon the working class movement.

To broaden this defense so as to develop in connection with a mass movement of the workers to re-establish the right to strike, the right to picket, the right of assemblage and freedom of press and speech. To make part of the defense campaign an attack upon criminal syndicalism laws and similar laws directed against the working class movement and to secure their repeal.

To raise the funds necessary for the legal defense as well as for the agitation and propaganda against infringements on the rights of the workers.

The immediate steps to be taken is for each city central committee where such exists and for each branch where there is no city central committee to:

1. Elect a committee to initiate the work of organizing a Labor Defense Council.

2. This committee should send an invitation to other local working class organizations to send delegates to the Labor Defense Council. This invitation should not be sent in the name of the Workers' party but by the provisional committee as a provisional committee of the Labor Defense Council. If possible, some well-known trade unionist should be included in this committee.

3. The Local Defense Council should at once begin a campaign of agitation and money raising. It should hold public meetings, have resolutions introduced in the unions and in every way possible stir the workers to the need of a united stand against the capitalist attack.

The headquarters of the Labor Defense Council was established at 166 West Washington Street, Chicago, and the "provisional National Committee" was made up of the following members: Roger N. Baldwin, American Civil Liberties Union; Dennis M. Batt, Proletarian party, Detroit; Robert M. Buck, editor, *New Majority,* Farmer-Labor party; Eugene V. Debs, Socialist party of America; Elizabeth Gurley Flynn, Workers' Defense Union of New York; Moritz J. Loeb, formerly of the Civil Liberties Union of Chicago, now with the Workers' party of America. The "Cooperating Committee of Defendants" of the Council included Earl R. Browder, assistant secretary of Foster's Trade Union Educational League; William F. Dunne, labor editor of *The Worker,* official English-language organ of the Workers' party, and candidate for governorship of New York; William Z. Foster himself, as secretary-treasurer of the Trade Union Educational League; and Charles E. Ruthenberg, national executive secretary of the Workers' party, who sent out the orders quoted above. Foster was national secretary of the Council, and Loeb, assistant secretary. The purposes of the organization were set forth by it in a secret report in a single paragraph as follows:

> To unite all radical, liberal and conservative organizations to form the Labor Defense Council. The purpose of this council is to defend the Reds arrested in Michigan, to raise bail money, to hold defense meetings and to carry on agitation in their behalf.

One of the first things done by the organization was the appointment of a publicity department to flood the daily newspapers of the country with propaganda for the movement. "Press releases" were issued and spread broadcast. Much of the material thus furnished was printed in reputable newspapers ignorant of the fact that they were printing appeals for a movement aimed at the overthrow of the country. One such release, one of the first sent out, was entitled, "Defense Is the Need of the Hour!" It was marked for "immediate release," and read as follows:

LABOR DEFENSE COUNCIL

FRANK P. WALSH, Chief Counsel for the Defendants

For the defense of the Michigan criminal syndicalist
defendants prosecuted at the instance of the Federal
Secret Service in its drive against organized labor.

To carry on in connection with the legal defense a campaign against
all infringement upon the right of free speech, free press and freedom
of assemblage and all measures restricting the rights of the workers.

ROOM 434
80 EAST ELEVENTH STREET
New York City

National Secretary
WILLIAM Z. FOSTER

Telephone STUYVESANT 6616

April 6, 1923

Dear Friend:

The press has brought you information of the progress
of the trial of the first of the so-called Michigan cases
at St. Joseph. Every day it is becoming clearer that
the issue in this trial is the right of free speech and free
assemblage in America, as well as such due processes of
law, as constitute the just basis of any democratic society.
Mr. Frank P. Walsh, attorney for the defense, has stated
clearly that the provisions of the Criminal Syndicalist
Acts, under which Foster and his associates have been
brought to trial, violate the Constitution of the state
of Michigan and the Constitution of the United States.
Evidence for this contention is fast becoming abundant.

A group of men and women met together peacefully to
consider the business of their party organization, contemplating no acts of violence and cherishing no intent
to promote or induce acts of violence, was itself treated
with utmost violence by the officers of the law. If ever
there was a trial involving persecution and tyranny, it
is this one. It comes as the last echo of the disgrace-
ful mania of governmental terrorism, which was one of the
plagues of the war.

The defense of these men and women, now on trial,
is an expensive one. Large sums of money must be raised
to guarantee them justice. This money can come only
from those who believe in the vindication of basic
democratic rights in this country. We appeal to you to
help us in this cause. Read the inclosed pamphlet giving
the story of the case and then send your contribution
in the inclosed envelope.

Sincerely yours,

[signatures]

BS&AU 12646

MAKE CHECKS PAYABLE TO THE LABOR DEFENSE COUNCIL
Accounts audited by Stuart Chase, C.P.A.

PRINTED ON UNION MADE PAPER

Circular letter sent out by the Labor Defense Council, organized to raise funds
for the defense of the communists arrested at Bridgman, Mich. Facsimile signatures
of John Nevin Sayre, Freda Kirchwey, Roger Baldwin, Capt. Paxton Hibben, Mary
Heaton Vorse, Rev. Norman Thomas, Rev. Percy Stickney Grant and Rev. John
Haynes Holmes appear at the bottom. The name of Father John A. Ryan of Washington appears conspicuously in the organization along with that of William Z. Foster.

Immediately upon the publication of the dastardly Daugherty injunction and the arrest of the so-called agitators at Bridgman, Michigan, the
progressive section of the labor movement united in a strong protest
against these intolerable attacks upon our fundamental constitutional
rights. Labor bodies all over the country condemned the proceedings in no
uncertain terms. Special mass meetings were called for Sunday, October 1.
The Chicago Federation of Labor denounced "the unlawful invasion of a
meeting," and "the indiscriminate arrest, without warrants or due process
of law, of men and women." The Minneapolis Trades and Labor Council
denounces the attack "of certain labor-hating, labor-baiting detectives" as
"the ever-present methods and tactics of tyranny, and of financial tyrants
and exploiters in control of Government."

New York will take its first decisive action against these attacks upon
the rights of labor at the huge protest meeting, arranged by the Labor
Defense Council, for Friday evening, October 6, at the Central Opera
House, 67th Street and Third Avenue. The speakers will include two of the
arrested men, William Z. Foster, the noted secretary of the Trade Union
Educational League, and C. Ruthenberg, secretary of the Worker's party of
America; Roger Baldwin, secretary of the Civil Liberties Union, and J.
Louis Engdahl, editor of *The Worker.*

The hand of William Z. Foster can be seen in this publicity. It was made to
appear that this was a spontaneous movement of the labor unions, and the
citations from the Chicago and Minneapolis federations were purposely designed
as a trap, for both of these organizations are extremely radical and have indorsed
much of the work of Soviet Russia, especially in this country. The fact, however,
that the Workers' party was back of the whole movement showed its connection
with the Communist party of America.

Trusted Communists were in charge of the organizing work of the Labor
Defense Council in the chief cities of the country. For example, in Philadelphia
the work was in the hands of Morris Kushinsky, whose party name is Hoffman
and who was district organizer of the third district of the Communist party.
Immediately upon receipt of the instructions from Ruthenberg, Kushinsky, alias
Hoffman, called a meeting, on September 19, of the City Central Committee of
the Workers' party to begin the work of organizing the Labor Defense Council of
Philadelphia. One of the first things done was to urge the foreign-born
Communist members of the party to become citizens of the United States to
save themselves from prosecution under laws which affect only alien agitators.
The famous Philadelphia "sucker list" was brought out and checked off with a
view to seeing how much cash could be raised from this source. This is the list of
the Workers' party and contains names of Philadelphians who, they say, may be
called upon for aid. In the list are the names of six members of the wealthy
Biddle family, which is connected with the Drexel interests; Mrs. George
Burnham, of the family which owns part of the Baldwin Locomotive Works;
Francis Fisher Kane, former United States district attorney, his sister, Mrs.
Walter Cope, and his niece, Miss Margaret Cope; Dr. Helen Murphy, a

well-known physician; Mrs. Gifford Pinchot, wife of the governor of Pennsylvania; David Wallerstein, prominent lawyer and member of the Civil Liberties Bureau; T. Henry Walnut, former assistant United States district attorney; and Asa S. Wing, who was in charge of the local work of relief for the Near East. There are several hundred names on this list.

Foster and Ruthenberg, both defendants in the Bridgman cases, were particularly active in organizing the local Labor Defense Councils as branches of the national body, and travelled over a great part of the East speaking at meetings in various cities. Practically all of these meetings were used to spread Communist propaganda as well as to raise money for the defense of Foster, Ruthenberg and the others.

The question of financing the defense on as large a scale as was planned presented a considerable problem. With lawyers' fees of unusual size to be paid, bail money to be furnished, anticipated fines and support of the families of the prisoners, as well as the providing of a kind of sinking fund for future contests with the authorities, the Communists were in difficulties to raise the money required. Large sums in the aggregate were raised in the meetings, held as often and in as many places as possible. The American Civil Liberties Union also contributed largely both with funds and legal advice — the services of 800 lawyers were offered by this organization — but in addition to this a call went forth to Moscow for additional financial aid. Moscow may be counted upon to provide the funds. This is the result of the carefully kept "sucker lists," collections taken at the meetings, and the funds which Moscow gets directly from the American public, including sums collected by Russian actors, dancers, and artists in this country, which were referred to in a previous chapter.

There are many means by which the Communists have planned to secure cash from citizens of the United States, this money to be used either in full or in part for the overthrow of this government by violence. Various industrial organizations are disguises for raising such funds. The connection of the Friends of Soviet Russia with the Moscow government is too well known to need repeating. This organization issued a circular which indicated that Sydney Hillman's organization, the Russian-American Industrial Corporation, was in very close touch with the Friends of Soviet Russia, and an interesting part of the scheme was to use the old plea of saving "starving" children. The circular reads:

> Friends of Soviet Russia starts big campaign for Russian-American Industrial Corporation and children's homes in Soviet Russia.
> The Friends of Soviet Russia, Local New York, has just opened a joint campaign for the Russian-American Industrial Corporation and the Children's Homes in Soviet Russia.
> The corporation, formed recently in the Amalgamated, has for its purpose the promotion of industrial activity in Russia by raising sufficient capital to start large factories. A million dollars is needed for the initial capital, and thousands have already purchased stock, which sells at $10 a

share. Every worker who wishes to see Soviet Russia prosper must lend his financial assistance to this project. Further details with regard to the corporation and the campaign to be conducted will be published later.

The second big item on the program of the Friends of Soviet Russia is the drive to raise enough money to support ten thousand starving children in Soviet Russia. As a result of the terrible famine millions of little children have lost their parents and are now helpless. To save them from starvation, and death from the freezing blasts of winter, an international drive is being conducted to rescue these millions of children. The quota allotted to the Friends of Soviet Russia to support is ten thousand. The method of raising money is as follows:

Organizations interested in saving these children can do so by adopting one or more of them. Five dollars down and two dollars a month for twelve months will support one child for a whole year. This means $290 for ten children per year. Those interested in adopting children should at once communicate with the local office, 208 East Twelfth Street. To carry both of these drives over the top the Friends of Soviet Russia will call a general conference of labor organizations interested in Russian Relief and Reconstruction.

The "Amalgamated" referred to in this communication is the Amalgamated Clothing Workers' Union of America, which is closely associated with the Communists in the Russian regime. That fact, and the fact that the Friends of Soviet Russia is a Moscow-controlled organization, show plainly enough the destination of funds raised in this way. In addition to these facts, however, is the fact stated by Litvinov, among other Russian officials, that there is no longer any danger of famine in Russia.

Among documents found at Bridgman at the time of the raid on the illegal convention of Communists was one on *Work Among Women,* in which it is set forth that "the famine appeal is the most practical means for penetrating women's clubs, leagues, etc." And already work has been directed by the Communists to win support of their cause among women's organizations of all classes. An elaborate program for this work was adopted at the Bridgman convention, going into such detail as the canvassing of cities, block by block, and block organizations for the Communists. The thesis adopted reads as follows:

The interest of the working class demands the recruiting of women into the ranks of the proletariat fighting for Communism.

Wherever the question of the conquest of power arises, the Communist parties must consider not only the great source of weakness to the proletarian struggle of an uninformed mass of housewives, farmers' wives and women workers in the industrial field, but also the fact that on the other hand, proletarian women once awakened are among the most tenacious fighting elements in the class struggle.

The experiences of the Russian Soviet Republic proved in practice the importance of the participation of women workers and peasants in defense of the Republic as well as in other activities of Soviet construction. This alone must serve as a lesson in all countries; while here in America we have recently had several thrilling examples; notably in the part working-class women played in the Chicago packing strike and the miners' struggle in Kansas, in Pennsylvania and West Virginia.

Communism, which alone affords women economic and social equality, and the necessary conditions for motherhood without conflicting with woman's social obligations or hindering her creative work for the benefit of society, should be the aim of all women fighting for emancipation. But Communism is also the final aim of the entire proletariat. Consequently, the struggle of the proletarian woman must be carried on in the interests of both the men and the women of the proletariat under a united leadership "one and indivisible" to the entire proletarian movement.

With Karl Marx we affirm that there is no specific women's question and no specific women's movement. But in present day society there are hundreds of thousands of working-class women in separate women's organizations and millions of workers' and farmers' wives with a lower status than a wage slave's, isolated from the general stream of organized endeavor, who must be reached and drawn into the struggle for Communism by specific methods of approach.

It is therefore imperative that women's committees be created to devise and carry into practice the specific methods that will win the women of the working class to the Communist ideal and that will unite them for and link them up with the general proletarian struggle.

Women's work that immediately presents itself may roughly be classified in four categories.

1. Work among the women organized in trade unions or organizations affiliated with trade unions.

2. Work among unorganized women.

3. Work in women's organizations other than trade unions: mothers' clubs, housewives' leagues, cooperatives, nationalist groups, whether social or cultural, etc.

4. Emergency work, such as work among strikers' wives, etc.

In this field the most important work presents itself. The Women's Trade Union League proposes to reorganize the former "Women's Auxiliaries" of the wives of trade unionists into industrial housewives' leagues.

The Women's Trade Union League is at present jogging along. With the introduction of new blood it could be made a powerful weapon. Much of our first activities should be directed to this work wherever possible. Were we to carry on a successful campaign, eventually capturing the leadership, we would be in a peculiarly strategic position for furthering women's work of all kinds, including emergency work.

Some of our best women are fortunately already very active in the organization.

In order intelligently to lay the ground-work in trade unions and other categories of women's organizations the questionnaire prepared by the Women's National Committee should be filled out with care and thoroughness.

The famine in Russia places not alone a solemn duty upon us but also offers us an unparalleled opportunity to reach the great unorganized masses of proletarian women; to crystallize their sentiment and win them for the proletarian struggle.

To realize permanent gains from the use of this opportunity the block system is proposed for adoption for all women's committees. The following is offered as a method upon which to proceed:

1. Organize a women's block committee of no less than three.

2. Select a block for activity, operating in one block at a time upon the follow-up plan.

3. Secure a small hall or store soliciting its free use for relief work.

4. Print simple, attractive tickets admitting two to hear stories and see pictures of Russia, promising also other entertainment.

5. Make house-to-house canvass several consecutive days before meeting, discovering the women sympathizers and leaving one or two tickets in exchange for a promise to use them.

6. In the course of the canvass discover block talent in children or grown folks. Arrange to utilize it, no matter how crude or untrained, in the block meetings, thus providing the promised entertainment and creating a basis for local interest in future block meetings of a similar nature under the same auspices.

7. One-fifth of those receiving invitations to attend may be relied on to be present in a meeting. Tickets should be issued with the usual result in mind.

8. Slides and lanterns can be supplied by local relief centers or obtained through application to the B (legal branch of the Communist party) national office. Instructions for their use are simple. Any member of the block committee wishing to use the outfit could learn to operate it "straight," while the simple explanations of the pictures can be made by anyone, as there is a certain easy system that a child could learn, that comes with the slides.

9. At the meeting, which should be given a neighborly, friendly atmosphere, enlist the women as members of the block committee to help the famine-stricken mothers and children of Soviet Russia. All who join should be recorded in the Women's Division of the B.

10. The Working Class Women's Block Committees should be adopted as the official name of these groups throughout the country.

11. Arrange for the next committee meeting in the home of one of the women where work, entertainment, collection of clothing, money, food, etc., sale of literature, block meetings and talks may be planned in harmony with local needs, etc.

12. In these activities pride in local talent must be utilized to knit the hopeful elements more closely together that the clarifying process may go on in a friendly, social atmosphere.

It is necessary to point out future possibilities. It should be clear to all our comrades that the block committees can become a vital force in the general proletarian struggle.

Third, work in women's organizations other than trade unions.

Again, among the organized women generally, the famine appeal is the most practical means for penetrating women's clubs, leagues, etc. These women's organizations are very numerous.

It is suggested that when our data concerning women's organizations are returned with the questionnaires we choose those whose proletarian character is best fitted to our aim, gradually widening our activities as we build up our forces.

Fourth, the Women's National Committee should at all times have its eyes fixed on the industrial horizon. When great industrial conflicts present themselves it should have its plans perfected for prompt emergency work among those working women more clearly involved in the conflicts. With the organization of the Women's Committees completed, work in the industrial districts will be greatly facilitated.

These four types of work will be all that our present forces will be equal to: the work in the Women's Trade Union League, organization of the unorganized, penetration of other women's organizations through famine relief appeals, etc., and emergency work. This is an ambitious program.

Sub-committees for each category could be named to facilitate the work in the first three types of activity, while emergency work could be assigned to a sub-committee appointed when an emergency arises or is anticipated.

In an interesting article, published May 1, 1922, *The Woman Patriot* says that "the so-called 'Pan-American Conference of Women' at Baltimore called by Mrs. Carrie Chapman Catt, president of the International Woman Suffrage Alliance and honorary president of the National League of Women Voters, was in reality 'The Women's Third International.'" The article is too long for quotation here, but seven short paragraphs give all loyal Americans food for thought. It is not charged here that the women interested in this meeting, the first of its kind held in the United States, are working for Communism directly, but it behooves all loyal American women, and men as well, to "watch their step" in these times surcharged with danger. These paragraphs read:

> The two former internationals were held in Zurich, in 1919, and in Vienna, in 1921, under the names, "International Congress of Women" and "Women's International League for Peace and Freedom."
>
> "Frequent changes of name," as advised by Nicolai Lenin, are resorted to by the International feminist-pacifist bloc as often as necessary, but the entire movement originates with the International Woman's Suffrage Alliance.
>
> The work is divided up, like an army's artillery, cavalry and infantry, into three mobile divisions:
>
> The political, under Mrs. Catt and her "International Woman Suffrage Alliance" and "League of Women Voters."
>
> The pacifist, under Miss Jane Addams and her "Women's International League for Peace and Freedom."*

---

*That the Woman's International League for Peace and Freedom is closely aligned with the Third International in interest and objective is clearly shown in an advertisement which recently appeared in *The World Tomorrow* and was cited by *The Woman Patriot*, in which it is stated that Miss Jane Addams of Hull House, Chicago, is listed as a stockholder in the Russian-American Industrial Corporation (Sidney Hillman) along with Nicolai Lenin, Eugene V. Debs, Charles P. Steinmetz, and Congressman La Guardia. *The Woman Patriot* also quotes the *Federated Press Bulletin* as stating that Anna Louise Strong, for many years Moscow correspondent of the Federated Press and of the official American Communist organ, *The Worker*, expects to fill numerous lecture engagements during the winter and can be reached at Hull House, 800 South Halsted street, Chicago. Press dispatches from Moscow recently indicated that some of the funds of the Russian-American Industrial Corporation in Russia had been misappropriated.

The industrial, under Mrs. Raymond Robins and her "International League of Working Women" and "Women's Trade Union League."

The three branches are employed precisely as a wise general would engage artillery, cavalry or infantry; using all three together wherever necessary and each one alone for special objectives.

Voluntary organizations which are carrying on agitative propaganda or which have objectives to a greater or less extent in harmony with the program of the Communist party of America are so numerous that it would be impossible to list them. They may be found in every state of the union, and several of the larger ones with headquarters in metropolitan centers are active in every state. In some instances, the work of such organizations is of so much value to the revolutionary forces that recognition is freely and officially accorded by the Communists. In other instances, the objectives are praiseworthy, the personnel is above suspicion, and it is only on pausing to analyze that the adherence to collectivism as opposed to individualism, or the tendency toward dependency on the state which is so characteristic of socialism, becomes apparent. Between the two extremes all grades of variations are to be found. As an example of the more radical type, the Women's Trade Union League may be mentioned. The League was originally started by Mrs. Raymond Robins, who was until quite recently, and for many years, its president. Miss Agnes Nestor and Miss Rose Schneiderman, the latter of whom is now president, figure prominently in its activities. Its object is to organize trade unions composed of women, and to federate those in existence. Its work is so much in harmony with that of the Communist party of America that at the Bridgman convention the latter adopted a thesis which obviously looks upon it as occupying an important strategical position in the united front of its lawful and open machinery. So far as is known the leaders of the Woman's Trade Union League have never repudiated this overture on the part of the Communist party, but on the contrary, from time to time in its annual conventions, the League has adopted resolutions indicative of its sympathy with the Moscow Soviet government, and in accord with the program of the Communist party, it "demands" among other things that public utilities now run by the state be turned over to workers' control. In view of these and many other facts, the Women's Trade Union League may be considered as a part of the united front of the open and legal machinery of the Communist party of America, regardless of whether the League or its leaders would desire such a designation. On the other hand, it would be unjust to regard all individual members of the League as communists. Obviously, they are not. Many of them have a purely nominal connection with the League, or, though working for its organic interests, are ignorant of the uses to which the League is being put.

The same is found to apply on appraising the nature of the activities of some other organizations. From the stand-point of hypersensitive humanitarianism, many of them have objectives which are excellent and desirable, provided we do not take into consideration the cost either in money or destructiveness to the state. It should be noted, however, that in almost every instance, some individual or group among the leading spirits of any particular society can be found having direct or indirect connections with the Communist party of America, while the numerical majority are quite above suspicion. For instance, in such a class undoubtedly belongs the American Association for Labor Legislation. It beseeches legislators for the adoption of social insurance by the state. To it we owe the present workmen's compensation laws which are on the statute books of the various states. Compulsory health insurance is a part of its legislative program but up to the present, largely owing to the bitter opposition of physicians and the administrative difficulties encountered in England, the Association has failed to achieve this end here. *En passant,* it should be said that these measures were born of revolutionary socialism in the decade following 1860. The effect of its adoption means a lightening of responsibility on the part of labor in the maintenance of a healthy well-balanced society, and quick adaptation of the working classes to the idea of dependency on the state. Samuel Gompers, at one time a member of the A.A.L.L., resigned, repudiating all its words and works. Social insurance legislation is class legislation and socialistic. The Soviet government of Russia has attempted with more or less show of success to establish a complete system of social insurance.

The most conspicuous generality which could be deduced from a study of the names of those connected with the management of the American Association for Labor Legislation is the fact that aside from Andrew Furuseth, radical president of the Seamen's Union, probably not one includes in his personal experience a history of having worked continuously for any length of time at manual labor, certainly not Thomas Chadburn, its president, nor Adolph Lewisohn, its treasurer (1923).

Doubtless many people who have contributed to the support of the American Association for Labor Legislation are far above the charge of consciously desiring the success of a subversive movement. If we subtract these from the membership and leaders of the organization, there remain a large number who are prominently connected with the radical movement and in some instances indirectly with the Communist party of America. It is still an inexplicable mystery how the Lusk Committee failed to give this organization due consideration. Among its conspicuous officials are or have been in the past such well-known radicals as Mrs. Raymond Robins, organizer and president of the Women's Trade Union League, which has just been considered and which is an important part of the lawful open machinery of the Communist party of America, and her associates Miss Agnes Nestor and Miss Mary Anderson; the Rev. John Haynes Holmes, the radical pacifist, and his friend and co-worker, Rabbi Stephen S. Wise; Owen Lovejoy, of whom more anon; Miss Lillian Wald, of the Henry Street Settlement, known as a member of the interlocking directorate of radical organizations; Miss Jane Addams, famous for her interest in the Women's International League for Peace and Freedom; and a host of others of like thought.

In general, there is a mutual sympathy for the objects which this class of organizations desires to attain, an interlocking personnel in the directorates, and programs which dovetail into each other, suggesting common inspiration and mutual financial resources. They present the appearance of a united front, and might be deemed the shock-troops of an insinuating army of borers, whose province it is to wedge ignorant inertia aside and make room for advancing communism. To call such organizations "socialistic" as opposed to communistic is in reality a distinction without a difference. These systems differ in degree and not in principle.

Among the papers uncovered by the raid on the convention of the Communist party of America at Bridgman was one entitled, "Next Task In The Communist Party Of America," consisting of orders from Moscow, signed by the Executive Committee of the Communist International, Bukharin, Radek, and Kusinen. It is quoted in full in Chapter Twelve. The careful reader will be amazed at the progress which this program has already made, not as the result of the open support of the Communist party of America, but as the result of ceaseless propaganda by this type of voluntary organization. The scar resulting from the repercussions of the Russian Bolshevik revolution on American social and political life is already a permanent one. As one glances over the names of those who make up the personnel of these non-communistic radical groups, there will always be found the name of the isolated individual or group of individuals whose connections and friends may be classed as dubious, or as having associations with those who are known Communists.

As for the "pale gray" organizations, the kind which bear all the earmarks of respectability, in number they are multitudinous. Also the clever way in which recognized organizations may be used by the radicals for their purposes is in many instances instructive. To attempt an enumeration would be outside the scope of this book, and to designate any definite organization as a part of the united front of the lawful propaganda machinery of the Communist party of America by examination of its personnel and objectives would in many cases only raise a debatable question. But that many are made use of with or without their official wish in the matter is apparent. Of such is the "National Information Bureau," which will be considered for a space inasmuch as it has been of assistance to some of the disloyal organizations.

According to its literature, the National Information Bureau was established in 1918, and at present has offices at One Madison Avenue, New York, the office building of the Metropolitan Life Insurance Company. The Bureau says, in its Bulletin No. 8, 1921: "Special reports are issued to members on request, on any organization within the field of the Bureau's formal approval. The Bureau also reports to members, as far as possible, on any enterprise in such related fields as the following:

Civic Reform	Soldier Magazines
Americanization	Child Welfare Magazines
Health Work	Semi-fraternal organizations, labor
Religious Work	unions, etc., seeking support from
(non-sectarian)	non-members.
Propaganda	Miscellaneous semi-commercial enter-
(non-political)	prises with a genuine or spurious
Negro Schools	humanitarian appeal.

"Reports are now available to members on approximately 1,600 agencies. New investigations will be made promptly on receipt of inquiries . . . .

"By arrangement with the Charity Organization Society of New York, the Bureau is enabled to secure, for its members only, reports on local New York agencies." This fact places the National Information Bureau in direct connection with what is generally known among social workers the country over as the "New York Charity Trust."

"The Bureau also issues exclusively for its members a special cautionary bulletin," Bulletin No. 8 continues.

"Organizations are approved on the basis of (a) *complete information supplied by the organizations themselves and supplemented by necessary investigation;* (b) compliance with the standards adopted by the Board of Directors of the Bureau." (Italics in this quotation added for emphasis.)

The Board of Directors has established a set of standards expressed in ten items, most of which, if not all, are entirely laudable. Two are here reproduced to show that in these respects the standards are so flexible that approval or disapproval, in any particular instance, will rest not so much on the standard as on *the interpretation of the standard* by the Bureau's Board of Directors:

2. A legitimate purpose with no avoidable duplication of the work of another efficiently managed organization.
3. Reasonable efficiency in conduct of work, management of institutions, etc., and reasonable adequacy of equipment for such work, both material and personal.

The Bureau also states itself to be "an impartial investigating agency, does not express a judgment concerning the purposes of organizations where the value of these purposes is open to legitimate difference of opinion," palpably a standard which has wide latitude of interpretation.

The Bureau apparently seeks to gain its financial support from organizations, firms and individuals willing to pay for the service, who desire investigations made of "national, social, civic or philanthropic organizations soliciting voluntary contributions." There are naturally many people both among the wealthier and the well-to-do classes who desire to be satisfied that any funds which they contribute will be properly disbursed, and the National Information Bureau is apparently the organization, from its point of view, which is able and equipped to give them satisfaction. Presumably, then, the Bureau is constantly receiving applications from such people, and in time would have listed large numbers of those who are philanthropically inclined. "Over 1700 investigations have been made; forty per cent show undesirable conditions" (1921).

In detailing the scope of the work of the National Information Bureau, attention has been called to certain dangerous potentialities, and it remains to examine the personnel of its organization as shown by its reports. Mr. Paul Cravath was apparently one of the earlier officials. He is widely known in New York as an attorney, and it is a matter of common knowledge that he has acted in a professional capacity for the banking firm of Kuhn, Loeb & Co., or for some of its partners as individuals. He appeared for Mr. Otto Kahn, for instance, before the Federal Trade Commission, at hearings appointed to investigate the facts as to the possibility of the existence of a moving picture trust. Literature describing the work of the Bureau in the year 1921 presents a list of names of the officers and directors, many of which are quite above the suspicion of being consciously involved in any subversive organization. There are two divisions of the Board of Directors, the first "representing the contributing public," and the second "representing organized social work." Of the names in the former division, that of Robert W. DeForest is perhaps the most conspicuous. He is a well known attorney in New York City, an official in the Metropolitan Life Insurance Company, and a trustee of the Sage Foundation, etc., etc., etc. Among radicals he is widely and favorably known because of the fact that he is or was president of the corporation which publishes *The Survey*, a magazine which the Lusk Committee Report very conservatively classifies as "a Liberal paper, having the endorsement of Revolutionary Groups." Its editorial policy exhibits a *tendresse* for Soviet Russia which approaches in an intellectual way that which is exhibited by the verbal brass knuckles of *The Communist*. The Lusk Committee brought out the fact that *The Survey* was "subsidized by the Russell Sage Foundation and has been receiving at the rate of $13,000 a year for the past nine years."

The Lusk Committee Report also records the fact that *Freedom*, a paper published by the Ferrer group of anarchists at Stelton, New Jersey, and advocating the "principles of anarchist communism," had this to say editorially: "It may well be asked, 'Why another paper?' when the broadly libertarian and revolutionary movement is so ably represented by Socialist publications like the *Revolutionary Age, Liberator, Rebel Worker, Workers World*, and many others, and the advanced liberal movement by *The Dial, Nation, The World Tomorrow*, and to a lesser degree, the *New Republic*, and *Survey*. These publications are doing excellent work in their several ways, and with much of that work we find ourselves in hearty agreement."

The explanation which has been advanced in defense of Mr. DeForest, to the effect that as a busy business and professional man he hardly has time to give detailed attention to the many activities to which he lends his name, is a specious one. He alone is responsible for the use of his name.

Among those given as members of the directorate of the National Information Bureau "representing organized social work" is the familiar name of Owen R. Lovejoy, general secretary of the National Child Labor Committee of New York. It should be noted that Lovejoy is secretary of the Bureau (1921), presumably indicating his lively interest in the work. By radicals of every hue from the Atlantic to the Pacific, Lovejoy's name is always hailed with satisfaction. He was formerly active in the American Association for Labor Legislation. He is listed in the Lusk Committee Report as a member of the executive committee of the Civil Liberties Bureau, of which Roger N. Baldwin was director. This Bureau afterwards merged into the American Civil Liberties Union, a part of the open or legal machinery of the Communist party of America. The roster of that Executive Committee reads more or less like the membership of a New York Local, among the members being: Jane Addams, Emily Greene Balch, Frank Bohn, Max Eastman, Zona Gale, Rev. John Haynes Holmes, Paul U. Kellogg (editor of *The Survey*), Agnes Brown Leach, Alice Lewisohn, James R. Maurer, Prof. Scott Nearing, Rev. Norman M. Thomas, Oswald Garrison Villard (owner of *The Nation*), Dr. James P. Warbasse, and Rabbi Stephen S. Wise. Mr. Lovejoy also wrote the so-called "Dear Gene" letter to Debs at the time when the latter was sentenced to Atlanta Penitentiary; in this letter Lovejoy analyzed his feelings at this event by comparing them with the falling shades of night.

As general secretary of the National Child Labor Committee, Lovejoy has been welcomed in at least one high school of the City of New York, where, after making a speech, he solicited pennies from the students for the support of the Committee.

In Bulletin No. 8 issued by the National Information Bureau, a list of the societies approved (1921) is given, and among them are the names of two, the American Association of Social Workers and the National Child Labor Committee, of which Lovejoy himself is an official.

In this approved list there are of course many societies and organizations which are far above criticism as to both their functions and the personnel of the officials. There are, however, some of which quite the opposite is true. For instance, approval has been extended to the American Civil Liberties Union, an important constituent organization in the open legal machinery of the Communist party of America, for all practical purposes a continuation of the old Civil Liberties Bureau, an organization which caused much anxiety to the government during the war, and of whose Executive Committee Lovejoy himself was a member. Approval has also been extended in a 1923 list to the Women's Trade Union League, of which, as stated, Mrs. Raymond Robins was the organizer and president, and which was discussed with more than friendly spirit in the documents seized during the raid on the convention of the Communist party at Bridgman. As has been shown, this organization is a part, and not an unimportant part, of the united front of the open legal machinery of the Communist party of America. Also approved in the 1923 list is the American Association for Labor Legislation, an organization which has also been considered and of which Mr. Felix Warburg of the banking firm of Kuhn, Loeb & Co. is or was a vice president, along with Ernest Freund, Miss Lillian Wald, and Rabbi Stephen Wise. In the approved list are also societies of all stripes, among them the American Union Against Militarism (1921); the American Jewish Committee (1923), organized to "protect and prevent the infraction of civil and religious rights of Jews throughout the world"; the Federal Council of Churches of Christ in America (1923), about which whole books have been written; the Foreign Policy Association (1923), which stands for "a liberal and constructive American foreign policy"; the League to Enforce Peace, "organized to promote an effective League of Nations with the United States as a member"; the National Association for the Advancement of Colored People (1923), an agitative pro-Soviet organization for propagandizing Negroes; the National Consumers League, of which Mrs. Florence Kelly (formerly Wishnewetsky) is the general secretary, and John R. Shillady, also on the directorate of the National Information Bureau, is the executive director; the Voluntary Parenthood League, which specializes in the propaganda of birth control, and which from an examination of its personnel and objectives may be regarded as in the periphery of the radical movement; the American Relief for Russian Women and Children, of which the pro-socialist and pacifist Jane Addams is the chairman; the Committee for the Rescue and Education of Russian Children; the American Jewish Joint Distribution Committee, of which Mr. Felix Warburg is the chairman; and many others.

If letterheads are to be believed, the National Information Bureau has extended its seal of approval, within the recent past, to the Friends of Soviet Russia, the open, legal branch of the Communist party of America. It has also set the seal of its approval on the many constituent organizations of the Friends of Soviet Russia and upon the American Committee for the Relief of Russian Children, of which Captain Paxton Hibben is the executive secretary; of him much has already been said.

Information of the type which the National Information Bureau collects and correlates is lifeblood to those who are actively engaged in the work of propaganda, good or bad. "Sucker lists" such as were uncovered in the raid upon the convention of the Communist party of America at Bridgman must be constantly replenished, and if a mechanism does not exist capable of supplying them, it must be organized.

CHAPTER TWELVE

The Negro Program;
Future Plans Of Communists

The Communists' earliest program in the United States included the use of the Negro masses in its campaign to bring about the overthrow of the government of this country by violence. This program recognized that the Negroes had many grievances, that race hatred was strong among them, and that they were easily inflamed to violence. Accordingly it was decided to use them in the great conspiracy. The Left Wing Socialists and the I.W.W., from which came the nucleus of the Communist party of America, had drawn no color line and had repeatedly urged the Negroes to meet violence with violence, to "fight back," and to demand their "rights" of the government and of individual whites, with threats of uprisings unless these "rights" were granted. Thus it was that the Negro program became one of the prime vicious plans of the Communists.

During the first year of organized activity by the Communists in the United States a great deal of attention was paid to the Negro question. A number of educated Negroes, most of them from Harvard, were found sufficiently discontented and sufficiently unbalanced to make good Communists. They were enlisted in the work, and from that time on have been preaching violence on every occasion. The race riots of 1919 came at the height of this radicalism among the Negroes, who were secretly supported and urged to greater violence by white Communists and the radical Negro leaders. The Communists made capital of these riots and the coincident racial feeling that was aroused. Soon after this, however, the Communist leaders turned to other features of the conspiracy against the government, and the interest of the mass of Negroes waned. But more recently the Communist leaders, acting under instructions from Moscow, have again turned their attention to this question, and their activities have resulted in renewed Communist expression by the Negroes, through their radical press and in committee work among them.

The Negroes came back from Europe, and from service in camps in this country, with renewed desire for betterment. They had also, by their experience in the Army, learned the use of organized force. The radicals in this country were quick to seize upon this feeling among the Negroes to preach violence and urge them on to take by force what they wanted. By every means this class consciousness was cultivated by the radicals, and later by the Communists. The dissatisfied Negroes were aided in starting newspapers devoted to urging the Negroes to join the radicals. When the Communist party appeared, the preliminary missionary work among the Negroes had been done in the name of "Bolshevism," which became a common term among the Negro agitators. Inflammatory cartoons and sketches appeared in the Negro radical press and gradually but surely this press became Communistic, openly and avowedly. Many of the radical Negro papers are now officially recognized by the secret, illegal Communist party.

One of the most inflammatory cartoons that have appeared in the Negro press depicted a Negro in the uniform of the United States Army standing, armed with sword and rifle, on the soil of France, his feet upon a rope that leads to the background of the picture where the United States of America is portrayed by a tree, against which is a Statue of Liberty and by which is a figure of the devil, entitled "Obstruction." At the Negro soldier's feet is a large severed head of a white man — "Obstruction" — with labels of "Jim Crow Him" — "Burn Him" — "Lynch Him" — "Kill" — "Mob" — "Starve." The general caption of this cartoon is, "Must He Carry On?"

Inflammatory reading matter is also furnished to the black readers. A single paragraph from *The Messenger,* one of the radical papers for Negroes, reads:

> As for social equality, there are about 5,000,000 mulattoes in the United States. This is the product of semisocial equality. It shows that social equality galore exists after dark, and *we warn you that we expect to have social equality in the day as well as after dark.*

Communist agents carefully sought out the various Negro organizations in this country, consulted with the leaders, and studied the motives behind each organization and leader as well as the methods used to attain the desired end. For several months these organizations were watched, and finally, acting upon the reports of their agents, the Communist party formally gave approval to the African Blood Brotherhood. This is the most radical of the Negro organizations, and while the door is not barred to others who may later prove that they are radical enough to unite with the Communists, this is the only one thus far formally approved. A document found at Bridgman, after the raid of the illegal Communist convention, included "a brief statement of the Program and Aims of the African Blood Brotherhood." This began with an enumeration of the aims, eight in all, which included "a liberated race; absolute race equality — political, economic, social; the fostering of race pride; organized and uncompromising opposition to Ku Kluxism; *rapprochement* and fellowship within the darker masses and with the class-conscious revolutionary white workers; industrial development; higher wages for Negro labor; lower rents; a united Negro front." In discussing these aims this statement, which was in the form of an official report, or thesis, to the Communist party, says:

A liberated race — in the United States, Africa and elsewhere. Liberated not merely from political rule, but also from the crushing weight of capitalism, which keeps the many in degrading poverty that the few may wallow in stolen wealth.

Absolute race equality. In this question are inextricably bound the issues of political equality, social equality and economic equality. Let one be denied and the whole principle of racial equality is denied.

The fostering of race pride by the dissemination of the true facts concerning the Negro's contributions to modern civilization and the predominant part played in the ancient world by this great race of ours.

Organized and uncompromising opposition to the Ku Klux Klan and all other movements or tendencies inimical to the interests of the Negro masses. To effectively oppose the bigotry and prejudice of the Ku Klux Klan we must (a) organize the Negro masses; (b) create a strong Negro federation out of the existing organizations that we may present a United Front; and (c) for the purpose of fighting the Klan ally ourselves with all groups opposed to its vicious activities, viz., the workers, including the Jewish and Catholic workers. As, for the purpose of throwing off our oppression, the enemies of the capitalist system are our natural allies by virtue of being in the same camp and opposed to the same enemy, so the enemies of the Klan are our friends in that they fight the foe we fight. Not love or hatred, but identity of interests at the moment, dictates the tactics of practical people.

Rapprochement and fellowship within the darker races and within the class-conscious and revolutionary white workers. For the purpose of waging an effective struggle and of weakening our enemies, we must (a) establish fellowship and coordination of action within the darker masses and (b) between these masses and the truly class-conscious white workers who seek the abolition of the capitalist system that oppresses and exploits alike black and white workers, and must, therefore, necessarily work toward the same end as we, whether they consciously will to help us or not. By seeking the abolition of the capitalist states, which are instruments of the capitalist-imperialists for the exploitation of the workers in the colonies and at home and the maintenance of the supremacy of the capitalist class, the class-conscious white workers must perforce contribute to our complete liberation, even as in 1863 the white workers in the Northern States of the United States contributed to our partial liberation because of their fight against the slave power competition of the South, and in fairness to large masses of revolutionary workers who acknowledge the leadership of the Third International, it is well to state that the Third International has emphatically ordered its members to help the darker races and all other oppressed peoples in their struggles for complete liberation.

Industrial development along genuine cooperative lines whereby the benefits will be equally distributed among the masses participating, and not hogged by a few big stockholders and dishonest and inefficient officials drawing exorbitant salaries. The African Blood Brotherhood is sternly opposed to the grafting of individuals and corporation enterprises upon mass movements for the reasons that (a) such procedure is manifestly dishonest and misleading. Enterprises supported by mass movements should be of such a nature as to equally benefit every one in the movement, not merely a handful of officials; (b) The African Blood Brotherhood does not consider any commercial enterprise good enough to base the second liberation movement upon the mere chances of its success or failure. No movement so based can long survive the collapse of its commercial enterprises. We believe in fostering and encouraging cooperative enterprises that will benefit the many rather than the few, but without basing the movement upon them.

Higher rewards for Negro labor, lower rents. To gain for Negro labor the full reward of its toil and to prevent capitalist exploitation either on the job or at the source of supplies we must encourage industrial unionism among our people and at the same time fight to break down the barriers which capitalist-stimulated prejudice has created against us in the trade unions. These barriers are already meeting the attack of the radical and progressive element among white union men and must eventually give way before the united onslaught of black and white workers marching to attack with the stirring slogan:

"Workers of the world, unite! You have nothing to lose but your chains! You have a world to gain!"

A united Negro front with which to oppose the united front of the white capitalists organized under the guise of chambers of commerce, Ku Klux Klan, American Legion, American Defense Society, etc. This can be done only by bringing all Negro organizations into a federation with a program to which any decent Negro organization could subscribe. Their identity could not be lost. Their autonomy practically unimpaired.

This interesting document was read to the convention on August 20 and discussed. A special committee had been previously appointed to consider the Negro question and its work, and after deliberation it drew up on a single page a program for work by the Communist party, with official approval, giving an interesting light on the methods employed by the illegal organization in stirring up strife and cementing radicals. This program reads as follows:

Victory of the workers can be achieved only by genuine and effective solidarity. Such solidarity is impossible of attainment as long as race antagonism befuddles the minds of the workers, dividing them into hostile camps, thus rendering them an easy prey to the machinations and tyranny of their capitalist oppressors.

Race prejudice is an evil and menaces the workers' cause. It must, therefore, be combatted resolutely and persistently in all of its baneful forms. The leaders of the working class must wage a relentless war against race segregation, disfranchisement, peonage and lynching.

The Negro masses should be led to see the similarity between their race struggle and the struggle of the entire working class. The white workers, on the other hand, should be shown that the class struggle of the workers regardless of race is one great battle against a common enemy, and that to win, they must support the oppressed races in their struggle against race persecution and aid them in their fight to secure political, industrial and social equality, without regard to race, color or creed.

At the present time, an organization is gaining a foothold in this country whose avowed purpose is to keep the Negro down, and whose unavowed object is to combat the revolutionary, radical and progressive elements of the working class. The Ku Klux Klan is a decided menace to the working class, and especially the Negroes. This organization is receiving official recognition in that candidates openly espousing its program are running for public office. It becomes imperative, therefore, that steps be taken to expose and fight this organization.

In order that the Negro may be reached with education and propaganda and that he may be organized for activity, the following methods are recommended:

1. Nuclei shall be established in all existing Negro organizations, such as fraternal, religious and labor organizations, cooperatives, tenant farmers' leagues, etc.

2. Colored organizers and speakers shall be sent among Negroes in order to inform them and win their confidence.

3. Newspapers and publications shall be established or, when this is not feasible, news service shall be established by friendly cooperation with colored newspapers of liberal tenets.

4. Friendship of liberal-minded Negro ministers shall be sought, as these men are at the present time the leaders of the Negro masses and many of them are earnest but lack scientific knowledge.

5. Conferences on the economic conditions among Negroes shall be held from time to time with these ministers, educators and other liberal elements, and through their influence the party shall aim to secure a more favorable hearing before the Negro masses.

6. By means of its membership the party shall penetrate the existing forums, literary societies, lyceums, schools, colleges, teachers' institutes, etc., of the colored people, and establish forums of its own for the enlightenment of the Negro population.

7. Where other forms of activity are impossible or impracticable as in certain Southern districts, cooperatives may be formed.

8. The party shall penetrate existing anti-Ku Klux Klan organizations and shall form organizations wherever none exist. As this is one of the most violent forms of suppression of the Negro at the present time, the formation of such anti-Ku Klux Klan organizations shall be fostered with all energy.

As a result of this attitude on the part of the Communist party of America and the natural desire of the radical Negroes who seek limelight and association among whites, there has been a marked increase in activity among the Negro masses. The agitators are now touring the country, nuclei are being established in whatever organizations of Negroes are found, religious, political or social, and the red gospel of Communism is being preached. A similar movement had been carried out just before the race riots that startled the country a few years ago. An Associated Negro Press was swung into line to carry inflammatory racial articles to the various radical Negro newspapers. Some of the papers are not actually organs of the Communists but are trying desperately, by assuming a radical attitude, to become the recognized organs in order to receive some financial support from the Communist funds. Recently an editorial was printed in one such paper, which could have no other purpose than to stir up strife exactly as the Communists wish.

This editorial was entitled, "An Eye for an Eye," and read in part:

> The truth about conditions in the South is coming out bit by bit. Lynching must go. The news agencies dare not tell the truth. Back of every lynching, as expert investigators of lynchings and race riots know, is a cause traceable to the corrupt moral and political system of the South. There is hate and poison and venom in every one of us — and it is just hate and poison and venom! . . . What Southern Negroes should do is to repay the crackers in their own bloody coin. An eye for an eye and a tooth for a tooth! Fight and agitate and lynch back, if need be!

Another radical Negro paper prints an article on "The Passing of the World Robbers," referring to the Christian Caucasian races which adopted "a topsy-turvy philosophy of life, out of harmony with nature," namely, the Christian religion. After two thousand years of this, the article says:

> . . . The long road reaches a turn, and indications are that the hideous nightmare of twenty centuries is drawing to a close. From the ends of the world the whisper runs that the day of European vandalism is nearing its end and the children of the Far East, together with such of Europe's sons as are susceptible to reform, will again administer the affairs of mankind and the civilization that was founded upon fraud and deception will be one with Nineveh and Tyre. Beyond the Carpathians, Russia, mother of the New Day, sits nursing the Infant Era . . . . World brigands, humanity greets your passing with a sigh of relief. Good-bye, good luck, G******* you!

Another paper prints a paragraph, reading: "Hail the Revolution! Long live the people! Down with the capitalist domination and exploitation of Africa and Asia! The dawn's in the East!"

As a result of the Bridgman raid there came to light an interesting document from Moscow, signed by the Executive Committee of the Communist International, Bukharin, Radek, and Kusinen, and entitled "Concerning the Next Tasks of the Communist Party of America." It was carefully marked "Not for Publication." In this document the Communists are instructed to stir up racial strife, not only among the Negroes, but between nations. It urges the Reds to foment distrust between the American nation and the British, the Japanese, the French, and between any two or all four, in the hope that this will lead to war and thus to destruction of capitalist nations, which will open still wider the way for Communism. It orders that the class struggle be continued with increasing intensity in order, among other things, to relieve the pressure upon Soviet Russia. It insists that new and more impossible demands be made upon the government of the United States, not in the hope of their being granted, but that they may furnish additional grounds for propaganda and attacks upon the government, and thus intensify the class struggle. Suggestions are made for subjects upon which the demands may be based and the fight waged.

This document, smuggled by an authorized Soviet courier into this country for the guidance of the Communists here as commanded from Moscow, is cleverly constructed, full of suggestive hints; orders the establishment of what has become the Workers' party; contains reprimands for mistakes made by the Communists in the past and plans for the future. It was taken to Bridgman by J. Lovestone. It reads as follows:

Concerning The Next Tasks Of
The Communist Party Of America

In the earlier stages, the Communist movement usually lacks the broad, directing viewpoint from which can be found the guide-posts for its various steps. Inexperienced Communists, for example, attack imperialism only in general, in its universal aspect, without exact information and minute attention to the unique manifestations of imperialism within the given country. They do not in any way direct their attacks for the purpose of playing up against each other the antagonistic interests of various imperialistic groups. Also, the representatives of false tendencies in the labor movement they attack in general terms, with indiscriminate battle cries having perhaps the desired application to some, but having in regard to others perhaps the exact opposite of the desired result. In a word, they strike around with their eyes closed, against all opponents of Communism in the same manner as against all opponents of their own narrow Communist groups. They fight as a little sect fights against the entire outer world.

Such primitive methods of battle, even when combined with the greatest zeal and heroism, are not dangerous to the enemies of Communism.

The Communists begin to be effective in the political struggle only when they adopt concrete strategic aims for their movement based upon a thorough examination of the facts. With a determined, purposeful drive to these aims, with the subjection of every phase of our movement to this principle, our movement begins to be effective.

In order to assist the American comrades in working out and formulating their line of action, the Executive Committee of the Communist International proposes for their examination the following main points:

1. As the greatest force opposing the proletarian world revolution appears at the present moment to be the counter-revolutionary world

alliance of American, English, French and Japanese capitalism, it is of vital interest to the proletarian revolutionary movement to work against the establishment and consolidation of this alliance, to attack its advocates most ruthlessly, to cut its tap root, if possible, to disturb its growing unceasingly, and adroitly to make use of the conflicting interests within it. The narrow nationalism of the American Japano-phobes and Anglophobes is not liberal or humanitarian nor friendly to labor, and is not in the slightest degree more acceptable to us than was the attempted bourgeois nationalism of the League of Nations. And yet, to the extent of its own cupidity, it really hinders and disturbs the process of uniting the counter-revolutionary forces in the capitalist world. To the extent that this narrow nationalism (Japanophobia and Anglophobia) attacks and tends to smash the outside world-robbers (and also, let us hope, to smash itself) — to this extent it is doing the historic work of self-destruction of the capitalist world system; and in this work it must not be hindered by us. Therefore, though we will not, in the *role* of social-patriots, help the chauvinists in their predatory ventures, we will make use of chauvinistic blindness on behalf of the proletarian revolution.

2. Soviet Russia, as the mainspring of the international revolutionary movement of the proletariat, must be supported in every way. It must be supported with economic help through the self-sacrifice of the workers of all countries. And, most of all, it must be helped through the class struggle of the workers in all capitalist countries against their own bourgeoisies. The fiercer the class struggle of the American proletariat rages, the less will be the pressure of the international counter-revolution upon Soviet Russia. In this respect the Communists must learn how to make use of the conflicting interests of the various factions of the bourgeoisie, how to turn the greed of the bourgeoisie for profits, and how to exploit the various tendencies growing out of greedy speculation, to the advantage of the Russian Revolution, and thus to the advantage of the proletarian world revolution.

3. The prerequisite of victory for the working class is that the working class unite itself for the class struggle. To bring about this unification, isolated action participated in solely by Communists will not suffice. It is necessary to bring about common mass action of workers who are not yet Communists. For this purpose the Com-munists must penetrate the working masses to the utmost, must work together with them, must live and fight with them and lead them forward in both major and minor battles. The uniting of the workers in general class-struggle organizations, and the joining of the various ones of those organizations into close relationships — this and not merely to attain Communist purity and perfection of program — is the task now facing the Communist party of America. The con-sciousness of the working masses is naturally very unclear at this time, half-bourgeois, and undeveloped from the standpoint of the revo-lutionary vanguard. But, generally speaking, it will develop more clear-

ly only during the process of the struggle itself against the bourgeoisie and through experience in the general class struggle organizations.

As a matter of course, not all organizations to which workers belong can be used as instruments of the proletarian class struggle, just as not every action of the worker can further the struggle. But the question of the possibilities of given organizations must be examined and judged on its own merits in each case. It is unthinkable, for instance, that a colossal trade union organization such as the American Federation of Labor could be composed entirely of enemies of the working class, as are such capitalist organizations as the Ku Klux Klan or the various professional strike-breaking bodies. Here a distinction must always be made between the reactionary, traitorous leadership and the unconsciously petty-bourgeois-minded mass which we have to win. And just so, one must not consider any mass movement of the unemployed, no matter how primitive, faltering and unclear, as being hopelessly and permanently under bourgeois influence. The general elections, in which hundreds of thousands of workers take part, cannot be rejected as being merely a peaceful movement with which the Communists will have nothing to do. Further, certain mass organizations, which not only are not communistic, but are not proletarian in composition, must be utilized by Communist strategy for the benefit of the proletarian class struggle. As, for instance, the existing mass movements of small farmers (who are, in a sense, semi-proletarian), and even movements of middle-class farmers under some circumstances. Another instance is the Negro mass movement for racial betterment, which movement often attempts deliberately to avoid proletarian class character but must include great masses of toilers. Communist strategy must utilize these movements as auxiliary forces, or, at least, must win them to benevolent neutrality in the class war.

4. In the present period of the dissolution of the capitalist system, the most important task of the Communists of all capitalist countries is the revolutionizing of the proletarian class struggle. The fighting proletariat is to be led from one stage to another in the revolutionizing process by means of suitable slogans. They must help the proletariat to free itself from the illusions and false traditions that limit its vision and fetter its activities and to counteract the fossilizing influence of the trade union bureaucracy. One must organize the proletariat for the historic training school, in which it will learn to become the conqueror of capitalism.

Only the Communist party can do this. The organization and training of the Communist party as leader of the revolutionary movement is, therefore, the fundamental task of the Communists.

The Communists must now take the lead in the struggle against the reduction of wages. This struggle, in its various forms, is especially adapted for uniting the largest masses of workers in one organization for the common struggle. The conservative labor leaders will find themselves placed in a most difficult position through this struggle, where they will soon be forced plainly to unmask their cowardly wobbling and their treacherous *role*, and where they will bring upon themselves the wrath of the struggling workers. In America almost nothing has been done so far in this direction, but it must be done thoroughly before one can ever think of the victory of the working class in the revolutionary struggle.

The organization of the unemployed is an equally important and difficult task. In this movement, just as much as in all other minor battles, the Communists must select their slogans according to the circumstances, and intensify them as much as possible, from the immediate needs of the day to the general worker's control of capital-industry. Right now they must make a special demand for state support of the unemployed out of the military budget.

The Communist party must remember that it is not its purpose to reform the capitalist state. The purpose of the Communist is, on the contrary, to cure the working masses of their reformistic illusions, through bitter experience. Demands upon the state for immediate concessions to the workers must be made, not after the fashion of the Social-Democratic parties, which try to make those demands within the limits which the state can grant them while retaining its strength intact. Communist demands for immediate concessions to the workers are formulated, not to be "reasonable" from the point of view of capitalism, but to be reasonable from the point of view of the struggling workers, regardless of the state's power to grant them without weakening itself. Thus, for instance, a demand for payment out of the Government treasury, of full union standard wages for millions of unemployed workers is highly reasonable from the point of view of the unemployed workers but damaging from the point of view of the capitalistic state and the capitalistic wage competition which the state defends.

We suggest a few examples of the type of demands that may be made. It must be clearly understood that these are merely examples for illustration, and are not binding, nor are they to be concretely regarded even as advised by the Comintern.

1. That all combinations or agreements having the purpose of reducing the rate of wages or the purpose of common action against labor organizations, shall be made in law a criminal conspiracy.

2. That no injunction shall be issued against workers for activities toward raising the rate of wages or reducing the hours of labor.

3. A constitutional amendment forbidding such laws as the Kansas Industrial Court Law.

4. A constitutional provision guaranteeing the unlimited right of peaceful picketing.

5. For disarming of all private detective cops in strike regions, or elsewhere. All organizations for the purpose of forming armed bodies to engage in activities against strikers to be declared criminal conspiracy.

6. That no process of law, criminal or otherwise shall be allowed forcibly to detain any regularly elected labor union official from his union duties during the process of a labor dispute.

7. Constitutional amendment forbidding the use of military or naval forces in any matter connected with a labor dispute.

8. Legal provision for the maintenance of order in strike regions by the appointment of members of the labor unions involved, such members to be nominated by the labor organizations, and armed from the public supplies for the purpose of maintaining order during the period of the strike.

9. Constitutional provision abolishing the United States Labor Board and prohibiting the Executive to interfere in labor disputes.

10. Favoring a close alliance of the United Mine Workers of America with the railroad brotherhoods and all other unions, for common action to raise the standard of living of all workers in both industries.

11. General amnesty for all persons imprisoned as a result of strikes or other incidents of the labor struggle. General amnesty for all persons convicted of crime in any way relating to the labor movement, or into whose criminal trial any evidence was offered against the defendant regarding the latter's views of the class struggle or political views. General amnesty for all prisoners convicted of political offences.

12. For the Plumb plan, amended to give labor a majority of directors.

13. Immediate bonus of $500 to every soldier or sailor enlisted in the United States forces during the World War; $1000 to those having been granted wound stripes. A payment of $5000 (in addition to all payments otherwise provided for) to the dependent of every soldier or sailor who died in the service during the war period. Funds for this purpose to be taken from military and naval budgets, respectively.

14. For the unrestricted rights of soldiers and sailors to organize in unions. Immunity for all grievance committees of private soldiers or sailors. No private soldier or sailor to be judged by a court-martial except composed entirely of private soldiers or sailors elected for the purpose within the military unit concerned.

15. Absolute prohibition of foreclosures upon farm property for debts.

16. For national credit, to the full value of his farm, to every farmer holding less than $20,000 worth of farm property, the money to be advanced out of the national treasury at interest to cover the cost of the loan transaction.

17. For national credit, to the full extent of their holdings, to all farm cooperatives, on the same basis.

18. National monopoly, and operation at cost, of all grain elevators except those in the hands of bona fide farmers' cooperatives, or which in future may be established by such organizations.

19. The liquidation of the Ku Klux Klan, invoking the criminal conspiracy laws in prosecuting all persons connected with the organization.

20. Condemnation of the Washington Conference as a preparation for a new World War. Condemnation of the imperialistic partitioning of the Far East and other regions for exploitation.

21. Warning of World War to grow out of secret and other arrangements made in Washington Conference, condemnation of this in advance as imperialistic War.

22. For the immediate recognition and unrestricted trade with Soviet Russia. For the re-establishment of postal agreement with Russia.

These and other similar demands must be considered only as starting points for broader, sharper, more universal slogans. In their agitation the Communists must point out that the problems will not be solved through these measures, but that we support these demands of the masses so that the very course of events itself may unmask the capitalist state and the opponents of the working class, and prove to the masses the necessity of the final struggle for power against the capitalist state itself. In this unmasking process, the Communists must make use of every device to discredit the opposition. At times they must develop a direct attack, brand every mistake, every crime, every refusal of the demands of the toiling masses and constantly demonstrate the solidarity and identity of the capitalist class with the capitalist state.

The Communists must participate as revolutionists in all general election campaigns, municipal, state and congressional, as well as presidential. Not in the same manner as the social-traitors and centrists, not in order to avoid violent revolution and substitute parliamentary activity for revolution, but, on the other hand, in order to use even the election campaigns to revolutionize the workers and lead them forward, to sharpen their class consciousness and to bring them together and unite them under Communist leadership. Class conscious, courageous and wise Communists, as elected representatives of the worker, can always find the possibility in the various institutions of the bourgeois state, in one way or another, to give effective object lessons to revolutionize the working class. Besides the Communist party can conceal its underground apparatus and develop it very effectively within the outer framework of the legal campaign organization and the election activities.

In all these minor struggles, as well as in the final revolutionary battle of the proletariat, the party organization must be the leader of the struggling workers.

Its weapons are manifold and vary, according to the situation, from entirely legal propaganda, from election campaigns, from modest movements for increase of wages and from peaceful demonstrations to the revolutionary strike and to the various forms of revolutionary class struggle.

In agitation and propaganda Communists cannot be satisfied with mere dogmatic presentation of Communist principles of the propa- gandizing of the armed struggle under all circumstances. They must not permit themselves to appear to the masses as fanatic bomb enthusiasts who know nothing about the realities of life. They must understand how to lead the working masses from the struggle for the satisfaction of their first concrete needs on to such a battle that the struggling masses themselves will begin to believe in success and victory.

The legal party press is under all circumstances a most important weapon to the Communist party. Just as the political movement of the workers of America has remained very backward in regard to matters of organization, so the revolutionary labor press is also as yet very weak. Its development is at the present moment the most urgent task of the party. As long as the party does not possess at least one or two legal dailies in the English language it is still crawling around on all fours. The party must do everything in its power in order to secure decided influence and direct or indirect control over as many existing papers of various labor organizations as possible. Especially it must try to win control over the labor union press. In addition, the party must publish an illegal official organ.

All good possibilities of both the legal and illegal activities must be utilized by the party energetically. He who wants to liquidate the illegal activities is no Communist at all, and neither is that type of conspirator who does not want to know anything about legal activities.

Under existing circumstances it is impossible for the Communist party in the United States to be a legal party. Of course the party can develop open labor organizations. It can even build a legal revolutionary Labor party. It must launch also such legal party, with the purpose that the Communists can openly enter its ranks without permitting the police to know which of the members are Communists and which are not. But the underground organization whose membership consists entirely of Communists must not be liquidated. On the contrary, it must be built ever firmer and stronger. It must guide and control the legal revolu- tionary party through its members. Every Communist, that is, every member of the underground party, must submit to an iron discipline and must act in accordance with the directions of the leading organs of the underground party in all legal as well as illegal activities.

As a matter of course, all real Communists in the United States will subscribe to this. The Executive of the Communist International knows that the Minority of the Party Executive does not deny the advisability of taking advantage of legal opportunities, although this Minority opposes the rapid and energetic procedure of the Majority in founding the legal revolutionary party. The distinction is, in the judgment of the Executive Committee of the Comintern, without good ground. The fact that the Party Executive is proceeding rapidly and energetically with the formation of the legal party organization is not a fault. It would have been a fault to wait with the launching of the legal party until the underground organization had developed "sufficient strength." The development of the underground organization can best be furthered through these very activities of its members in the ranks of the legal party. Historic progress is not such a simple matter as to leave us the liberty first to complete the development of the underground party apparatus, and only then to begin the building of the legal party organization. In this manner the very best opportunities for the launching of the legal party would be lost.

The centrists would have a free field for their efforts at founding an independent opportunist party. This opportunity must not be left to them. The Communist party must take the initiative in the formation of the new legal party and must take the control firmly into its own hands. It must be careful to assure itself the actual control over all the leading organs of the legal party. For this reason the legal organization must take the permanent form of a party organization. Some other loose organization form would be very much more difficult to control and to guide. Furthermore, the development of a solidly organized legal party, in which members of the Communist party have at least the majority on all important committees, will make possible the control of still other anti-capitalistic organizations through this legal party.

For the foregoing reasons we draw your attention to the following for your guidance:

1. The Communist party of America is as yet far from having satisfactory connections with the masses. The means of contact must be constructed with the greatest possible speed.

2. Connection with the masses essentially implies a public operation. Secret operations, even with the widest possible ramifications, cannot be satisfactory mass operations. The means of public contact with the masses must be principally:

　a. A legal press, including at least one daily English legal newspaper, acting with the necessary disguise as a central party organ.

　b. Organized grouping of sympathizers within the trade unions.

　c. An overground political party.

3. Certain indispensable accompaniments to the highest developed capitalist form of society leaves weaknesses in the capitalist structure that have to be taken advantage of by a Communist party of action. The Government of the United States will not now permit a "Communist Party" to exist but it is compelled to permit "parties" to exist in an almost unrestricted variety, for the purpose of its own preservation. The capitalist class builds its regime upon the rock foundation — the mass illusion — that social questions are solved in the sphere in which these parties operate. The state attempts, wherever it can, to exclude a truly proletarian revolutionary party from the public field. It attempts first, to exterminate the revolutionary party if possible, or second, to terrorize and corrupt the revolutionary party into subservience to capitalist law which makes revolution impossible, or third, at least to

confine the revolutionary party's operations to the narrow sphere that can be reached secretly.

A Communist party must defeat all these attempts. It must not be exterminated. It must unequivocally refuse to obey capitalist law, and must urge the working class to the violent destruction of the entire legal machinery. It is equally the duty of a Communist party to defeat by any means that may be necessary, the capitalist government's attempt to confine the revolutionary party to the underground channels in which it is even more concealed from the masses than it is from the government.

4. The program of the Legal party will have to be somewhat restricted. Special measures and slogans which, while not stating the illegal Communist purpose, will objectively have the revolutionary effect upon the masses, must be adopted. The Legal party must at all times, go as far toward the Communist program as possible while continuing a legal existence.

5. The entire membership of the underground party, the real Communist party, must join the open party and become its most active element. Communist party members must, at all times, hold the positions of leadership in the Legal party. In addition to the entire Communist party membership, the Legal party should admit to its ranks the more advanced workers who accept the principle of the class struggle, and the abolition of capitalism through the establishment of the workers' power. Working class organizations that subscribe to these principles can be admitted to or affiliated with the Legal party, as a body, within the judgment of the Central Executive Committee of the Communist party.

6. The Executive of the Communist International has resolved to support the position of the majority of the Central Executive Committee of the Communist Party of America in favor of the immediate construction of a legal political party on a national scale, which will act as an instrument of the illegal Communist party for participation in legal activities, such as the electoral campaigns, etc. The executive of the Comintern takes this position after having been informed that the Minority of the Executive Committee of the Communist party of America accepts "in principle" the tactic of the legal work of various sorts at the present time, but rejects the tactic of the immediate construction of a legal political party on a national scale with the Communist party membership as its nucleus. The ruling of the Communist International must be accepted as obligating every member of the Communist party of America, minority or majority, to work diligently in the immediate construction of a legal political party. As a rule, party members who fail to participate whole-heartedly in the legal work, or who sabotage that work must leave the party.

7. But in carrying out these instructions, the party must guard itself against the tendency to repudiate or neglect the illegal work — the tendency to become legal in fact as well as in outward appearance. This tendency will be found especially among "intellectual" party members who have little experience in the brutal physical phases of the class

struggle to which the rank and file workers are always exposed, but from which the intellectuals engaged in legal political work are sometimes shielded. Upon finding themselves in the easier life of legal activities, many will forget that no matter what manoeuvres may be made upon the public stage, the final class struggle must be, until its end, a brutal fight of the physical force. A certain element of the party membership will inevitably forget this fundamental principle (which no humble worker in the class struggle is allowed to forget) and will come forward with *naive* proposals for liquidating the illegal machinery of the party. Such tendency is very dangerous to a proletarian revolutionary party. The actual liquidation of the underground party would mean the liquidation of the revolutionary movement. Party members who persist in such a view must be ruthlessly expelled from the illegal party.

8. The underground organization of the Communist party must not sink into disuse, but, on the contrary, must constantly extend its illegal machinery further and further, in proportion to the growth of the illegal party. While coming out in the open, the Communist party must not make the mistake of being trapped in the open by exposing its national or district Communist party headquarters, records or illegal machinery, its underground printing arrangements or the personnel of its Central Executive Committee. The Central Executive Committee headquarters (of the party proper) must continue to be guarded in secrecy (and even the problem of redoubling its security from discovery should be constantly studied). The underground machinery of the Communist party is not merely for emergencies, but for constant and permanent use. Down to the lowest unit — the group of ten — every branch and stem of the party structure must continue to keep its secret addresses and meeting places and to use these in constant underground functioning. Every member, no matter what his work is in the legal party, must also perform his duties in the underground organization.

9. The party underground press must continue. The means of publishing unknown to and in spite of the capitalist authorities must be always kept in hand and in use. Under bourgeois rule, no matter how "liberal" it may be, a Communist party must never relinquish its facilities for underground press and, under the circumstances now prevailing in the United States, the active functioning of the underground press cannot be abated. But it would be foolish to print any considerable amount of literature underground that could be printed legally. The legal political party will be able to take upon itself the printing of a large portion of the literature that is not definitely illegal. It may also be made sponsor for a great many legal Communist newspapers. Legal newspapers must form a very large part of the work of a mass party. The illegal press must carry the propaganda that the legal press cannot carry, thus making sure that the full Communist message is made clear at all times.

10. The intellectual workers in these legal institutions of the party must be subject to the same discipline, wage scale and regulations as underground party workers. It must always be remembered that the real

revolutionary party — the American section of the Third International — is the Communist party of America and that the Legal party is but an instrument which it uses to better carry on its work among the masses. Only through membership in the American Section — the Communist party of America — can American workers become members of the Communist International.

Dear Comrades: It would be entirely useless to quarrel over the question whether extensive or intensive methods are preferable in your Communist work. You must learn how to make a practical combination of both of these methods under all circumstances. Unite for your common work, not for the liquidation of either the legal or illegal revolutionary activity but for the liquidation of the really damaging liquidation tendencies of the labor movement.

It is, as a matter of course, very necessary that you make all preparation in your underground party convention for the public convention at which the legal Revolutionary Party is to be launched. But before as well as after the party convention the minority members of the party executive must submit to the decision of the majority loyally and without question. Without this party discipline, Communist party activities are impossible. The Party Central Committee must, of course, understand how to train the party membership sensibly and practically for the observance of the party discipline and, generally, for the centralization of party activities. It must understand and it must constantly learn still better how to lead the entire organization. On the other hand, it is the duty of every member to support the authority of the party executive. It is foolish and harmful, for instance if factional opposition accuses the party executive of oppressing the foreign language organizations. You must make an end of such accusations, comrades.

We hope that in your coming party convention, all of you will give evidence, in your resolutions and actions, of firm, organic unity, and that your party will prove its ability to measure up to the great responsibilities that stand before it.

With Communist greetings,

Executive Committee of the Communist International,

> N. Bukharin
> K. Radek
> O.W. Kusinen, *Secretary.*

CHAPTER THIRTEEN

Present Status Of The Bridgman Cases

$\mathbf{A}$fter a number of delays and postponements the first of the cases arising out of the Bridgman raid, that of William Z. Foster, was called at St. Joseph, Michigan, March 12, 1923. Nearly the first week was devoted to securing a jury. The trial ended on April 6th. After being out a little over 31 hours, the foreman advised the court it would be impossible to arrive at a decision and the jury was discharged. It had stood six to six from the first ballot.

The second case, that of Charles E. Ruthenberg, was called for trial April 16th. Less time was required to secure a jury and less time for the trial of the case. The jury, after being out for a few hours, returned a verdict of guilty. The defendant filed notice of an appeal, and pending decision of the Supreme Court was admitted to bail. The main contention upon which appeal was based was that the criminal syndicalist law of Michigan, under which Ruthenberg was found guilty, is unconstitutional. Up to this time (February 1, 1924) the Supreme Court has not handed down its decision.

The question has often been asked, "Why was conviction secured in the case of Ruthenberg and not in the case of Foster?"

The State probably had a weaker case against Foster than it did against any of the defendants. In the first place, Foster was arrested not on the grounds, but later, in his Chicago office. He insisted then and on the witness stand that he was not a member of the Communist party, and Ruthenberg, who was on the stand as a witness in Foster's defense, swore Foster was not a member of that organization. It was shown by evidence that while Foster was at the Bridgman convention, held by the State to have been an illegal gathering under the law, and took part in the proceedings by making an address, he left the convention before the adoption of the resolution which the State largely depended upon to show the character and purpose of the meeting.

To understand the contentions of the prosecution, the following, from the opening statement of the Honorable O.L. Smith, assistant áttorney general of Michigan, who headed the State's counsel, is apropos. Mr. Smith said:

> That the members of the jury may have clearly in mind at the outset of this case the fact issues involved in the prosecution, I desire to make a statement, as short as possible, of the facts upon which the prosecution will ask the conviction of the defendant, William Z. Foster. I wish to call attention to the statute under which this prosecution is brought. Criminal syndicalism is defined as the doctrine which advocates crime, sabotage, violence or other unlawful methods of terrorism as a means of accomplishing industrial or political reforms. Advocacy of this doctrine is the crime prohibited by the statute. Under the statute it is our contention that this prohibited doctrine may be advocated:
> First, by word of mouth or writing;
> Second, by printing, publishing, editing, knowingly circulating books, papers, documents or written matter in any form containing and advocating the prohibited doctrine;
>
> * * *
>
> Fourth, by organizing, helping to organize, becoming a member of, or voluntarily assembling with, any society, group or assemblage of persons formed to teach and advocate the prohibited doctrine.
> It is under the fourth method of advocacy of the prohibited illegal doctrine that the defendant, William Z. Foster, is charged with violating the Michigan law.

The defense took the position, and brought evidence to sustain that position, that Foster was not a member of the Communist party of America, which taught the proscribed doctrine; that he was not a delegate to this convention; that he was there as an invited guest and to make an address; and that the reason for his accepting the invitation and making the address was to secure the support of the gathering for his magazine, *Labor Herald*. Further, that Foster's whole work was in the interest of the working people; that he had been recognized as an able leader of the wage-earners; and to sustain this, considerable stress was laid on the fact that he headed the organization of the steel workers for the American Federation of Labor and was put in charge of the activities of that organization when the strike was called.

Again, the State, up to the taking of testimony, was deceived as to the probable nature of the defense. For some weeks previous to the calling of the case, the defense had taken a large number of depositions throughout the country, all of which were to sustain the allegation that the raid and finding of the illegal and incriminating documents was a "frame-up" on the part of the government and private detective agencies. Much publicity was given to all these depositions. However, when the case was called, no such depositions were offered in evidence, and the defense based its whole case on the grounds that Foster was not a member of the Communist party; that even if he was, the Communist party was not an illegal organization but was merely a group of people who believed in carrying government ownership to its ultimate conclusion, that is, the "socialization" of all industries. The defense took special care to leave the impression that in the "socialization" process, the lands of the small farmers were not to be involved. This was done because a majority of the jury were farmers. The defense laid great stress on the fact that the prosecution was only "persecution of a well-known labor leader." The contention, no doubt, had great weight with a number of the jurors.

Then again there was a woman on the jury. This is not to question the honesty or integrity of this woman juror, but she was evidently more or less emotional. Her sympathies were successfully aroused. She was made to believe that Foster was a high-minded person, working at great personal sacrifice, to aid the "struggling masses." Because of her training, her environment, her surroundings, her innate honesty of purpose, she was unable to grasp from the mass of testimony that Foster was heading a great conspiracy against civilization and Christianity. Because of her high-mindedness, she was wholly incapable of grasping the fact that there could be such a conspiracy.

The prosecution was not so well-versed in Communism, its purposes, methods, plans, and ideas, as was the defense. This enabled the defense, often skilfully, to steer clear of dangerous ground and to avoid the injection of dangerous utterances. The rather verbose and weighty language employed by the average Communist writer went over the heads of a large number of the jurors. One must not overlook the fact that the jury was composed of twelve honest, sincere, loyal persons whose contact with the world had not been sufficiently extensive to enable them to grasp the seriousness of the plans proposed by Communism. Being honest themselves, being loyal and patriotic, they could not be made to understand the utter dishonesty and disloyalty of those who were guiding the destinies of the Communist party and all of its allied movements.

In view of these facts, that there was a "hung jury" in the Foster case is not surprising. The taking of testimony had not proceeded for two days before it was the unanimous belief at the press table that a "hung jury" would result.

With but a week intervening, the case of Charles E. Ruthenberg was called. Here the evidence was stronger for the prosecution. Ruthenberg was arrested on the grounds. He admitted he was not only a member but an official of the Communist party of America, and while he disclaimed any purpose to change the government by "force, violence, and acts of terrorism," he clearly indicated by his rather frank method of testifying that he believed a "revolution" would be necessary to establish communism.

The jury, composed largely of farmers, was a most intelligent body of men. They were alert, were not swayed by emotion, and were ready to render their decision on the facts as they gained them from the evidence, and in accord with the law as laid down by the judge.

In the Ruthenberg case the State was acquainted with the character of the defense. It had found the weak points of the defense in the Foster trial, and through more complete examination of the documents secured in the raid, was able to present this incriminating evidence in a manner which was more intelligible to the jury. As stated, the result was conviction of Ruthenberg after a few hours.

In both cases the State was ably represented by the Honorable O.L. Smith, Assistant Attorney General; Charles W. Gore, County Prosecuting Attorney; Charles Bookwalter, Assistant County Prosecuting Attorney; and Max Burger, a government expert on the doctrines of Communism, whose knowledge of this subject was of material aid to the State. Credit should also be given to the government agents who took part in the raid and were called as witnesses for the State. Special credit should go to Frank Morrow, known as "K 97," whose cleverness enabled him to become an accredited delegate to the convention and who was able to convey information to the government that the meeting was to occur. The raid and prosecutions followed.

CHAPTER FOURTEEN

The Shortcomings Of Our Laws

An effort has been made to show, from documents of the Communist party of America and the "legal" branches of this organization, in what manner the Communist International of Moscow is endeavoring to bring about the overthrow of the government of the United States by force of arms, and to what extent this conspiracy has progressed. There can be no misreading the aims and objects of this conspiracy, for the documents themselves frequently refer to the necessity for using "armed force," "armed insurrection," and "violence" as the only means of attaining the end at which the Communists aim. The endeavor has also been made to show that many non-Communist organizations and individuals have aided and are aiding the movement through agitation, through contribution of funds, through supporting trouble-makers and interfering with efforts to suppress radicalism.

The Communist party of America has been declared officially to be an illegal organization. Because of this it has been necessary for this party to hold its annual conventions in secret, hiding in the woods, as was the case at Bridgman, with lookouts posted to give warning of the approach of officers of the law. It has been necessary to use codes for communicating with one another in order to escape detection, and for each member of the illegal organization to have and use a fictitious name in order that identities may not be known. In view of the facts as they are known and provable with unimpeachable evidence, the question has naturally arisen, why doesn't the government wipe out this nest of vipers? The answer is simple: the government has no power to do so.

The Communists and radicals of every hue seek refuge under the very laws they deride; they appeal to the laws they are trying to overthrow for protection from punishment for violations of those laws. Certain senators and members of Congress, certain judges on the bench, even the federal bench, and countless citizens of no official position, obsessed with the theory of "free speech," are unable, or unwilling, to recognize the difference between free speech and a conspiracy to overthrow the government by armed revolution. Bills introduced in Congress are killed by an opposition which suddenly develops when any proposal is made to give the officers of the law adequate authority to protect the government from conspiracies to effect its downfall. The Communists boast that they have members of Congress working for them and that they can prevent the passage of laws designed to curb radical activities. Senators are threatened with being reported to Moscow unless they act thus and so. And known Communists go to Washington with perfect immunity and consult with senators and congressmen in their offices at the Capitol.

Members of the government at Washington, and representatives of the people in both branches of Congress, have known of the inadequacies of the laws ever since Red radicalism first raised its head in this country. Loyal officials and earnest congressmen have made recommendations and introduced bills looking to the strengthening of laws of the country in order that this international blight may be prevented from finding root in the soil of the United States. And these recommendations have been ignored and these bills have been killed.

It will be a surprise to most loyal Americans to know that anyone, provided he be an American citizen, may manufacture a bomb in the city of Washington (or in any other federal territory), take that bomb, and walk down Pennsylvania Avenue, announcing to all who will hear that he intends to blow up the Capitol as a part of a project looking toward the overthrow of the United States government, and have committed no crime beyond disturbance of the peace, a violation of a municipal police regulation. What is more, he may actually blow up the Capitol and destroy it, all the while proclaiming his purpose to be the violent overthrow of the government — and all he can be arrested or prosecuted for is destruction of government property. This is legally the same offense that may be committed by any boy throwing a stone through the window of a government building. For there is no federal law which will touch an American citizen who joins the Communist party and endeavors to carry out the purpose of that organization — the overthrow of this government by force and violence.

If an alien does the same thing he may be deported under the existing laws. Or rather, the law provides for his deportation, but by a curious twist of the law even the alien is saved from punishment. For the same law that provides for his deportation also specifies that before being deported he must be provided with a passport approved by the representative in the United States of the country to which he is to be deported. And as no country wants radicals who aim at the destruction of all so-called "capitalist" governments, the securing of a passport for the accused alien is difficult and often impossible. For example, England and France have refused to permit those of their nationals who are Communists to be dumped upon their shores by the United States; and even Russia, after a hectic experience with the shipload of Reds deported on the *Buford,* refuses to accept any more of that brand. So it is seen that the law which provides for the deportation of aliens also forbids, in effect, their deportation.

The law under which the government functions in the handling of this situation today is Section 6 of the Criminal Code, which reads:

> If two or more persons in any State or Territory, or in any place subject to the jurisdiction of the United States, conspire to overthrow, put down, or to destroy by force the Government of the United States, or to levy war against them, or to oppose by force the authority thereof, or by force to prevent, hinder or delay the execution of any law of the United States contrary to the authority thereof, they shall each be fined not more than five thousand dollars, or imprisoned not more than six years, or both.

This law would seem, at a casual reading, to be sufficient to enable the government to crush the conspiracy of the Communists, for example, which aims at the destruction "by force" of "the Government of the United States." But many times courts have interpreted this section of the Criminal Code to mean that an overt act against the government must be committed before any offence has been perpetrated. Therefore, the conspirators in the woods at Bridgman, who were met in secret convention to plot the overthrow of the government, would be considered, under these interpretations of the law, to have been entirely within their rights. Fortunately, however, a number of states, and Michigan is one of them, have stringent anti-syndicalist laws to protect the government of the United States, which seems unable to get a law through Congress to protect itself.

Some of the men arrested in connection with the secret, illegal Bridgman convention, notably Ruthenberg and Foster, have repeatedly referred to the typewriters and mimeograph machines as the weapons the Michigan authorities captured at Bridgman, and have slurringly asked if it was thought that they were planning to overthrow the government with those "weapons." And yet one of the results of the late war in Europe was the tremendous increase in the use of propaganda as a weapon. It was used by the Communists to destroy the efficiency of the army of Russia under the Czar, and is being used today by the Communists to influence even the highest officials of this government so that the danger of Communism will not be understood or appreciated. Propaganda is now recognized by military authorities as a distinct and very potent military tactic. Our own military authorities assign it a very definite place in the category of warfare, beside gas, liquid fire, and other methods that had to be combatted in the World War. The Italian campaign, the retreat of the demoralized Italian armies, was the definite result, first, of a weakening of morale effected by carefully planned and cleverly placed propaganda.

One of the features of the operation of the laws under which the government is striving to counteract or crush the Communist movement is the confusion of authority. The immigration question comes under the Department of Labor;

undesirable aliens may be kept out by the immigration authorities legally, and a few are so kept out. The passport problem is in the hands of the State Department, which may refuse to grant a passport to whomever it pleases; and it sometimes does refuse passports. The Treasury Department has to do with smuggling, and the Post Office Department has to do with the mails and their misuse by radicals. The Department of Justice is the legal branch of the government, to be called upon for advice and information. But there is no law that compels one department to ask for the records of the Reds, native or foreign, before they are admitted, or granted passports, or tried for the misuse of the mails or for smuggling. In fact, it has happened frequently that Americans and aliens have been permitted to go freely about their plotting against the government, armed with passports, admitted freely by the immigration authorities, when in the various files of the different departments was enough evidence, if collected and used, to convict the man or woman affected of nearly every crime short of murder — and sometimes actually of murder. Communists have no trouble getting passports to use going back and forth to Moscow. These passports are frequently forged and used by other messengers of the Communists. The Department of Justice must have a vast amount of information regarding the activities of individuals connected with the Communist party of America, and its information is available to other departments of the government if asked for; but there have been cases, it is reported, where even after information has been furnished upon such request it has not been regarded.

Many times efforts have been made to strengthen the law so that the government could handle the Red menace effectively without waiting for bombs to be exploded or persons slain. Almost invariably such efforts have come to naught because of opposition in Congress and because of the activity of the propagandists of the Communist Party and of those whose work plays directly into the hands of the Communists. Lawyers loving limelight have a habit of appearing and defending "free speech," which with them means nothing but unrestrained license. Hundreds of people rally to fight any bill that has a patriotic motive back of it, such as a measure designed to prevent the overthrow or the attempted overthrow of this government by violence. Such was the fate of the Sterling bill, which passed the Senate but was defeated in the House. The writer holds no brief for this particular bill, but many loyal lawyers have studied it carefully trying to find a reason why any real red-blooded American would oppose it. But it was opposed so strenuously that it was defeated in the House of Representatives. It was entitled, "A bill to prohibit and punish certain seditious acts against the Government of the United States and to prohibit the use of the mails for the purpose of prompting such acts," and read as follows:

> Be it enacted by the Senate and House of Representatives of the United States of America in Congress assembled, That it shall be unlawful for any reason to advocate or advise the overthrow, or to write, or knowingly to

print, publish, utter, sell, or distribute any document, book, circular, paper, journal, or other written or printed communication, in or by which there is advised the overthrow, by force or violence, or by physical injury to person or property, of the Government of the United States or all government, or advise or advocate a change in the form of the Government or the Constitution of the United States or resistance to the authority thereof by force or violence or by physical injury to person or property; and it shall be unlawful for any person by force or violence to prevent, hinder, or delay the execution of any law of the United States or the free performance of any of its officers, agents, or employees, or of his or their public duty, or to attempt by force or violence to overthrow the Government of the United States.

Sec. 2. That the display or exhibition at any meeting, gathering or parade, public or private, of any flag, banner, or emblem intended by the person or persons displaying or exhibiting the same to symbolize or indicate a purpose to overthrow by force or violence or by physical injury to person or property, the Government of the United States or all government, is hereby declared to be unlawful.

Sec. 3. That every document, book, circular, paper, journal, or other written or printed communication in or by which there is advocated or advised the overthrow by force or violence or by physical injury to person or property of the Government of the United States or all government, or in or by which there is advocated or advised the use of force or violence or physical injury to or the seizure or destruction of persons or property as a means toward the accomplishment of economic, industrial, or political changes, is hereby declared to be non-mailable and the same shall not be conveyed in the mails or delivered from any post office or by any letter carrier; provided, That nothing in this act shall be so construed as to authorize any person other than an employee of the Dead Letter Office duly authorized thereto or other person upon a search warrant authorized by law to open any letter not addressed to himself: Provided further, That any author, publisher, or party affected or aggrieved by the action of the Postmaster General in excluding materials from the mails under this section shall, upon filing a bond to cover the actual cost of such proceeding, be entitled to a hearing *de novo* before a judge of the Federal district or circuit in which the party affected or aggrieved resides. The court shall have power during the pendency of proceedings in court to suspend the order of the Postmaster General; Provided further, That no such court proceeding shall bar or interfere with any criminal prosecution under the terms of this Act.

Sec. 4. That it shall be unlawful to import or cause to be imported into the United States or any place subject to its jurisdiction any matter declared by section 3 of this Act to be non-mailable or to transport or cause to be transported any such matter from one State to another or into any place subject to the jurisdiction of the United States.

Sec. 5. That whoever shall use or attempt to use the mails or the Postal Service of the United States for the transmission of any matter declared by section 3 of this Act to be non-mailable or who shall violate any other of the provisions of this Act shall be fined not more than $5000 or imprisoned not more than five years, or both, and if an alien, shall be, upon the expiration of his sentence, deported from the United States and forever barred from re-entering the United States or any Territory under its jurisdiction.

Sec. 6. That every foreign-born person who has become a naturalised citizen of the United States who shall commit any of the acts forbidden by this Act shall, upon conviction thereof, forfeit his citizenship in the United States; and any foreign-born person who has declared his intention to become a citizen shall, upon his conviction of any offense under this Act, forfeit his right to become such citizen, and all proceedings had in the matter of naturalization of any such person shall be cancelled and become null and void, and he shall thereafter be ineligible for naturalization in the United States, and shall be subject to deportation as in the case of other aliens, as provided by law.

There was little opposition to this proposed act when it was brought out of the Senate Judiciary Committee and presented to the Senate. But when it came up in the House, the opposition was active both on the floor and among the lobbyists. Perhaps the most active opponent at this stage was Jackson H. Ralston, a Washington attorney who represented the American Federation of Labor and who had also acted as counsel for Louis F. Post, former Assistant Secretary of Labor, at a hearing before a congressional committee on charges against Post arising out of his actions and policies in connection with deportation proceedings. And yet the passage of this act or one of similar import is necessary, and is known to be necessary, if the government is to be able adequately to handle such individuals engaged in Communistic activities directed toward the overthrow of this government by force and violence.

A certain group of lawyers, not always having the same personnel but invariably including many of the same individuals, seems always to be seeking ways to embarrass the government and interfere with its functioning when it attacks radicalism in any of its forms. These lawyers do not seem concerned as to the merits of their case, as was shown when they brought charges of illegal practice against the Department of Justice, charges which were quickly shown to be utterly without foundation, a fact that the veriest tyro would have known upon cursory examination of the "evidence" they presented. The make-up of this particular group of lawyers, whose activities seem to have been directed to hindering instead of helping the government in its fight to protect itself, a right inherent in every government, is interesting.

This self-appointed committee of lawyers, which signed the charges against the Department of Justice, included Felix Frankfurter, Ernst Freund, and Frank P. Walsh. These men were identified with the American Civil Liberties Union, an organization, as has been shown, which includes on its committees known Communists working directly and constantly for the overthrow of the government of the United States by force and violence. Frankfurter, from his chair at Harvard, became so active in his work in behalf of the radicals that Theodore Roosevelt wrote that he had taken "an attitude which seems to me to be fundamentally that of Trotsky and the other Bolsheviki leaders in Russia."

The American Civil Liberties Union was also active in this movement with which its members were identified. Of this organization, as has been seen, it has been said that the effect of its activities "is to create in the minds of the ill-informed people the impression that it is un-American to interfere with the activities of those who seek to destroy American institutions. They seek to influence legislators and executives to repeal or veto any law calculated to protect the State or the Federal Government from the attacks of agitators."

Frank P. Walsh is the lawyer who, on his return from Moscow, was reported in Communist circles to have been retained for a fee of $50,000 to defend the Bridgman conspirators. Zacharia Chaffee Jr., a colleague of Frankfurter at Harvard and the man who advocated in print and in public declaration that there should be no law against sedition and anarchy, was also one of the lawyer-signers of these charges. Another was Francis Fisher Kane of Philadelphia, whose name is on the Workers' party "sucker list" and who was formerly United States attorney in his district. A Senate committee report declared that Kane's statement before the committee "gives the impression that his tendencies are strongly Socialistic." Yet another signer was Swinburne Hale of New York, who resigned as captain in the Army, in the Military Intelligence Section, when official information was sought regarding Ludwig C.A.K. Martens, the "Bolshevik Ambassador."

Dean Tyrrell Williams of the Washington University Law School, St. Louis; Jackson H. Ralston, mentioned above; R.G. Brown of Memphis; Alfred S. Niles of Baltimore; Roscoe Pound, another Harvard professor; and David Wallerstein of Philadelphia, were the other members of this particular group. Some of them are almost invariably found on the side of the criminal whose activities the government is trying to curb.

APPENDIX A

COORDINATION OF COMMUNIST ACTIVITY IN THE AMERICAS

**Thesis Presented To The Illegal Communist Convention
at Bridgman, Michigan, August 22, 1922**

If the workers of this country would fight American capitalism on all fronts, they must make common cause with the Latin-American masses. In Mexico, Cuba, Chile the exploited masses are fighting out a class struggle which is part and parcel of our own. There is a fundamental interrelation between the proletarian movements of the Western Hemisphere. The sooner the working class of the United States, as well as of Latin-America, becomes conscious of this interrelation, the more quickly will it be able to utilize the power arising from it.

American Imperialism

The United States is no longer a national State: It is an empire, in which the chief foreign field for exploitation is Latin-America. The capital with which Latin-America is exploited is American capital. The Standard Oil Company, the Harvester Trust, the Copper Trust, the United Fruit Company and other combines hold enormous fiefs in Mexico, Central America, the West Indies and South America. Back of these is the Money Trust.

Of the $5,000,000,000 that American capitalists have invested abroad, $3,188,000,000 is in Latin America. This has given the American capitalists the power to inspire or frustrate Central American revolutions, seize control of customs, issue currency and completely dominate the policies of national governments in many Latin-American states.

When direct pressure fails, the capitalists have always at their disposal the services of the State Department and the military forces of the United States. United States marines maintain "law and order" in Haiti and Santo Domingo for

227

the National City Bank. In Nicaragua, American troops patrol the streets and the American flag flies over the National Palace. General Crowder, as the representative of the United States Government, is forcing upon the National Government of Cuba a loan of $50,000,000 in defiance of both houses of the national legislature. There is not a country in Central America of [or] the West Indies over which does not hang constantly the threat of American invasion.

Wall Street Extending Its Sway

With a large part of Latin-America already in its grasp, American capital is steadily fastening its grip upon wider and wider areas.

Before the war the interests of American capitalists in South America were negligible. In 1916 they involved $285,000,000; today the investment in municipal and government bonds alone exceeds $600,000,000. Wall Street has already become master of the destinies of Venezuela, Colombia and Peru. Native Latin-American capital has never been a factor in any of the Latin-American countries. It is true that before the war European capital, principally British, predominated in Argentina and Uruguay, and was a serious competitor in other South American countries. But this has all been changed. The United States now leads the field and is increasing its investments, while European investments fall off.

Danger To American Workers

Latin-America supplies an outlet for surplus capital and enables American capitalists to derive added strength to resist the demands of workers in this country. The oil, copper and fibres of Mexico, the copper of Chile, the beef and grain of Argentina and the many other raw materials of Latin-America constitute a fund on which American capitalists could draw in an emergency, as in case of strikes.

At present gangs of Latin-American workers are brought into this country on a system of contract labor, or *engancho*, to work in scab industries. With the spread of American imperialism, this system is bound to grow.

Moreover, to hold in subjection the ever increasing masses of Latin-American workers that are falling under American exploitation a strong military machine will be built up, which will be used against the American working class.

Strike-Breaking In Latin-America

A short time ago there was a general strike in Cuba. American battleships sailed into Havana harbor and under the threat of armed intervention, the strike was broken. In Venezuela, the brutal dictatorship of Juan Vicente Gomez, backed and supported by the approving United States Government, crushes every liberating impulse of the toiling masses. A similar condition prevails in Guatemala, where the amiable Orellana rules. At the point of the bayonet, American marines compel Haitian and Dominican laborers to toil in chain gangs out on the hot roads. The method of the exploitation of the ragged Mexican worker by American industrial magnates is more akin to the system pursued here and in addition it counts with the whole hearted co-operation, sometimes more or less disguised, of the Obregon Government.

The Latin-American Workers Cannot Fight Alone

The introduction of an exotic capitalism into Latin-American countries has opposed to a backward and unripe proletariat the highly developed bourgeoisie of the most powerful capitalistic nation of the world, with all the military resources of the United States at its command. The fight is unequal. Isolated, the Latin-American workers cannot hope to defend their interests successfully against their mighty adversary. They need us as well as we need them. A proletarian revolution anywhere in Latin-America is well-nigh impossible until there is a revolution in the United States. Wall Street, with its billions of dollars, imperilled, would crush it immediately. American imperialism, economic and political, is the instrument of exploitation throughout the western world. In Latin-America, as in the United States and Canada, the Class Struggle is a struggle against Wall Street.

A United Front Against Wall Street

What the workers of this country know from contact with capitalism must be supplemented by the actual experiences of the workers who have endured these hardships to which colonial people are subjected. The proletariat of all the Americas must be welded into a fighting unit to combat American capital wherever its influence extends.

The objective forces of the struggle have already called forth several rather inadequate attempts at common action, and both in Mexico and Argentina there have been repeated moves toward All-American unity. However, the only real organization claiming to speak for this country and Latin America is the Pan-American Federation of Labor. Being in reality a barefaced effort on the part of Samuel Gompers and his machine to exploit the impulse toward solidarity, the Pan-American Federation of Labor has never won the confidence of the Latin-American masses, who, in fact, regard it suspiciously, as another instrument of the Monroe Doctrine. It has been used by the Gompers machine to thwart the Latin-American workers in their efforts to combat the American imperialism.

The Pan-American Federation of Labor has failed, hitherto, because it did not truly voice the aspirations of the Latin-American proletariat. There can be no successful joint movement except on the basis of the Class Struggle and a militant fight against American imperialism. An organization must be built up that will fight American imperialism at every step, as well as carry on the struggle against capitalism, through joint strike action, international agreements, etc., under the leadership of the Red Labor Union International. This means that the militant minorities in the few labor organizations that now belong to the

Pan-American Federation of Labor must try to win over their separate national bodies to such a program as will assure the participation of the great mass of Latin-American workers now on the outside. In this work the Communist parties of the various countries must take the leading part.

The Communist Parties

But this is only one phase of the Communist task. The struggle is political as well as economic. The Communist parties will have to educate the workers to an understanding of their common interests, give them political directives, prevent them from wasting their energies in futile pseudo-revolutions engineered by political adventurers, and marshal them for the overthrow of capitalism and American imperialism. The Communist parties of all Americas should be in constant touch with one another. They must formulate an all-American program and function as a unit in its support. The Communist International is and must remain the head and center of the revolutionary proletarian movement in all countries, but the needs of the unified struggle in the Americas require supplementary contact with the Communist parties directly involved. This does not imply autonomy, but is merely an administrative measure made necessary by the unity of capitalism in the west.

Why American Workers Must Lead

The United States is the radiating center of western capitalism as well as imperialism, a circumstance which gives the American working class the advantage of a central perspective. Furthermore, the forces of capitalism not being so highly developed in Latin-America, the Latin-American proletariat, while often finely militant in temper, is inexperienced and immature as a class. The frequent revolutions in Central and South America have often little to do with the Class Struggle, although this cry is raised at times by political opportunists whose purpose is to gain personal support by playing upon the feelings of the masses. Socialist parties appear that are socialist only in name. Although there do exist splendid revolutionary parties in Latin-America, the proletarian movement is in many respects perverted and distorted, beyond anything we know in the United States. With some notable exceptions, the Communist parties are numerically insignificant and all have been out of contact with the stream of the world movement.

To achieve all-American Communist unity, it falls naturally upon the Communists of this country to take the lead.

All-American Communist Conference

The first step is for the Communist Parties of all the Americas to get together in conference. The Communist party of America should send out a call for a conference to be held in Moscow following the Fourth Congress of the Communist International.

The conference must not be interpreted to mean merely a gathering of these comrades who happen to be delegates to the Fourth Congress, but a serious effort should be made to secure a full representation of all Communist parties in the Western Hemisphere, even if it is necessary for the Comintern to pay traveling expenses.

The following is proposed as a tentative agenda:

1. Role of the all-American proletarian in the World Revolution.

2. United action against American imperialism.

3. The Pan-American Federation of Labor and the Red Labor Union International.

4. The tempo of the revolutionary movement in the Americas.

5. Special tasks of the proletariat in each country.

6. The united labor front in the Americas.

7. Co-ordination of the Communist activities.

8. An all-American technical committee, for translation and distribution of literature, etc.

APPENDIX B

RELATIONS OF ONE [ILLEGAL BRANCH] AND TWO [LEGAL BRANCH]

**Thesis Written by J. Lovestone, Executive Secretary,
Communist Party of America
Adopted By The Illegal Communist Convention
At Bridgman, Michigan, August 22, 1922**

I — Necessity Of A Communist Party

All experience in the modern class struggle proves that the working class can emerge victorious only after developing an organ of leadership in the form of a highly disciplined Communist party, thoroughly conscious of revolutionary principles and tactics. The first task of Communists is, therefore, to develop such a party.

II — Action Of Masses

While the Communist party is the organ of leadership and bears the heaviest brunt of the fight, the revolution is an action of broad masses of the exploited sections of the population extending far beyond the limit of the numerical strength to which a highly conscious disciplined party can be developed. The final struggle for power by the working class is not the result of a revolutionization of the minds of the masses through merely theoretical propaganda, agitation and education. It develops out of the irreconcilable conflict of the interests of the classes. This conflict is first shown in the minor struggles of the workers for their existence. The minor struggles clarify the fundamental conflict of class interests, thus bringing class consciousness and leading toward the major struggle for power. Education and propaganda, though necessary to build the revolutionary party, would, if taken alone, build a sterile sect, utterly impotent to deal with mass action. The major task of the

233

revolutionary party in regard to the broad masses of workers is, therefore, not abstract propaganda and abstract theoretical education, but participation in all the struggles of the workers as the most active force.

III — Contact With The Masses

The leadership of the masses of the exploited can be attained only by directly engaging in all their struggles, together with the masses of the workers. In a country where political conditions permit the possibility of mass political organization of the working class, the revolutionary party can not secure leadership without securing a powerful, and finally dominant position among such mass political organizations of the workers. This essentially implies a *public* contact with the masses. In America, it has become the most urgent immediate task of the Communists to secure a public, open, so-called "legal" existence as an organization.

IV — A Legal Party

A truly revolutionary (i.e., Communist) party can never be "legal" in the sense of having its purpose harmonize with the purpose of the laws made by the capitalist state, or its acts conform with the intent of capitalist law. Hence, to call a Communist party "legal" means that its existence is tolerated by the capitalist state because of circumstances which embarrass the capitalist state's efforts to suppress it. The revolutionary party can avoid suppression into a completely secret existence only by one or both of two means:

a. By taking advantage of the pretenses of "democratic forms" which the capitalist state is obliged to maintain. By this means the Communists can maintain themselves in the open with a restricted program while establishing themselves with mass support.

b. (Later stage) By commanding such mass support among side [wide?] masses of workers that enable them to proclaim publicly their final object in the revolutionary struggle and manoeuvre openly to attain this object regardless of the desire of the capitalist state to suppress it. It is necessary at the present time (and circumstances make it the most urgent immediate need) to resort to the first of the before-mentioned methods of open contact with the working masses; which means to maintain an open political party with a modified name and restricted program. The second of these two conditions must be reached by the Communist party of America. We seek to have an open Communist party as soon as this can possibly be attained.

As to whether a legal Communist party is possible the test is whether the Communist party program including the advocacy of the principle of mass action and violent overthrow of the capitalist state together with affiliation to the Communist International can be publicly advocated without being suppressed.

V — Number Two

A legal political party with such restrictions can not replace the Communist party. It must also serve as an instrument in the complete control of the Communist party, for getting public contact with the masses. It must mobilize the elements of the workers most sympathetic to the Communist cause, with a program going as far toward the Communist program as possible while maintaining a legal existence. It must, with a course of action in daily participation in the workers' struggle, apply Communist tactics and principles and thus win the trust of the masses and prepare them for the leadership of the Communist party. It must organize the sympathetic workers into a framework that will later become the framework of an open Communist party, taking care systematically to educate the workers in the "legal" party in principles, tactics and discipline, so as to fit them to become members of the Communist party. Thus the building of a legal political party with a modified name and program will prepare the field for an open Communist party strong enough to stand in the open and capable of leading in the revolutionary struggle.

VI — Future Suppression

The overthrow of the capitalist system can only come through the violent overthrow of the capitalist state. To accept this view is to accept the certainty that the capitalist state will find itself in violent conflict with the masses led by the Communist party. While the capitalist state retains the governmental machinery, and as the struggle grows sharper in approaching the final struggle, the capitalist state will inevitably strike again and again at the revolutionary party in the effort to destroy it. After the Communist party shall have established itself in the open, it must be prepared for, and must expect to be driven out of a "legal" existence from time to time. The Communist party must at all times be so organized that such attacks can not destroy it. It must perform its functions of leadership in the class struggle no matter what tactics the ruling class adopts — open as far as possible, secretly as far as it must.

VII — Underground

The underground machinery of the Communist party is not merely a temporary device, to be liquidated as soon as the Communist party with its full program can be announced in the open. The underground machinery is for permanent use. It is not a machinery to be used only as emergency occasions. It is for constant use. It must continue to operate not only while the legal party operates under a restricted program, but also at all times, before and after the Communist party, with a full Communist program and shall not exist in the open. There is never a time, previous to the final overthrow of the capitalist state, when a truly revolutionary party does not have to perform a considerable amount of work free from police knowledge and interference. The Communist party will never cease to maintain its underground machinery until after the establishment of the dictatorship of the proletariat in the form of the Workers' Soviet Republic.

VIII – Control

Throughout the Communist movement of the world, the system of "Presidiums" prevails, by which matters of necessarily secret nature are kept in the hands of the most reliable and most trusted members of the party. This is a necessary feature of a revolutionary organization. As the Communist party of America grows to dimensions containing many thousands of members, it will be necessary to maintain this principle. At times when the Communist party as such maintains itself in the open, the membership which constitutes the present Communist party within the Number Two [the legal branch – Ed.] will, with some variations, constitute the older and best known, and most disciplined membership, to be entrusted with the more confidential matters and the illegal work of the party generally. This does not mean that the whole party membership will not be required to do work that conflicts with the capitalist law, but that the work of the most secret nature must be kept in the most trusted hands.

During the time when the Communist party operates, not under its own name and program in the open, but through a "legal" political party with restricted program and different name, the same principle is applied by having full control of such legal party in the hands of the Communist party. This is accomplished by having a majority of all important committees composed of Communist party members, and by means of regular and compulsory caucuses of all the Communist party members within any legal unit, bound by the unit rule, a principle which will prevail in some effective form when the Communist party is itself in the open. As the membership develops loyalty to the party and respect for its discipline it will be possible to lessen the purely mechanical control and avoid the small friction that is inevitable for the present. There is an unsatisfactory feature in the present condition. Committee members, persons in responsible positions, and all especially active members of such legal party should be, practically without exception, members of the Communist party. The party must make systematic efforts to bring this about. Definite efforts must be made to bring every member of such legal party who shows himself to be equipped with Communist understanding and capable of leadership, into the Communist party. Every such active member must be tested as to his readiness to accept the Communist party program and discipline, and the decisions of the Communist International, and upon passing the tests, must be brought into membership of the Communist party.

IX — Executive Committees

The party must endeavor to reach at the earliest reasonable time the condition where all members of responsible committees of Number Two [the legal branch — Ed.] such as the Central Executive Committee, District Executive Committee, sub-District Executive Committee, etc., shall be members of Number One [the illegal branch — Ed.]. The personnel of committees of Number Two should consist of its majority of the personnel of the corresponding committees of Number One. The remainder of the personnel of the Number Two committees should generally be Number One members wherever possible. The organizers and officials of Number One and Number Two committees shall generally not be the same.

X — Industrial

We must hold before ourselves as a goal to be attained at the earliest possible time the functioning openly of Communist party caucuses in the trade unions, known as such inside the respective trade union meetings.

Keeping this in mind as a goal, and that the framework and human material being organized into an open party, at present existing legally, is intended ultimately to be welded into an open Communist party, it is a logical course to form now wherever practicable nuclei of Number Two in the trade unions, one of the purposes to be the training of trade union members of Number Two in the principle of discipline.

However, it is not always practicable to operate by the method of Number One and Number Two nuclei in the unions meeting regularly as two distinct systems. And in a large proportion of cases, the circumstances of actual life compel that:

a. Caucuses of Number Two can no more be announced openly in a union than could be caucuses of Number One, and that:

b. In some cases the existence in a union of a substantial number of unionists willing to go a long way with us but holding anarchist or syndicalist views, makes it necessary to hold the greater number of caucuses *with* such elements under a name other than the name of a political party, for the purpose of defeating the "right wingers" and for the additional purpose of training such anarchist and syndicalist elements in the principle of disciplined action as a first step toward making Communists of them; and

c. In other cases where the general conditions in a union make it necessary for the Number Two members to operate together with non-member sympathizers as a disciplined caucus under a name of *another* legal instrument of the Communist party.

These conditions make necessary an adjustment of the caucus system, which will generally assume the following course of development. While the machinery of Number One nuclei is being established, their caucus meetings take precedence over all others. After the Number One nuclei have been firmly established and the members have learned to function unitedly, they will begin to give more and more attention to Number Two caucuses, and Number One caucus meetings will take precedence only when new issues or crises arise and are to be called as frequently as these conditions make necessary. Between such meetings the Number One nuclei function through the Number Two by means of a steering committee.

The standard open caucus of the left section of the union must be held under names and slogans of immediate significance, which will win the greatest possible mobilization of the left section of the union against reactionaries, on issues of the daily struggle.

APPENDIX C

ADAPTATION OF COMMUNIST PARTY OF AMERICA
TO AMERICAN CONDITIONS

As you look at our party (both Number One and Number Two) you can easily observe that something is wrong. It does not function as it ought to. It does not function as a party must in order to fulfill its aim of leading, or if not strong enough, participating in every political and economic struggle of the working class of this country. In short, our party as it is today is a mechanical instrument which will function as a dead machine at any time, but it is unable to carry on any activity which needs life, thought and interest and arouses the enthusiasms of the comrades so they will come asking for a chance to work whether easy or hard.

If you go through the history of our party and especially if you study its functioning in the recent past you will find that every step which has been taken was a mechanical procedure. Any instruction coming from anywhere that in being carried out needed to be spiritualized with the fire of real sincerity was only executed in a technical manner. To see that clearly take the instance of the election campaign in New York or the instruction concerning the opposition. In both cases the comrades distributed the leaflets (if they did) without participating in any of the campaign. This clearly shows that the membership of which our party is composed is actually stranger to the vital functioning of the party organization.

After a long period of organization work, after clearing up our main tactical differences (the latter being accomplished by the few comrades who understand the American stituation and who really strive to fight in America which the general membership does not) we arrived at the point where every ounce of our energy should be concentrated to start our activities, that is to fight in the open American capitalism and participate in every such struggle of the workers. If we

239

dare to face the facts we find that we are unable to do so and although we go forward in our decisions and although a very small group of comrades do all in their power the membership in general does not move and does not understand and *care,* about the decisions. What the membership in general does is to obey an imaginative military discipline (which satisfies their romanticism) and carry out every decision without mentally taking part in it. That is the situation in general and if we were to give a few more facts the matter would be clear for further study.

Many comrades say the chief reason for this situation is because the vast majority of the party are foreign speaking comrades. If we would accept that we would sanction this situation as unchangeable unless we would get enough English comrades in the party. The cause of this situation is not that we are composed of foreign speaking comrades but the reason is that *our membership is not mentally present in America.* They didn't join the party, or better they did not create the party as a working class defense and fighting organization, but they created it under the strange influence of European happenings. The party membership gets its spirit and its hope, not from America where they ought to fight, but exclusively from Europe and it is this foreign spirit and hope that keeps them in the party. Once losing that, the party would not be able to keep them together. The party itself is a strange thing to them. They join it like they would join any other club. They don't have the conception that the party belongs to them and that the party's interest is their interest, but on the contrary they have no interest in the party so far as the fight in America is concerned. They pay their dues to be entitled to call themselves Communists. Their conception is an abstract one, which satisfies itself in being purely a Communist. Later, that means that men with such conception are individualists and so we dare to state that our party is composed in a great majority of members with such an individualistic conception. The members don't understand the political structure of the American state and so they don't understand the political situation in America. As a matter of fact they are not interested in the things they do not understand.

This, then, is our party membership. Must we say that the party which is created (as Trotsky says) "by the proletariat for its defense and struggle for emancipation" can not and will not fulfill this aim, unless the conditions in the party (the conceptions of the party members) are changed? Today we have romantically inclined members in the majority who do everything mechanically to justify themselves as Communists, because they have not been shown how to function as a live part of the American movement. Because of this conception the members don't see any chance for fighting American capitalism and they wait for the coming of the revolution from abroad.

Our party is not able to lead and to influence the masses. These are rather hard words but true, nevertheless. The influence we have and we will gain, will be the influence of our program in general and we, the party, will not be able to make any use of it.

Every one of us feels this situation but it seems we wait for some unknown force to bring about a change. We know that our party membership is not capable of leading the masses and is not capable of carrying out the party's program with spiritual participation in it. Those of us who are waiting for the coming of the English elements into the party are overlooking the fact that if the party as it is composed today is not capable of action then it will always be (unless it is changed) a dead part of our body which will hinder us in our work. The fact is that our party will always be composed of a majority of foreign speaking comrades. Why? Because the basic industries of our country are operated by foreign speaking workers and as these workers are the most oppressed elements of the American working class they are nearest to us. On the other hand, the English speaking population of the country compose the middle class and among the workers they are in the easier industries. So we can not base our future on the coming of the English element but we have to use every effort that our party as it is composed today shall be able to function.

At the time of the outbreak of the various revolutions in Europe the party developed rapidly and after the passing away of the revolutionary wave the party lost in its influence and lost in its membership. This is clearly shown in the case of the Hungarian movement. At the time of the revolution in Hungary the Hungarian Federation in America had 4000 members and the paper 15,000 subscribers. Today the federation has 600 members and the paper has but 7,000 subscribers, although the readers were not raided.

As our party membership has no political aim in this country, they take without any interest the political moves or programs of the party, and without any sound fighting or aim any looseness of membership is justified.

The Communist party is not organized for itself and for the satisfaction of idealists but we are a rough fighting organization, aiming to bring about a mass movement in this country led by us. Can we do that with our forces? Yes, if we first develop change in the mental attitude in the minds of the general membership toward the problems as they exist here in America. Today, we are merely a propaganda organization without functioning even as a propaganda organization should. We have only extended our propaganda to those who have come to us, but have not reached out to the great masses awaiting the message. The slogan *"To The Masses"* was carried out by us only by taking a step nearer to the masses and we are now standing gazing at them.

The activities of our membership are the unconscious reflex of European influences.

The main cause of this situation in our party is that our members have not the slightest knowledge of the political state and industrial machinery. Yet no one has told them that to be a real Communist means to fight there where you are; that they must get acquainted with the conditions prevailing there.

Solution Of The Problem

The most important step in the solution of the problem is a correct and thorough understanding of the problem itself by the membership. Without a clear knowledge of the difficulty by the rank and file it will be impossible to accomplish the solution. The comrades must make up their minds to tackle the great obstacles and master them. They must see clearly the fact that the revolutionary movement and its development in this country depends on them and that means that their policy should not be to wait until we have enough English comrades and let them do the work. Rather the very fact that they are here compels the members as Communists to assume full responsibility for the movement here in America that membership in the Communist party in the other places of the world demands.

The second step should be to dissolve the federation organization and have nothing else than propaganda committees.

The kind of federation organizations we have today was the result of a compromise between two groups at the Unity Convention, one of which had no federation whatever and the other with federations having autonomy. It was hoped by this compromise that the control of the federation members (that is, party members) would be taken out of the hands of federation leaders, and the federation organization would serve simply as language propaganda organs of the party. But this has not been the result.

What are the facts concerning the control of the members? Who really controls the membership, the party or the Federation Bureaus?

The members of the various federations are entirely inactive except when they get instructions from the Bureau concerning some work in their own language organization or concerning work in some other organizations of their own language.

Being organized for several years in language federations, they know little or nothing about the party leaders. While their ignorance of the party leaders causes a terrible indifference toward the selection of party officers, the members engage in bitter factional fights inside the federations over the selection of federation officers.

Most of the federations have large property interests which serve as a strong means of control in the hands of the federation leaders in the control of the federation membership.

Reflect on these important facts and consider them carefully and see what ties there are that bind the members of the federation to the party.

The following are the ties that bind the membership to the party:

1. The federations belong to the party.
2. Their interest in the international movement.

We do not wish to make a detailed argument regarding these facts but we feel that everyone who reads this, realizes that the federations have much stronger control over the membership than the party. As our party is composed of several federations and inasmuch as they have greater control over the members than the party, the party therefore has no direct moral control of the membership but can only exercise its control indirectly through the federation bureaus. That is what we call a highly centralized party.

For the successful prosecution of the work of a revolutionary party, it is necessary that the moral control of the membership (which after all is the only real control) must be in the hands of the central executive body of the organization, which in the light of the facts is not true of our organization at the present time.

The function of the language federation bureaus should be only to act as a means of communication between the central executive body of the party and the membership in the language they understand and to carry on propaganda to the masses in the tongue they know. There is no other good reason for their existence.

In proposing the dissolution of the federation organization we advocate the dissolution of every phase of their organization (which gives them direct connection and leading power). This means also the transfer of all institutions and property belonging to the federations over to the party.

We offer in the place of federation organizations, propaganda committees and editorial boards and an advisory committee. The function of the last named is to prepare plans for the work to be done in their language in organizations like Sick and Benefit, etc. We propose no national propaganda committees but only district propaganda committees which shall carry on the work according to party instructions, as a sub-committee in the district, adapted to the conditions in the various districts. The translation of party instructions can be done by translating secretaries in the national organization and sent down through party channels.

The United States is so large that there are whole sections with problems peculiar to themselves that seriously interfere with the efficient operation of the organization and which it is next to impossible to solve from the national organization. The establishment of district propaganda committees would solve this perplexing question. There are many other reasons that favor the establishment of these committees and insure a much more efficient organization than could ever be the case under language federation bureaus.

Summary

In closing we can emphatically state that the future of the party is hopeless unless this situation is changed. The question of tactics can be decided upon by a few comrades who are at the convention, but they will not have the backing of the members. This is so vital that we can not expect any real results from our work in this country until it is solved. A Communist party, not even in possession of its own members, can not hope to exert the slightest influence over the masses.

In the course of discussion there might arise some other problems for solution, but every one of us must agree that this one is the main problem confronting the Second Convention of the Communist party and the Communist party itself.

Finally, the solving of this problem will not be accomplished simply by dissolving the federation organizations. The members must realize and feel this problem in all its seriousness, and with the dissolution of the federation organizations must break the mental ties with other parts of the world and become rooted and grounded in the movement in *America.*

APPENDIX D

**Sent August 4, 1922, from "National Office,
Communist Party of America, Section of Communist International"
Marked "Rush One To Every Group"**

The Executive Committee of the Communist International has informed us that Comrade Cook, member of the Presidium of the Comintern and the Presidium of the Red Trade Union International has been ordered to return home immediately with full instructions from the Communist International regarding the various problems confronting the American party. All districts are strongly urged to hold themselves in complete readiness for immediate arrangements of meetings to listen to the report from the Comintern.

The special representative of the Comintern, Comrade Brooks, is now working actively with the Central Executive Committee and is proving of great aid to us.

Reports from every district are very favorable regarding the return of opposition members to the party. We must not lose sight of the fact that it is the duty of every party member to do his utmost to help liquidate the opposition and get them back into the party.

The Executive Committee of the Communist International has instructed us to postpone holding the convention until the arrival of Comrade Cook with its instructions. The Central Executive Committee acted on this matter and by a vote of five to five decided not to delay holding the convention. All efforts are being exerted to have Comrade Cook arrive here on time so that at least the delegates may have an opportunity to listen to the report and instructions from the Executive Committee of the Communist International.

On the recommendation of Comrade Brooks, the Central Executive

Committee elected the following new special committees: (1) A committee to prepare a report on the prevailing political and economic conditions in the United States. (2) A committee to prepare a new thesis on the relations between One and Two. (3) A committee to revise the agenda for the convention.

After listening to the Central Executive Committee discussion on the postponement of the convention, Comrade Brooks, Special Representative of the Comintern to the Communist Party of America, proposed the following resolution to the Central Executive Committee:

> The thesis adopted by the Third World Congress on the subject of organization explicitly prohibited the formation of closed factions within Communist parties. I have ascertained here in America that two existing tendencies in the Communist party have already crystallized into definite factional structures which are waging against each other war to the knife on questions big or small. I am convinced that the actually existing differences of opinion do not by any means justify such factional formations and merely represent the continuation of the worst traditions within the ranks of the American Comrades, traditions which are repeatedly condemned by the Communist International. I am convinced that this situation can lead to complete paralysis of the party's activity and to new splits, fatal to American Communism.
>
> Basing myself on the above mentioned thesis of the Third Congress and acting in the spirit of all the decisions of the Communist International bearing on the American question, I call on the comrades of both factions immediately to take proper steps for the factional regime and to create real guarantees for party unity which is so extremely endangered. For this work I am entirely at your disposal.
>
> (signed) Brooks
> Special Representative,
> Executive Committee of the Communist International

A motion to approve this declaration was carried unanimously. Furthermore, a committee of seven, three members of which are representatives of the Comintern in various capacities, was chosen to present plans for the unification of the party to the convention and recommend methods as to the selection of Central Executive Committee material. This committee is now busily engaged in its work.

Comrades, this declaration must be accepted in letter and spirit by every member of the party. *Apropos* of this situation in the party the District Executive Committee of District 4 [the Cleveland District — Ed.] has several weeks ago unanimously passed the following resolutions in the "National Caucus," commonly called the "Goose Caucus."

> The District Executive Committee of District 4 has been informed of the existence of various caucuses and particularly of the so-called

National Caucus and the nature of propaganda they are conducting. This propaganda is not based on any ground of principles but purely on personalities, and confines itself to attacks on the party's Central Executive Committee and this not even intended to bring any good to the movement as a whole.

From all their communications and theses, only one conclusion can be drawn which is at the same time their only argument, viz., — The Central Executive Committee does not think the way it acts, we are the only ones who force its hand in the proper direction. Such arguments can only come from positively misguided and insincere people who have no consideration for the welfare of the movement but see only their own ego and calculate how to aspire to power.

That such rubberneck, backstairs stuff is injurious to the movement there is no doubt in the minds of the Committee. It lowers the morale of the membership and weakens the discipline in the party.

Furthermore, taking into consideration the call of the Central Executive Committee to suggest and criticise the theses and propositions of the Central Executive Committee and as these caucuses refused to have their hand in this work and so reject the invitation of the Central Executive Committee to help build the movement through the regular party channels;

The District Executive Committee of District 4 goes on record condemning these caucuses as harmful to the movement and wishes to remind the same not to waste their time looking for support in this district where you will not find it.

We advise those caucuses not to squander their money in mailing their stuff to the members in this district where it will bear no fruit, but rather to use the regular party channels and so really help build the organization in the only way this can be done.

We call upon our members to maintain the discipline of the party; without discipline we cannot build an organization of the revolutionary workers.

The National Office will make every effort possible to keep the membership fully informed as to the situation in the party and the Comintern. All districts are requested to send district news promptly and regularly to the National Office of the party.

(signed) L.C. Wheat [Lovestone]
Executive Secretary,
Communist Party of America,
Section of the Communist International.

APPENDIX E

THE WORKERS' PARTY ON THE UNITED FRONT

Thesis Presented by J. Lovestone To Communist Convention At Bridgman, Michigan, August 22, 1922

1. A United Front of Labor, a solid phalanx of the working class drawn up in battle line against the forces of the capitalist class and the capitalist state is the prerequisite of a victory of the proletariat. The creation of this phalanx is the task of the hour. Groups of workers organized in various organizations as well as groups of hitherto unorganized workers must be united in support of a common aim and in common action. Many organizations of labor though ostensibly formed to fight the battles of labor are tied up by their treacherous leaders to the interests of the capitalists thus breaking the united front of labor and strengthening the front of capital. The problem is to break these groups of workers away from the army of capital and line them up with the army of labor thus establishing a united front of labor against capital.

2. The working class as a whole is not conscious of having class interests in irreconcilable conflict with the interests of the capitalists. They are conscious, however, of immediate problems that demand solution as a condition for their existence, questions of wages, working conditions, etc. These questions must form the basis for a United Front of the workers, for united action. It is through these struggles and only through them that the workers can learn the political character of their struggle. It is in these struggles that the betrayers of the workers in the position of leadership must be exposed in their true character as enemies of the proletariat and the tools of the capitalists. It is in these struggles and only in them that the Communists can establish their leadership in the class struggle and develop this struggle into a revolutionary

battle for the overthrow of capitalism and the establishment of the proletarian dictatorship as an instrument of Communist reconstruction.

3. In pursuing the policy of uniting larger and larger masses of the workers on the basis of a common struggle the existing organizations of the workers must be made more and more effective instruments of these struggles. The experience the workers will gain in these struggles will help us to gradually eliminate all dualism in the field of economic organizations of the workers. Trade lines must be gradually eliminated and step by step the organizations of the workers must be welded together into industrial unions closely united in one great body.

4. While the creation of the United Front can be accomplished on the field of economic organization through amalgamation of existing bodies, it must be accomplished on the field of political organizations of the workers by elimination of the influence of such parties and groups whose program and action mislead the working class. The economic struggles of the workers are carried on by organizations including in their ranks most of the participants of the struggle. Working-class political parties can not organize within their ranks a majority of the working class. These organizations serve rather to give leadership to the workers' political struggles. Those parties misleading the workers must be eliminated from such leadership. On the basis of immediate issues the workers must be led into political struggles in which the Communists prove the superiority of their tactics, their slogans, their aims and their leadership as compared with the tactics, slogans, aims and leadership of other political groups or parties claiming the support of the workers. Thus the Workers' party will gradually win away the masses of politically active workers from the political organizations that betray the workers. It will discredit and destroy them and win complete leadership in the political struggles of the workers.

5. In creating a united front for the working class for their economic struggles, the existing labor unions must remain the instrument of these struggles while the members of the Workers' party must be the instruments to unify these economic organizations.

The plans for the general campaigns are formulated after consideration of recommendations by party members in the unions. The Central Executive Committee of the party formulates the slogans and sends its corresponding instructions through the industrial department to the membership. At the same time all means of publicity are used by the party for propagation of the action contemplated. The unity of action must be established on a basis that can be realized immediately and the action must then be developed and led on step by step to the climax. In the process of the struggle the weakness of the existing craft union form of organization will become apparent. The experience of such struggles, developing these weaknesses must be utilized to drive home the criticism of the present form of organization and advantage must be taken of the situation to advance constructive proposals seeking to eliminate these weaknesses. Thus the amalgamation of craft into industrial unions becomes an issue dictated by the necessities of the struggles and ceases to be an abstract theoretical bone of contention. The main criticism of treacherous or inefficient leaders and the fight against them must be based on their shortcomings in the actual struggles. Thus the abstract and invariably ineffective criticism on the basis of differences in the theoretical conception of the class struggle or the state will give way to concrete issues on the basis of which an alignment of the workers can be effected.

6. In cases where dual industrial organizations are involved in a struggle the party must not only take the initiative to offer its services for the creation of a unity of purpose, unity of tactics and a united front in action, but also the creation of organizational unity. While in such cases the party addresses itself to the leaders, the executives of the organization, it also propagates the membership of such bodies to the same so that the leadership that stands in the way of unity will be discredited and eventually eliminated. But in all such cases, elimination is not the sole object of the application of the tactics of the United Front of Labor, but only one of its purposes.

7. Not only those workers who have immediate interests in a struggle should compose the United Front. All issues of importance must be made class issues and the working masses rallied to the support of the workers immediately concerned. Only by thus broadening the struggle will the working masses become class conscious.

8. Separate delegated bodies, councils, etc., for the organization and direction of the united working class action on the economic field must be organized only if there is no danger of serious conflict with existing bodies of the same character. In all cases where such directive bodies are created they should be formed, if at all possible, on the initiative and by action of the unions involved. Our party organization will supply the initiative where the forming of such bodies becomes necessary. No basis for even a shade of suspicion or dualistic intention must be given.

9. The creation of a United Front of Labor on the political field in the United States is the problem of the development of independent political action of the working class. The working class of Europe has for a long time participated independently in political activities. Not so in the United States. Here the problem is not to unite existing political groups and organizations for common action, but to awake political class consciousness among the workers. The class struggle has reached such a degree of intensity here that every battle of the workers reveals the political character of the struggles that is teaching the proletarian masses the necessity for class conscious political action. The numerous efforts of all kinds of labor organizations to form a labor party in the United States is evidence of this fact. These struggles indicate a step forward in the progress of the class struggle toward revolutionary working class action. To oppose this tendency toward the formation of a labor party would be folly.

10. The capitalists realize the potentialities of even a tame and not in the least revolutionary independent labor party for the development of the class consciousness of the workers. Their tools in the labor movement have, therefore, consistently opposed its formation. But when its formation can no longer be prevented these capitalist tools will assume the leadership of the movement for a labor party and will exert every effort to reduce such a party to a mere machine for their election, and to prevent it from becoming a real weapon for the workers in the class struggle. To make the labor party an instrument of the class struggle and the revolution the participation of the Communists is an imperative necessity. It is not in the interest of the proletarian revolution nor can the Workers' party assume responsibility for the largest political power of the workers remaining dormant. The party must not oppose the coming to life of this power because it has not yet the standing and influence among masses to set it at work in the name of and for the purpose of Communism.

11. To promote the development of the political action of the working class into revolutionary action the Communists must become a factor in the Labor party that may be formed. We can achieve this end only if we anticipate the formation of such a party and now adopt a policy through which we will become established as a force in the political struggle of the workers and thus an important factor in the labor party. The participation in a United Front in local political struggles will give us a strong position in relation to the labor party.

12. Attempts to misuse the name of Labor party in the formation in some sort of a "workers' non-partisan league" must be guarded against. Such a party would merely exploit the growing desire for independent working class political action to get endorsements for some misleaders of labor on capitalist party tickets, on the principle of Gompers: "Reward our friends and punish our enemies." It is the work of the Communists to also guard against the formation of such a labor party as is forecast in the work of the Conference for Progressive Political Action. This conference includes not only representatives of labor, but progressives and liberals of every shade. A party such as forecast by this conference would not mobilize the political power of the workers for the immediate struggles against the capitalists but would dissipate that power in election campaigns fought on the basis of petty ameliorative reforms and of schemes for minor changes in the form of the capitalist government. Such a party would be merely a larger but weaker edition of the Socialist party, which has for two decades misdirected the political energies of the workers supporting it through its program of reforms and limitations of the political struggle of the workers to mere participation in election campaigns. The Communists must fight to make the labor party a real instrument of the class struggle, fighting the immediate battles of the workers on the political field and engaging in political action, from election campaigns to mass strikes with political objectives and their logical developments in revolutionary struggles.

13. The Workers' party must not artificially force the development of a labor

party. It must through educational work win support of the masses of the workers for the movement of the labor party.

14. The work of education can best be carried on through establishment of the United Front on the basis of political issues growing out of the intense economic struggles of the workers. The party must use its influence and strength in the trade unions to form delegated conferences of labor organizations. Such conferences decide on a general political campaign including all forms of political action. Through these tactics the Communists help to awaken the political consciousness of the proletarian masses, broaden the conception of these masses as to the meaning of political action and establish themselves as a force in the political activities of the workers. The party must be the most ardent champion of all such action and must identify itself with all its phases. Our members should initiate such action through the unions. The position which we will thus gain for our party will attract the revolutionary forces of the workers of the United States and they will rally around our banner. These tactics will make us a force which will have to be considered in the event of the formation of a labor party and we will be able to influence its character and its activities and win leadership in it.

15. The United Front tactics can not be interpreted to mean organization unity with any other organization. The Workers' party must exist as a distinct organization with a disciplined, educated membership acting upon a revolutionary platform to give leadership to the struggles of the workers. In all its activities the party retains its full independence, its right of criticism and its freedom of action. The Workers' party must be the left and the most active section of the labor movement on both the economic and political field. By its unceasing activities, by its correct interpretation of problems and situations and by its qualities of a fighting advance guard of the workers, it must gradually eliminate all other parties and groups claiming the support of the workers as a factor in leadership. It will win leadership in all the phases of the struggle of the working class and lead the solid phalanx of the proletariat into the last decisive battle against the capitalist class, the capitalist state and the capitalist system.

Program For Coming Elections

1. The United Political Front embraces political action from election campaigns, mass demonstrations to mass strikes with political objectives and their logical development in revolutionary struggles. The basis for a United Political Front which will embrace the working masses has not yet been created in the United States. To enter into a political federation with existing political organizations, none of which have the support of the masses of the workers, would be to negate the possibility of creating a real United Front of the workers politically. The Workers' party will, therefore, as a rule nominate its own candidates in the coming elections and carry on its campaign independently.

2. However, wherever the Central Labor body of a city votes for independent

political action by the organized workers, thus indicating that the movement for independent political action has the support of the organized workers, or the fact that the movement for independent political action has the support of the masses is otherwise indicated, the Workers party will support this action by joining, as an autonomous body, into a federation to carry on the struggle. It will take the initiative in those cases where it considers conditions ripe for such action. The conditions for such participation are the following:

a. All working class organizations ready to participate in the United Front campaign must be accepted as part of the federation.

b. The platform must raise as the issues of the campaign immediate questions of the class struggle such as unemployment relief, the open shop, the use of the injunction against the workers, opposition to industrial courts, etc.

c. The United Front federation should adopt as the name under which the candidates are placed on the ballot and the campaign conducted, a name other than that of an existing political party, if the name "Workers' party" and its candidates are not endorsed.

Permission to place candidates on the ballot under the name of an existing working class political organization may be granted by the Central Executive Committee when technical conditions make that necessary; in such instances, however, the campaign must be conducted under the name of the United Front Federation.

3. In such political division where it develops that a candidate of another party claiming to be a working class party will be defeated through votes cast for the Workers' party candidate and a capitalist party candidate elected, the Workers' party will follow a policy appropriate to the situation. The unsound principles and tactics of reform parties can be demonstrated in action. Also, the Workers' party can best gain the confidence of the masses of the workers who support candidates of these parties in districts where there is prospect of their success, by not causing defeat and the election of capitalist candidates, but advocating their election and proving through their election the futility of their party program in action. The Workers' party in such instances may withdraw its candidates prior to the election, at the same time issuing a manifesto making its criticism of the candidates in whose favor it withdraws and stating the ground for its action.

APPENDIX F

"OUR BOLSHEVIST MOLES"

Series of Articles Published in *London Morning Post,*
December 1922 – January 1923

(Under this caption the London Morning Post *published in December 1922 and January 1923 a series of articles showing from authentic documents the activities of the Communists in Great Britain. By special permission of the editor of the* Post *the substance of the articles is herewith reprinted to illustrate the similarity of the Communist work in foreign lands with that in America, and as evidence of the international character of the gigantic conspiracy to bring the entire world down to the level of the workers when the "dictatorship of the proletariat" shall have been established.*

Just as the Moscow Communists hoped to make of the coal miners' strike in the United States the first step toward armed insurrection against the Government in the summer of 1922, so the same group planned to use the British coal strike at the same time. Following is, first, an editorial from the London Morning Post *of December 28, 1922, the date of the beginning of the series. Then, in sequence, the articles follow.)*

We are able to begin today the publication of a series of articles describing in detail the organization and the methods of what, we say deliberately, is one of the most dangerous revolutionary conspiracies with which this country has ever been confronted. The information we shall publish is drawn from the secret documents of the Communist party. That party is now the dominating force of the Labor party, which is numerously represented in Parliament. Those members of the Labor Party who are not either overtly or secretly Communists no longer exert any influence, nor do they possess a coherent policy. Unable to check the revolutionaries in the past, the men who are fond of describing their views as moderate and who deprecate methods of violence are now dragged impotently in the wake of the Communists. In the opinion of the Communists, the old-style Labor leader is no longer worth consideration, and accordingly the order has gone forth from Moscow that he is to be superseded by the genuine revolutionary. It must not be imagined that Communism is accurately represented in the House of Commons by the few noisy persons who have already earned the contempt alike of the House and of the public. Men much more formidable are directing the Communist party in this country, which, as we shall prove, take their orders straight from Moscow. We shall show, also, that the Communists are formed into a vast secret society, with its centers in every town and district, and its agents in every walk of society. There is here disclosed no ordinary manufactured political agitation, such as the elder Socialist movement, for which the Communists express the liveliest contempt.

In the documents from which we shall draw indisputable evidence, it is clearly shown that the great mining strike was initiated and directed by the Communists as the first step towards revolution; and the failure of that treasonable conspiracy was the subject of severe rebuke on the part of the notorious Russian Bolshevik, Karl Radek. It was, indeed, by reason of the defeat of the Communist plot on that occasion that the new Communist organization, of which we shall give a full account, was instituted. It was dictated from Moscow, and it is based throughout, as we shall show, on what is called the Theses of the Communist International. The Communist party in Great Britain is recognized by Moscow, and as a condition of that recognition every member of the Communist party must accept and carry into execution the instructions of the Theses. Members are bound to perform work both legal and illegal when they are ordered to do so. Those who fail in obedience "must be excluded from the party." The Theses of the Second Congress of the Communist International contain definite and minute instructions for the dissemination of Bolshevist doctrines, not only among the "proletariat," but in every grade of the community. Every convert to Communism becomes a potential or active agent of revolution, working under strict and detailed instructions. Groups of "nuclei" are constituted in all districts, which are under the direction of regional committees, which in their turn are guided by the central body, which is always in session in London. The scheme of organization has been elaborated, as our readers will perceive, with consummate ability. Its main purpose is to ensure incessant activity in every branch of revolution, from the teaching of children to the preparation for armed insurrection. The Theses demand practical results. The leaders of revolution in Moscow are no longer content with mere dissemination of doctrine or the issuing of manifestos. The central authority in this country is the Executive Committee of the Communist party; which, as we have observed, is the most active force in the Labor party; and the Executive Committee in this country is responsible to the Executive of the Communist Internationale at Moscow, and is bound by the decisions given by Moscow.

Such is the outline of the very dangerous revolutionary organization whose workings we shall expose. It should be remembered that we are here dealing, not with the wild project of a few half-crazed visionaries, but with the work of bold, cunning, and unscrupulous men, who have not only planned the revolution in this country but who, with the help of the Labor party proper, or at least with their connivance, have actually carried into execution the first measures of the revolutionary campaign. Indeed, so serious is the menace that we hope none of our readers will dismiss the information with the comfortable thought that the British people have too much sense to engage in revolution. Doubtless that consideration is generally accurate, but the Bolsheviks, who rule the Labor party, have provided against that contingency also by formulating the principle that, given time and opportunity, a resolute minority can always "stampede the majority." That is perilously true. The danger, some of whose secrets — but by no means all — we unmask, is a present and an active danger. It demands not only the strict attention of the Government but the lively consideration of every honest citizen. The Communist is the sworn and deadly enemy of society. Destitute alike of morals and of natural scruple, he is no more to be tolerated than a wild beast; and for the same reasons.

At a special Conference of the Communist party of Great Britain, held in London last March, a Commission was appointed "to review the organization of the party in the light of the Theses (of the Communist International) . . . and to make detailed recommendations to the Executive Committee and to the Annual Conference for the application of the Theses." The members of the Commission were Messrs. R. Palmer Dutt (editor of the *Labour Monthly*), M. Inkpin, and M. Pollitt (editor of *All Power,* an organ of the Red International of Labor Unions). The following were the terms of reference:

1. To draft such revision of the Constitution as may seem necessary to bring it into accord with the Theses.

2. To examine and report on the existing divisions, areas and other units.

3. To draw up a full scheme for the co-ordination and direction of groups and nuclei in the Trade Unions and other working-class organizations, and to make recommendations as to the first steps to be taken in the practical operation of the scheme.

4. To consider the organization of the party centre and make recommendations.

5. To bring under review the party press and other forms of propaganda in order to make possible a more effective fulfillment of the Theses in these respects.

The Report of the Commission has been represented to the party, and was adopted by the annual Conference, held at the Battersea Town Hall on October 7. It is a remarkable document, and is worthy of very careful study by employers, Trade Unionists, Co-operators, Government departments and by all who are fighting Bolshevism. Unfortunately, the report is only for members of the Communist party. It is, therefore, necessary for the writer to describe this document in detail, so that those who may be directly or indirectly affected by the underground burrowings of our Bolshevist moles will be familiar with their methods and plans. The report fills nearly seventy-nine pages, and it must be admitted that the plan of reorganization and the new methods of waging the Bolshevik war on society are diabolically clever.

The new organization and methods of the Communist party are, as the report indicates, founded on the Theses of the Communist International. These were issued in August 1920 and in December 1921. Extracts from the Theses have been published in the *Morning Post.* Every organization recognized by Moscow must accept and carry out the instructions of the Theses; and "members of the party who repudiate the conditions and theses adopted by the Communist International must be excluded from the party." Members must be prepared to undertake both legal and illegal work when required to do so by the party leaders or by the Communist International.

The form of organization which has hitherto been generally adopted by the Socialist parties does not lend itself to the kind of revolutionary activity desired by the Communist International. After the miners' strike last year the British Communists were severely criticized by Karl Radek because they had failed to obtain from the strike revolutionary results. The failure was explained as being due mainly to defective organization on the part of the Communist movement in this country. The new organization scheme to be described in these articles is the sequel to the criticisms of the Moscow Chiefs of the Communist party.

Before describing the scheme of organization recommended by the Commission — and now in process of development — it is necessary to look at the Theses of the Communist International, on which the new organization of the Communist party of Great Britain is to be based. The Theses of the Second Congress of the Communist International, Moscow, August 1920, contain the instructions that are of immediate interest. Clause 8 calls upon the Communists to replace "the old leaders by Communists in all kinds of proletarian organizations, not only political, but industrial, cooperative, educational, etc." Clause 9 states that: "Therefore, the preparation of the dictatorship of the proletariat must be begun immediately and in all places by means of the following method, among others:

"In every organization, union or association — beginning with proletarian ones first — and afterwards in all those of the non-proletarian workers and exploited masses (political, professional, military, co-operative, educational, sporting, etc.) must be formed groups or nuclei of Communists — mostly open ones, but also secret ones, which become necessary in each case when the arrest or exile of their members or the dispersal of the organization is threatened. These nuclei, in close contact with one another and with the Central party, exchanging experiences, carrying on the work of propaganda, campaign, organization, adapting themselves to all the branches of social life, to all the various forms and subdivisions of the working masses, must systematically train themselves, the party, the class, and the masses by such various work . . . .

"The masses must be approached with patience and caution, and with an understanding of the peculiarities, the special psychology of each layer or profession."

This extract from the Theses is a sample of the instructions of Moscow, and the study of the report of the Communist Commission shows that the orders have been obeyed in every detail. There is scarcely any organization or branch of social life to escape the open and secret attentions of our Bolsheviks when their new plan of attack on Society is complete and in working order. The scheme of organization to be described in this and the subsequent articles is most intricate, elaborate and costly; it penetrates every phase of social life.

The New Scheme

In the new organization of the Communist forces, every member of the party "has his own special work and responsibility." There are no idle or passive members; each one will have his allotted task and will work under strict orders and be subjected to the most rigid discipline. "The method of sharing out the work and responsibility is by making every member a member of a working group; that is to say, either of a special committee in charge of some special activity under the direction of the District or Centre, or of a nucleus which is carrying out party policy in some working-class organization." To unify the work of these groups there is a system of reports, "each group reporting regularly to the directing authority in charge of the work." It is further provided that:

Every activity has its leading committee or directing authority, appointed by and subject to the Executive Committee, which supervises the actual work and gives day-to-day instructions (not general instructions) on what to do and what is the correct party line to follow.

The three governing principles of the scheme are:

1. Centralized Direction. The establishment of strong directing centres in conjunction with the party centre.

2. Division of Work. The allocation of members to working groups for special tasks and the drawing of every member into the work by this means.

3. Organized Influence in the Working Class as the Aim. The concentrating of all activities of our groups, with a view to building up a network of influence throughout the working class and its organizations.

The Central Authority is the Executive Committee of the Communist party. This Executive is, as we shall see later, responsible to the Executive of the Communist International at Moscow, and must report to Moscow at regular intervals the results of its work in Great Britain. This will be understood by consulting the new "Statutes and Rules" of the party. Rule 1 says: "The Communist Party of Great Britain is a section of the Communist International, and is bound by its decisions."

The Immediate Aim

The Communist Party Executive in London is now forming District Party Committees. These Districts are not the old geographical divisions of the country into which the party organization has hitherto been divided. The new Districts are to begin with those industrial areas in which the membership of the party is mainly concentrated .... The Report states that "the District is the pivot of Communist organization," and it quotes the following from the Moscow Theses on Organization (para. 44):

"The thing to be aimed at is that every locality forming an economic, political, or transportation centre should spread out and form a net of organizations within a wide area of the surroundings of the given locality and the economic political districts adjoining it."

Bureaus And Departments

The District Organization Bureau contains, like the Organizing Bureau at Headquarters, seven departments. The following departments, with their numbers as given in the Report, are of public interest:

1. *Register Of Members,* with their qualifications and the work to which they are allocated. This register will enable the Committee to keep under review the disposition of members' activities, and to draft members for new work as needed. There will be a general register of individual members, with party record, record in working-class movement and personal record. In addition, there will be separate registers of the different organizations for each activity; Trade Union nuclei, factory nuclei, Trades Councils, and local Labor party fractions, propaganda committees, distribution groups, etc. Finally, there will be the special registers of members with certain qualifications and functions (speakers, instructors, linguists, etc.).

4. *Distribution.* Maintenance and control of the distribution apparatus of the party, through the groups in the localities and the factories, both for the sale of literature and for the rapid distribution of leaflets, Executive cables, etc.

5. *Transport And Communication.* Organization of ways and means of sending, receiving, and, if necessary, of accommodating literature, messages, individuals, etc., and of maintaining lines of communication with the Centre and also between localities and between workshops.

6. *Information.* Organization of all necessary information concerning the District through the local information groups and collection and transmission of information to the Centre.

This information from the District Committees is tabulated and classified by the corresponding departments of the Organization Bureau at the Centre. The District Political Bureau also consists of seven departments which correspond to the departments of the Political Bureau at the Centre. These include the following:

1. *Industrial Committee.* For the direction of the nuclei in the unions and the workshops and the fractions on Trades Councils and Local Labor Parties, in accordance with the lines laid down by the Central Industrial Committee.

2. *Elections And Municipal Committee.* For election work (Parliamentary and municipal) and direction of municipal representatives.

3. *Labor And Co-operative Committee.* For coordination of work inside Co-operative Societies and Guilds, Labor clubs, and miscellaneous local Labor organizations, and undermining and propaganda work in local Social Democratic organizations.

4. *Education Committee.* For arranging the training classes of candidates for party membership, special training of party's workers, organizers, etc., and instructions of workers outside the party . . . .

7. *Political And Supplementary Committee.* For propaganda and undermining work in Government and bourgeois institutions and special intelligence.

A Report To Moscow

The purpose of this elaborate machinery of organization is indicated in the above extracts. The main purpose is to obtain control of the industrial organizations of the workers. Before this scheme of organization had been devised, the Executive of the Communist party of Great Britain reported to Moscow that "the Party has 200 propagandists of Communism," and the party has nuclei almost in every trade union, and efforts are being pushed forward to bring these into touch with each other according to the industries, in the terms of the Theses of the Communist International . . . . All the members of the party are bound to take an active part in the unemployed agitation; it is very acute, and whatever has been done to turn the situation to account in a Communist sense is due to the work of the party. (The Communist International, Nos. 16-17.)

The members of the party in a locality are combined in small groups. These groups correspond to the German Zehnergruppen, or "Tens," and "are composed of members living within easy walking distance of one another." Where the party is strong "these group areas may cover a street or a block; in other words, a ward." There is a Group Leader, who will be responsible for his group and must see that the members are carrying out the instructions received from the Local Party Committee. This Committee directs and coordinates the activities of all the groups (also nuclei and fractions) in the locality, and reports to the District Party Committee. No slackness is allowed; every member is under strict supervision. He must be a working member, "since he could not be a member of the party at all unless he were a member of a working group. This is the vital secret of the Theses. . . . Every member has some special qualification, which can be used in some sphere of the party's work. It will be the business of the Party Committee so to organize the groups that they are composed of the members best suited to the work in hand." For this reason persons joining the party must serve a period of probation before being admitted to membership.

The Communist Press

Before coming to the actual nature of the work which the Committee's groups and nuclei of the Communist party will have to do, it is necessary briefly to summarize the plans for the entire reorganization of the Communist press. The report of the Commission states that the main party organ must be "a mass organ, i.e., an organ of working-class life and struggle. Its object is not only to agitate, but to organize and train." The Communist organ "should be the newspaper of the working class, and not a small magazine of miscellaneous articles with a Communist bias." It must "report working-class life and struggle in such a way as to give every item an agitating and organizing value."

We now come to the vital part of the Communist organization. All the elaborate and expensive machinery of organization is for a definite purpose. This purpose has been shown in the extracts from the Moscow Theses and by the report of the British Communists to the Moscow Headquarters of the Communist International. What follows is concerned with this Bolshevist machine at work. Chapter 4 of the Report of the Communist Commission is headed "Party Activities," and section 1 of this chapter describes the work "in the Trade Unions." It states that (p. 36):

"The work of the party in the Trade Union movement and in the workshops (factories, mines, docks, railways, shipyards, or other places of work) is the principal activity before the party in the present period. It is here that we must build up the leadership of the party in the actual day-to-day struggle of the workers in order to have the solid basis to proceed to further struggles. That leadership will not be achieved by the issue of manifestos, but only by systematic and organized work over the whole field.

"The field is extremely complicated, and only the highest degree of organization will secure results. . . . We must never let the 'industrial side,' i.e., our activity in economic movement, become separate from 'party work,' since the whole direct object of our activity in the economic movement is not the separate economic struggle, but the common political struggle, i.e., the revolutionary struggle for power under the dictatorship of the party. Therefore all our work in these organizations must be primarily directed towards strengthening the party's hold; if we form any independent movement it must be only as a vehicle for the party's action, and all our work must be under the daily direction of the party."

The Commission explains that the work of the party in the Trade Unions, "despite its volume," has failed through lack of common direction. They had no "hold on the membership," and no channel through which the necessary reports and information could be obtained. To overcome these difficulties there must be organized and directed day-to-day work in the Unions, and "its aim must be to bring increasing numbers of workers under the direct leadership of the party. For this reason 'nucleus work' is not simply the creation of centres of agitation, but one of the most highly organized forms of the party's work."

The aim is to transform the Unions "into mass organizations of the revolutionary struggle under the leadership of the party. This plan is not a mechanical process of 'capturing' the Unions... The process is one of actually organizing the workers around the party, and by our organization from top to bottom of the Union, establishing a real and not merely a formal, hold upon it." This is to be accomplished by first organizing "our members in their 'nuclei' or groups of party members in each Trade Union branch." These nuclei must be "firmly welded together over the whole country," and must act under "central direction." This direction will come from the Headquarters of the party and the District Committees will "only act as transmitting centres for nationally decided policies in each Union to the nuclei affected in their district."

Manipulating The Unions

At the Central Industrial Department of the party in London there will sit a main Industrial Committee, assisted by "Special Advisory Committees from each of the provincial Unions or groups of Unions. The advisory Committee of a given Trade Union will consist of our best members in that Union ... it will receive the reports of our nuclei to the Union either directly or through local or district committees, as also reports of any officials, executive members, etc., we may have in the Union." This main Industrial Committee at the Centre will divide into sections for (1) Trade Unions; (2) Trade Councils; (3) Workshops; (4) Press. Similar Committees will meet at the District Centres "to receive instructions from the main Industrial Committees, work them out for the District, and pass them on to the Union nuclei concerned in their District." A nucleus must be formed in any Trade Union branch where there are one or more members of the party.

A Trade Union nucleus is a party organization working in a Trade Union branch, and consists of party members and candidates in that branch. A nucleus only exists when it has been organized by or reported itself to its Leading Committee, and is meeting, working, and reporting regularly. The nucleus will receive full instructions as to its work at the time when it is formed by the representative of the Leading Committee accredited for the purpose, and thereafter will receive particular instructions over any issue or campaign as occasion arises.

Espionage

It will be seen, and Trade Unionists should note, that these nuclei in Trade Union branches are an organized system of espionage, directed from the Headquarters of the Communist party. The average Trade Union member is to be surrounded by the organized spies of Moscow, and his Union is to be secretly "wangled" into the acceptance of policies devised by the chiefs of the Communist party and introduced into the Unions by the underground agents of the party.

The nuclei in several branches of a Union in a locality are to form "a Local Committee for that Union" in order to co-ordinate the work of the nuclei in its local branches. In the same way the nuclei in all the local Trade Union branches, workshops, and the fractions in the Trades Councils, etc., are to be combined in a Local General Committee. This Committee takes up any subject or agitation on which all the nuclei should concentrate. Communists on District Committees or the Executive of a Union will "be organized in definite party organizations (Fractions), which will meet and report regularly, and receive their instructions from the Leading Committee." Members of the Communist party who are officials in a Union will be separately organized for party purposes, and will have to furnish their own reports regularly on the work, together with any information obtained, and will receive their distinct instructions.

A Local Industrial Organizer will be appointed "to transmit instructions to the various nuclei" and to supervise their activities. The work of a nucleus in a Trade Union branch covers a wide field. In addition to the routine day-to-day work it will:

Organize the Left Wing opposition in all branches around all current questions . . . it will be prepared for each branch meeting with resolutions, movers of resolutions, discussions, etc. . . . it will endeavour to weaken the position of reactionary officials and leaders by pressing issues which force them to take up an unpopular stand; . . . it will work for the election of accredited Communist candidates as officials and delegates to conferences, etc.; during strikes its members will be active in the forefront and pressing for extension of the dispute, and greater solidarity; and it will be watchful to keep the Leading Committee informed of all developments, and to follow carefully the lead given in order to achieve uniformity in the party's action.

Control Of Industry

More important than the nuclei in the Trade Union branches are the nuclei in the workshops. The Report declares that:

"The factory or workshop is the real unit of the working class, and should be the main field of our activity. Here, far more than in the localities, is the basis of the Party's organization of the workers, and contact with the working class as a whole, whether organized or unorganized. The Trade Unions only bring us in contact with a portion of the working class . . . and only a minority of those who turn up at branch meetings, etc. The workshop brings us into contact with all the workers on the spot . . . . The Trade Unions can only initiate the struggle. Once the revolutionary struggle begins the workshop becomes the centre . . . . Upon our organization in the workshops will depend the success of the workers in the first phase of the revolutionary struggle and their readiness for organization under the dictatorship of the proletariat."

Whenever members of the party are employed in a factory or works, "they must be organized as a responsible party body or nucleus." The forms and activities of a workshop nucleus are "manifold and varied," and the duties include the distribution of "the party paper and literature," dinner-hour discussions, formation of social and sports organizations, taking up of grievances, etc. These are, of course, the general propaganda duties. Their special task is "to agitate for the formation of factory committees," especially during a crisis, as these committees tend to "develop into the conscious struggle of the working class for power."

Business Secrets

If a Factory Committee is formed, or if one already exists, "the nucleus must concentrate its efforts on securing and maintaining control of it. Our members must put before the Factory Committee the objective of the control of industry, and seek to develop the struggle for the control of industry into the struggle for the dictatorship of the proletariat."

The real purpose of these factory committees is revealed in a warning to the nucleus. They are reminded that "workers' control" is not "our objective." It is one of many demands "to develop the struggle and so carry forward our propaganda."

Breaking New Ground

The following instruction is given by the Commission for cases where the Communists wish to attack a works in which they have no members:

"Special attention will be needed if the party wishes to gain a foothold in a large and important factory or works where we have as yet no members. In such cases, when a decision has been taken to make the attempt in regard to some particular factory, a special campaign will have to be developed for the purpose, and militant groups will be needed to start the assault. As a first step there should appear in the party organ some report or news bearing on the factory question. At the same time meetings should be arranged outside the factory which would concentrate on matters of particular interest to the workers in that factory."

Leaflets, manifestos, etc., will be distributed, and the party organ pushed. "The number of readers of the paper obtained will indicate the measure of our success. Once we have obtained our contacts individual recruiting proceeds."

Space will not permit of more details concerning these workshop nuclei. But it must be understood that none of the groups, nuclei and local committees which have so far been described, is allowed to act on its own initiative. Everything is done by order and under careful direction. Each group or nucleus has its appointed leader, who acts under orders from its Local Committee. This Committee is responsible to the District Committee and the District Committee is acting on the instructions of the Executive Committee at the Centre; and this Executive is carrying out the orders of the Executive of the Communist International at Moscow.

The Co-operative movement, with its large funds, has in recent years attracted the Socialists, and now the Communists intend to penetrate this movement. The Report we are considering explains the importance of the Co-operatives to the Bolsheviks. It points out that "very active propaganda is being carried on by the Labor Party and I.L.P. members to organize their influence in the co-operatives." Communists must bring the Co-operatives into "the current struggle," and "finally to work to secure controlling positions in them for our members." For this purpose every Communist who is eligible must "join his local co-operative society."

Local Government Fractions

Considerable attention will be given by the new organization to "work in local government." This is "an immediate task before the party." The guiding principle is stated in the following terms:

The purpose of the party's work on Local Government bodies is clearly stated in the Theses. The Communist party does not enter on Local Government bodies to help in their work, but to expose and destroy them as part of the bourgeois machinery and administration. For this purpose the work on them must always be subordinate to the objects and tactics of the mass struggle outside. On the other hand, the work on them must never be merely negative, but must always have positive propaganda value. "We should not merely oppose demands, but should formulate demands the struggle for which will clearly expose the class character of local government and lead to open conflict with the Central Authority."

The policy and tactics on local government bodies depend on whether the majority is (a) Communist, (b) Labor, (c) Bourgeois. In all cases the aim of the Communists is the destruction of the machinery of local government. During strikes "the local government machinery" must be used "to serve the purpose of the strike." "In the actual revolutionary struggle any hold on local government should be used to stop its operation and replace it by revolutionary workers' councils." A section on this subject is devoted to the dangers of reformism. "The active participation in the administrative detail of a Local Governing body has a tendency to cool the revolutionary ardour of the Communists, and many revolutionaries are afraid of taking part at all for fear of coming reformists."

Prejudices Of Women

Chapter 6 of the Bolshevist Report is devoted to the work of the Communists among women. It begins by declaring that: "The role of women in the class struggle cannot be ignored by Communists in any country . . . . The seizures of power by the proletariat and the subsequent achievement of Communism can only be accomplished with the active participation of the wide masses of the proletarian and semi-proletarian women." It is admitted that the task of winning the support of women for Bolshevism is very great. There are many strong prejudices to overcome. The starting point must be in the working-class organizations with women members. These include Trade Unions, the Co-operative Societies, and Guilds. One of the prejudices to combat is the prevailing prejudice against the participation of women in the thick of the fight. "We shall have to fight relentlessly against a great deal of prejudice of this kind in our own ranks. Many comrades discourage their wives, sisters, and women friends from attending party meetings or from taking any part whatever in our work. This attitude must be overcome."

The women will be separately organized, and the Women's Propaganda Committee will organize "propaganda and agitation among proletarian women, such organization to remain completely under party control." At headquarters there will be the "Central Women's Propaganda Committee," with a General Organizer. The Report goes on to tabulate the duties of this Central Committee, one of which will be the "maintenance and continuous contact with the International Secretariat of Communist Women" (Moscow).

The work of the Central Committee and also of the District and Local Committees will be divided into sections in the manner described in connection with the Party Executive and the District Party Committees. The Report states that:

"Thorough division of the work among members of the Committee is most essential. One member should have charge of the work among housewives, another of that in the co-operative movement, and so on."

Functions Of Women's Groups

The local work will be distributed "among various small working groups with different functions or fields of activity (such as Co-operative Guild Groups, Literature Distributors' Groups, House to House Propaganda Groups, etc.)." Communist women in Trade Unions will join the party nucleus (where such exists) and will act "on the instructions from the Nucleus Management Committee or leader." They will get into personal contact with the women members of the Trade Union branch, and will endeavor to get them "to attend classes or instruction groups." Communist women are to join the Local Labor Parties "if individual membership of the Labor party is allowed." These women members must report to the Committee under whose direction they are acting. The procedure is the same as that already given in other cases.

Other activities of women Communists are the holding of street corner meetings in "proletarian shopping centres" to discuss "the cost of living — bread meetings — or the care and education of children," etc. Special attention must be given to literature for women. "A series of vivid, arresting short stories, with a strong agitational bias, would also be useful." Entertainments likely to attract women will be provided, but "propaganda should be judiciously mixed with entertainments."

The Money Mystery

Many proposals and technical details of the Communist reorganization scheme, for lack of space, have been omitted, such as the relations with Communist Schools for the young and the special features of the Communist Saturdays and Sundays when members will be called upon to do some special work for the Party. But the general features of the organization have been given, and it is scarcely necessary to remind the reader that the administrative expenses of the organization will be heavy. Where the money will come from is not explained in the Report — the subscriptions of members are quite inadequate to meet the cost of such an elaborate scheme. But as the plan of organization is based on the instructions of the Moscow International, it is not unreasonable to suggest that Moscow may be financing it.

"The final and culminating campaign," says the Report (p. 74), "to which the whole of the Party organization leads up is the open fight for power." Will this cleverly devised plan of the revolutionaries succeed? Not if the intended victims are made aware of the intentions and methods of the conspirators. Now we know the plans and policy of the Communist party and its precious International of Bandits at Moscow, it will not be difficult to frustrate their revolutionary designs upon society.

INDEX

Adaptation of Communist party to American conditions, 239

Addams, Jane, American Association for Labor Legislation, 192; American Relief for Russian Women and Children, 196; Civil Liberties Bureau, 195; organizer of anti-American bodies, 126; stockholder, Russian-American Industrial Corp., 189; Women's International League for Peace and Freedom, 189, 192

Adjustment Committee, Bridgman convention, 20

Advance (publication), 82f.

African Blood Brotherhood, approved by Communist Party of America, 198; program and aims, 31, 198-200; represented at Workers' party convention, 90

Agrarian program, cost, 120; Legal Agrarian Bureau, 120; of Communist Party of America, 115-116

Agricultural schools, students planted by Communists, 116, 120

All-American National Council, 53

All-American Technical Committee, 231

Allen, Governor (Kansas), 121

Allison, Elmer T., 90; Advisory Committee, Friends of Soviet Russia, 100

All Power (publication), 257

All-Russian Central Executive Committee, 74

All-Russian Jewish Relief Committee, 144

Amalgamated Clothing Workers' Union, affiliated with Friends of Soviet Union, 100; children's homes in Soviet Russia, 185; Conference for Progressive Political Action, 42; predominantly a Jewish organization, 44, 141; quote from report to Moscow, 138; report on, in Baltimore, 139

Amalgamated Metal Workers, 138

Amalgamated Textile Workers, pretended hostility to Clothing Workers, 145; represented by William Z. Foster, 97; strikes, aided by American Civil Liberties Union, 127

America, Communism in, 20; in counter-revolutionary alliance, 203-204

American Association for Labor Legislation, 191; approved by National Information Bureau, 196; personnel of organization, 191-192

American Association of Social Workers, 195

American capitalism, 240

American Civil Liberties Union, 14, 43, 44, 45, 121, 195; aids arrested Communists, 127, 180; approved by National Information Bureau, 195; charges filed against Department of Justice, 224; contributions to Labor Defense Council, 182, 184, 185; early history, 126, 127; funds, 128; Labor Defense Council, 182; linked with Communism, 121; opinions, 127

American Committee for the Relief of Russian Children, 109; approved by National Information Bureau, 196; four National Committee members in Moscow, 109; Russian Fair and Costume Ball, 159; represented by Captain Paxton Hibben, 109

American Committee for Russian Famine Relief, activities and propaganda, 103; organized by W.W. Liggett, 103

American Defense Society, 14; opposition of Negro Communists, 200; protests landing of Moscow Art Theatre, 151-152

American-Federated Russian Famine Relief Committee, 100

American Federation of Labor, 205; aids Communists, 180-181; Communists have difficulty gaining membership, 141; Communists working in, 20, 52, 140; Conference for Progressive Political Action, 42; Federated Press claimed as organ for, 86; Foster heads steel workers, 216; report on J.D. Cannon, 154; represented by J.H. Ralston, 224; trapped by Communists, 145

American-Hungarian Workers' Federation, 100

American-Jewish Committee, 196

American-Jewish Joint Distribution Committee, 196

American Labor Alliance, 90, 137

American League to Limit Armaments, 53, 126

American Legion, 128; opposed to Communism, 169; disapproved by World War Veterans, 69; opposition of Negro Communists to, 200

American-Lithuanian Workers' Literary Society, 100

American Medical Association, 103

American Neutral Conference Committee, 126

American Relief Administration, 107-110

American Relief for Russian Women and Children, 196

American Union Against Militarism, 53, 126, 196

American workers, danger to, 228; must lead Pan-American revolution, 230